WHO'S WHO

IN

CLASSICAL MYTHOLOGY

WHO'S WHO

— IN —

CLASSICAL MYTHOLOGY

JESSICA HODGE

SMITHMARK

This edition published in 1995
by SMITHMARK Publishers Inc.
16 East 32nd Street
New York, New York 10016.

SMITHMARK books are available for bulk
purchase for sales promotion and
premium use. For details write or
telephone the Manager of
Special Sales, SMITHMARK Publishers
Inc., 16 East 32nd Street,
New York, NY 10016, (212) 532 6600.

Produced by Brompton Books Corp.,
15 Sherwood Place,
Greenwich, CT 06830.

ISBN 0-8317-9362-7

Printed in Hong Kong

10 9 8 7 6 5 4 3 2 1

Page 1 Gold death mask of an Achaean
king, found on the acropolis of Mycenae
and hailed by the archeologist Heinrich
Schliemann as the mask of Agamemnon.

Page 2 Head of Neptune at the center of
the great silver dish which was part of
the Mildenhall treasure found in Suffolk,
England.

Page 3 *Above left:* Diana the huntress,
mosiac from Tunisia, second century AD.
Middle left: This sphinx is one of several
which line the avenue leading to the
temple at Luxor, Egypt.
Below left: Greek temple of Hera at
Paestum, southern Italy.
Right: Ariadne at Naxos, fifteenth-century
Italian medallion.

Far right Apollo with his lyre pouring a
libation, fifth-century BC Greek dish.

Contents

A

Abderus

Arm-bearer to Heracles. When Heracles goes to war against the Bistones, he leaves in the care of Abderus the flesh-eating mares of Diomedes, which he won as a result of his eighth labor. The mares have already devoured their original master, after Heracles defeated him in battle, and also tear the unfortunate Abderus to pieces.

Absyrtus

Son of Aeetes, king of Colchis and owner of the Golden Fleece. Absyrtus's sorceress sister Medea helps Jason and the Argonauts to steal the Fleece, and as she sails away with Jason, she kills and dismembers her brother and throws his limbs into the sea in order to delay her father's pursuit.

Acarnas and Amphoterus

Sons of Alcmaeon and Callirhoe. When Alcmaeon is murdered by his first wife's brothers, Callirhoe prays to Zeus that her baby sons should avenge their father. Her petition is granted; the boys grow to men overnight and kill their father's murderers.

Acastus

King of Iolcos, whose wife Astydamia falls in love with Peleus while he is living in banishment at Acastus's court. When Peleus refuses her, she falsely accuses him to Acastus of trying to rape her. Acastus is torn be-

tween the duty of hospitality and his wife's anger; rather than killing Peleus outright, he orders that he be taken hunting on Mount Pelion and there tied to a tree and left to be devoured by wild animals. Peleus is destined to be the father of the great Greek hero Achilles, however, and cannot be allowed to perish. Zeus orders Hephaestus to release him, and he returns to Iolcos, defeats Acastus, and puts Astydamia to death.

Acca Laurentia

Wife of Faustulus, shepherd to King Numitor of Alba, the city founded in Italy by Aeneas. She finds the twin babies Romulus and Remus, Numitor's

Above Seventeenth-century engraving showing Acca Laurentia receiving either Romulus or Remus from her husband, Faustulus.

grandchildren, on the banks of the River Tiber, where they have been abandoned by order of Numitor's evil brother, and brings them up as her own. She is so promiscuous that she is known as "*lupa*," or "she-wolf," hence the legend that the boys were suckled by a wolf.

Acca Laurentia

Legendary prostitute in Rome, in whose honor the Romans celebrated the annual festivals of Laurentalia. The keeper of the temple of Heracles plays the god at dice, on condition that if Heracles loses he should make him a present, but if he wins he shall be given a sumptuous feast and spend a night with Acca Laurentia, the most beautiful woman in Rome. Needless to say, the god wins. After his night with Acca, he tells her as a reward to go into the street and kiss the first man she meets. This is Tarrutius, an elderly unmarried man, who is so delighted with Acca's boldness that he makes her his heiress.

Achates

Faithful follower of the Trojan prince Aeneas throughout the Trojan War and Aeneas's subsequent journeyings. In Virgil's *Aeneid* he is invariably described as "*fidus Achates*," loyal Achates, and the phrase became a Latin cliché.

Achelous

River-god, son of the sea-god Oceanus and Tethys. He is one of the many suitors for the hand of the beautiful Deianira, whose father promises her to the strongest. Achelous is challenged to combat by Heracles, another of Deianira's admirers, and in his efforts to avoid defeat, changes himself first into a serpent and then into an ox. Heracles breaks off one of the ox's horns as a symbol of victory, and Achelous retires defeated and disgraced to his riverbed. The broken horn is filled with fruits and flowers by the nymphs, and presented to the goddess of plenty.

Achilles

One of the greatest of the Greek heroes, around whom center many myths; the main subject of Homer's *Iliad* is not so much the Trojan War as such, but rather the rivalry of Achilles with Agamemnon, and his duel with Hector. He is the son of the sea-nymph Thetis and the mortal Peleus, king of Thessaly. Thetis is so beautiful that both Zeus and Poseidon lust after her, but an oracle warns that her son will be greater than his father, and so they marry her swiftly off to Peleus, celebrating the wedding with spectacular pomp as compensation to her. Thetis has the gift of foresight and knows how Achilles will die, but she tries to prevent this by making him immortal. She anoints him daily with ambrosia, the food of the gods, and buries him in the embers of the fire by night, in order to burn away his mortal parts, but she is discovered and prevented by Peleus.

Below Greek red-figure vase painting of Achilles aiding the wounded Patroclus.

She then takes Achilles to the river of Hades, the Styx, and dips him in it in order to make him invulnerable, but the heel by which she holds him remains unprotected, hence the phrase ''Achilles heel.'' In her anger with Peleus at his interference, Thetis leaves both him and Achilles and returns to the sea, and Achilles is sent by his father to the centaur Chiron for his education. When he returns to Thessaly, he finds that the exiled Patroclus has taken refuge at his father's court; the two become inseparable friends and lovers.

In the *Iliad* Achilles, already recognized as a mighty warrior, goes voluntarily to the Trojan War at the invitation of Nestor and Odysseus and the urging of Patroclus, even though he was never a suitor to Helen. In later legend, however, he is persuaded by Thetis to adopt female disguise and hide at the court of Lycomedes of Scyros, where he fathers Neoptolemus with Lycomedes' daughter Deidamia. The prophet Calchas foretells that Troy will never fall unless Achilles joins the besieging army, and Odysseus is sent to find him. Suspecting the truth, Odysseus hides a sword among a parcel of presents he brings the ladies of the court, and arranges for a war trumpet

Below Achilles mortally wounded in the only vulnerable part of his body, his heel.

to be sounded just as the parcel is opened. While the real ladies run for shelter, Achilles seizes the sword and prepares to fight. He accepts the result of the stratagem and accompanies the Greek armada to Troy.

In Homer, Achilles brings 50 ships manned by the Myrmidons, who owe him allegiance. On arriving off Troy, the Greeks land on the island of Tenedos, where Achilles ignores a warning from his mother and kills Tenes, king of the island and son of Apollo, thus incurring the implacable enmity of the archer-god. In the first nine years of the war, during which Troy remains impregnable, he leads many forays against neighboring towns, and among many other prisoners captures the beautiful Briseis, who becomes his lover. When Agamemnon has to surrender Chryseis, daughter of Apollo's prophet Chryses, to her father on pain of Apollo's vengeance, he insists on taking Briseis for himself, and this is the cause of the fatal quarrel between the two men which almost loses the Greeks the war and leads ultimately to Achilles' death.

Bitterly offended, Achilles withdraws to his tent and refuses to fight, instead asking Thetis to persuade Zeus to favor the Trojans. Even when the Trojans threaten the Greek ships, and Agamemnon apologetically offers to return Briseis and marry one of his daughters to Achilles, the embittered hero remains obdurate. He does, however, permit Patroclus to borrow his armor and lead the Myrmidons into battle, as long as Patroclus does no more than raise the siege of the ships. Encouraged by the terrified withdrawal of the Trojans, who believe him to be Achilles, Patroclus ventures too far and is challenged by the Trojan prince Hector, who kills him after a fierce battle and strips him of Achilles' armor.

On learning the news of Patroclus's death, Achilles is rent with rage and remorse. Comforted by Thetis, he swears to revenge himself on Hector and longs for his own death, which Thetis knows is doomed to follow soon after the fall of Hector. She persuades the smith-god Hephaestus to make Achilles a new and divinely-wrought suit of armor, and Achilles, having reconciled himself with Agamemnon, cries his great war-cry, causing the Trojans to retreat in confusion. When he joins battle, his war-horse Xanthus, momen-

tarily endowed with the gift of speech, foretells his master's imminent death. Achilles kills so many Trojans that the god of the River Scamander, infuriated by the number of bodies thrown into his waters, emerges to take issue with the hero, who is saved by the intervention of Hephaestus. He also engages with Aeneas, but the latter is destined to found Troy and so the gods separate them by enveloping them in a cloud.

Finally, Achilles comes across Hector, at the very gate of Troy, and chases him three times round the city until the Trojan is inspired by Athena to stand and fight, and meet his doom. On the point of death, he asks Achilles to return his body to his father Priam, but Achilles' thirst for revenge is still unquenched, and on 12 consecutive days he drags the naked body of Hector round the walls of Troy and the tomb of Patroclus. Eventually, Thetis appears to him, bearing a message that the gods are angry at his lack of respect for the dead; when Priam comes to beg for the body of his son, Achilles receives him kindly, touched by the old man's grief, and gives him the corpse for proper burial rites.

Other stories about the exploits of Achilles before Troy that do not appear in the *Iliad* include his duel with the Amazon queen Penthesilea, who brings her warriors to help the Trojans. After a close-fought struggle, Achilles gives her a mortal blow and removes her helmet. On seeing her beautiful face, he falls passionately in love with her, kills Thersites for mocking his instant love, and gives Penthesilea full funeral rites. Another story concerns his epic struggle with Memnon, also the son of a goddess, and a more improbable one tells of his love for Priam's daughter Polyxena, which leads him to agree to desert to the Trojans in return for marriage to her. When he appears unarmed to ratify the agreement, he is killed by Paris from hiding.

In Homer, however, Achilles' end is suitably glorious. Apollo appears to him after he has penned the Trojans in their city and warns him to withdraw, but Achilles refuses. Apollo then guides the arrow of Paris to the one vulnerable place in Achilles' body, his heel. A fierce struggle takes place over his corpse, which is rescued by Ajax, son of Telamon, and his funeral lasts for 17 days. When Thetis and the

Nereids come to sing a dirge for him, the Greeks flee to their ships in terror. They then argue over who should be awarded Achilles' armor; Ajax claims it, but the Greeks award it to Odysseus, who in turn gives it to Neoptolemus. Achilles was widely acclaimed in the classical world as the archetypal warrior, and he was the hero most admired by Alexander the Great, but some later Greek philosophers saw him as dangerously violent and enslaved by his own instantaneous reactions, contrasting him with Odysseus, the man of judgment.

Acholoe

One of the harpies, winged monsters with vultures' bodies, women's faces, and clawed hands and feet. See Harpies.

Acis

Sicilian shepherd, the son of the Italian shepherd-god Faunus and beloved lover of the sea-nymph Galatea. The Cyclops Polyphemus, in a jealous rage after being spurned by Galatea, crushes Acis with a huge rock, and the gods in pity turn him into a stream which still flows down Mount Etna. Handel's opera *Acis and Galatea* gives the story an idyllic pastoral setting.

Acrisius

King of Argos, twin brother of Proetus, with whom he quarrels while still in the womb. Their quarrels continue, and after the death of their father Abas, Acrisius drives his brother from Argos and rules alone. He is told by an oracle that the son of his daughter Danae will put him to death, and so he imprisons her in a bronze tower to prevent any man gaining access to her. Zeus is more than a match for this ruthlessness, however, and visits Danae in the form of a shower of gold. When Danae gives birth to a son, Perseus, Acrisius sets them adrift in a rudderless boat, but Zeus protects them and guides them to the island of Seriphos, where Perseus grows to become a renowned athlete and warrior. He attends a funeral games at which, in demonstrating his skill at quoit-throwing, he accidentally strikes dead an old man who proves to be Acrisius, his grandfather, and so the oracle is fulfilled.

ACTÆON

Acteon changé en Cerf pour auoir vû Diane nue dans le bain, est deuoré par ses propres Chiens.
Euripide. Ouide. Metam. l. 3.
T. Mathan sculp.　　　　Auec priuilege du Roy.　　　　P. Mariette le fils excud.

Actaeon

A famed huntsman, grandson of King Cadmus of Thebes and son of the shepherd-god Aristaeus. He surprises the hunter-goddess Artemis and her attendants bathing naked in a forest pool, and is transformed into a stag and devoured by his own hounds in punishment for his temerity. Earlier versions of the story suggest that he offended the goddess by claiming to be a better hunter. The subject was a popular one with painters from the Renaissance onward.

Adamantea

Nursemaid of Zeus, who protects the infant god from his father, Cronos, by

Above Actaeon devoured by his own hounds after the offended Artemis has transformed him into a stag. Copper engraving, 1655.

suspending him in his cradle from the branch of a tree, so that he may not be found in earth, sea, or heaven. She also orders drums to be beaten and cymbals crashed so that Zeus is not betrayed by his crying.

Admetus

King of Thessaly and one of the Argonauts who sail with Jason in quest of the Golden Fleece. He wins the hand of Alcestis, beautiful daughter of Pelias, by fulfilling Pelias's condition that the successful suitor shall bring him a chariot pulled by a lion and a wild boar.

Above Admetus, threatened by death from which Alcestis delivers him.

Right This fresco from Pompeii shows Admetus raised from the dead.

Apollo tends Admetus's sheep for nine years while under sentence of banishment from Olympus. In gratitude for Admetus's kindness, Apollo persuades the Fates, or Moirae, that Admetus shall never die, as long as someone else can be found who will give up their life instead. The devoted Alcestis willingly makes this sacrifice.

Adonis

In Greek myth, a beautiful youth from Cyprus, lover of Aphrodite and son of Myrrha by her own father Cinyras. When he is born, already notably beautiful, Aphrodite removes him and gives him to Persephone, queen of the underworld, to look after. Persephone then refuses to return him, and either Zeus or the Muse Calliope arbitrate, decreeing that Adonis should spend some time each year with each. Aphrodite warns him of the dangers of hunting, but he ignores her fears and is killed by a wild boar, believed by some to be either Aphrodite's husband Hephaestus, or her lover Ares, in disguise. Aphrodite, in mourning, sprinkles nectar on the blood shed by Adonis, which becomes an anemone. As she weeps, the thorn of a rose pierces her foot, and stains the anemone red. In one version of the myth, Persephone restores Adonis to life on condition that he spends six months of the year, i.e. the winter, with her.

The story is linked with other regeneration myths of the mother-goddess and her mortal consort, such as the Phrygian Attis and the Egyptian Osiris. Adonis was a god of Asiatic origin, and entered Greek mythology relatively late; he was worshipped as a vegetation-god, and his rites usually began with lamentations and ended with rejoicing at his rebirth. The story has remained popular in both art and literature; one of Shakespeare's earliest works was a narrative poem, *Venus and Adonis*.

Adrastus

King of Argos, descended from Proetus, and leader of the Seven against Thebes. Polynices, son of Oedipus and rightful king of Thebes, and Tydeus, rightful king of Calydon, ask Adrastus for his support in regaining their respective kingdoms. Adrastus has been advised by an oracle to marry his daughters to a lion and a boar, and since Polynices wears a lionskin and Tydeus a boarskin, he gratefully accepts them as sons-in-law. Despite warnings from the prophet Amphiarus, Adrastus leads the assault of seven armies led by seven heroes against Thebes, described by the dramatist Aeschylus in *Seven Against Thebes*. The expedition is a failure, and only Adrastus among the leaders escapes. Ten years later he accompanies the children of the Seven, supported by Theseus, in another expedition, this time successful, but Adrastus's son is killed and he dies of grief soon after.

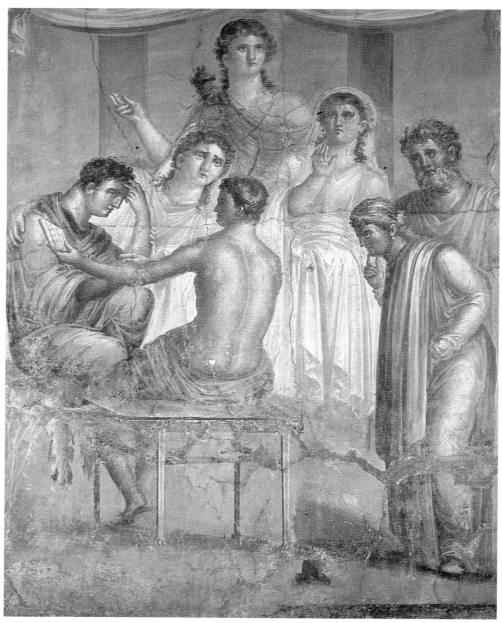

Aeacus

Son of Zeus and Aegina and ruler of the island which still bears his mother's name. When a plague kills all his subjects, he prays to Zeus to repopulate his kingdom, and Zeus turns all the ants inside the trunk of an old oak into men. Aeacus calls these new subjects Myrmidons, from the Greek word for ant. He becomes the father of Telamon and Peleus, and so the grandfather of Achilles and Ajax. He is a man of such integrity that when he dies he joins Minos and Rhadamanthys as one of the judges in the underworld.

Aeatus

A descendant of Heracles and brother of Polyclea. An oracle foretells that whichever of the two first touches land after crossing the River Achelous shall rule the kingdom. The ingenious Polyclea pretends to be lame and per-

suades her brother to carry her across on his shoulders. As he approaches the shore, she leaps from his back and claims the kingdom, but Aeatus subsequently marries her and they rule jointly. Thessaly is named after their son Thessalus.

Aeetes

King of Colchis and father of Medea, Absyrtus, and Chalciope. When Phrixus flees to his court on the back of a golden ram, Aeetes at first welcomes him and gives Chalciope to him in marriage. After Phrixus has sacrificed the ram to Ares and made its skin into the famed Golden Fleece, however, Aeetes grows jealous, kills his son-in-law and steals the fleece. He hangs it on a tree and sets a venomous dragon to guard it, but Jason and the Argonauts, with the aid of Medea, recover the fleece in one of the most famous tales of Greek mythology. See Jason.

Above In Titian's *Venus and Adonis*, the goddess of love tries to dissuade her lover from the fateful hunt.

Aegeus

King of Athens and father of the Greek hero Theseus. He wishes to father a son but is wary of his nephews, the Pallantides, who want his throne. He journeys to Delphi to consult the oracle, and on its instruction stops on his return at the court of Pittheus, king of Troezen, who gives him his daughter Aethra in marriage. When Aegeus returns to Athens, he tells Aethra that, if she has a son, she should send him to Athens to claim his patrimony when he has grown strong enough to lift the stone under which Aegeus has concealed a sword. By the time that Theseus has grown to manhood and come to Athens, Aegeus is living with the sorceress Medea, the divorced wife of Jason, and has had a son by her. Medea tries to persuade

Above Greek bronze plaque from the sixth century BC showing Aegisthus fleeing to the altar for protection as his lover Clytemnestra is killed by Orestes.

Aegeus that the stranger is dangerous and should be poisoned, but Aegeus recognizes his own sword in the nick of time and acknowledges Theseus as his son. Theseus subsequently sails to Crete to battle with the Minotaur, and promises to hoist white sails on his return as a sign of success. He forgets, however, and Aegeus, waiting anxiously on the cliffs of Sounion for news of his son, concludes on seeing black sails that Theseus is dead, and throws himself into the sea.

Aegiale

One of the sisters of Phaethon, who dies driving his chariot of the sun. His sisters mourn their brother's death so sincerely that they are turned into poplars, and their tears become drops of amber.

Aegisthus

King of Argos and a member of the doomed house of Pelops and Atreus. He is the grandson of Pelops, and the son of Thyestes by Thyestes' own daughter Pelopea. Pelopea subsequently marries Atreus, Thyestes' brother and thus her uncle, and Aegis- thus is brought up in Atreus's household. The brothers are conducting a long feud, and Atreus sends Aegisthus to kill Thyestes, but Thyestes recognizes his son by the sword which he had left with Pelopea, and in turn sends him back to kill Atreus. This Aegisthus does, and ascends the throne of Argos, banishing Agamemnon and Menelaus, the two sons of Atreus. With the aid of Tyndareos of Sparta, Agamemnon and Menelaus dispossess Aegisthus, but by the outbreak of the Trojan War they appear to be reconciled with him, for Agamemnon leaves Aegisthus as regent of his kingdom when he leads the Greeks against Troy. Aegisthus has his revenge, however, for he and Agamemnon's wife Clytemnestra fall in love, murder Agamemnon on his return from Troy, and jointly assume the throne. After ruling for seven years, they in turn are murdered inside the temple of Apollo by Orestes, son of Agamemnon and Clytemnestra.

Aegyptus

King of Egypt with 50 sons, Aegyptus rules jointly with his brother Danaus until a disagreement between them causes Danaus to leave for Greece with his 50 daughters. He settles in Argos and becomes king, which prompts Aegyptus's sons to follow, and they marry their cousins in a mass ceremony. By order of Danaus, however, they are all murdered but one by their wives that same night.

Aello

One of the harpies. See Harpies.

Aeneas

A Trojan prince, son of Anchises and Aphrodite, who is brought up by the centaur Chiron and marries Creusa, daughter of the Trojan king Priam. He does not figure much in the *Iliad*, Homer's account of the Trojan War, where he is said to feel aggrieved with Priam for not according him sufficient honor. It is in the Roman authors, and above all Virgil, that the story of Aeneas is fully developed, with the aim of pleasing the Roman emperors by tracing their descent from such an illustrious ancestor. In Virgil's *Aeneid*, Aeneas is always "*pius Aeneas*," a worthy warrior devoted to his father and his gods, and driven on by his sense of destiny.

The *Aeneid* tells how Aeneas is warned by the ghost of the Trojan hero Hector to flee Troy just before the final defeat. Aeneas sees his father Priam killed, and finds Helen, the cause of so much bloodshed, cowering in the palace. He is prevented from killing her by his mother, Aphrodite, who tells him instead to save his family from the doom of Troy. Aeneas carries his aged father Anchises on his shoulders, leads his son Ascanius by the hand and leaves the unfortunate Creusa to follow behind, which she fails to do and disappears in the chaos of the sacked city. Aeneas sets sail for Italy, where he is destined to found Rome.

During the seven-year voyage that ensues, his ship is driven by storm into Carthage, where he is kindly received by Dido, the Carthaginian queen, and sorely tempted to accept her offer of marriage and the Carthaginian throne, but the gods order him onward. He also lands at Cumae in Asia Minor, and is conducted by the Sibyl down into the underworld, to the Elysian Fields where the dead heroes live, and where his father foretells the glorious future that awaits his descendants. When he finally sails up the Tiber, he is welcomed by the local king, Latinus, marries his daughter Lavinia, and succeeds to the throne.

Aeolus

The Greek god of storms and winds, who rules the Aeolian Islands, off the coast of Sicily. In Homer's *Odyssey*, he gives Odysseus all the contrary winds tied up in a bag, to ensure that he has a swift journey home from Troy, but while Odysseus is asleep his sailors untie the bag and the ship is blown off course.

Aerope

Wife of Atreus, of the doomed house of Pelops. Aerope has an affair with her brother-in-law Thyestes and bears him twin sons. Atreus divorces Aerope and banishes Thyestes, but then summons him back to Argos on the pretext of reconciliation and entertains him to a magnificent feast, at which Thyestes is

Below Aeneas tells the story of his wanderings to Dido, queen of Carthage, in this nineteenth-century engraving.

served a dish made from the flesh of his own children and unknowingly eats it.

Aesculapius

See Asclepius.

Aeson

King of Iolcos, whose throne is usurped by his half-brother Pelias. He entrusts the upbringing of his son Jason to Chiron, the centaur, because he distrusts Pelias. When Jason grows to manhood, Pelias sends him on the quest for the Golden Fleece, in the hope that he will never return to threaten his position. In one version, Pelias murders Aeson during Jason's absence, but in another Jason returns with the witch Medea to find Aeson old and ill. At his request, Medea removes all the blood from Aeson's veins and replaces it with the juice of certain magic herbs, and instantly Aeson is restored to youth and vigor.

Aethra

Princess of Troezen and mother of Theseus. In some versions she is later carried off by Castor and Pollux when they rescue their sister Helen, whom Theseus has stolen and entrusted to his mother's care. She grows fond of Helen, stays with her when she marries Menelaus, and accompanies her to Troy when she elopes with Paris.

Agamedes and Trophonius

Two architects who build the entrance of the temple of Apollo at Delphi. In payment they ask the god for whatever gift it would be most advantageous for them to receive, expecting eternal life or untold wealth, or some such boon. Instead they are found dead in their beds eight days later; the god has granted them the ultimate gift, release from their mortal form.

Above Gold death mask of an Achaean king, found on the acropolis of Mycenae and hailed by the archeologist Heinrich Schliemann as the mask of Agamemnon.

Agamemnon

King of Mycenae and son of the accursed Atreus, he is the High King of all the Greek forces that sail against Troy. After the death of his father, he and his brother are dispossessed of their kingdom by Atreus's brother Thyestes, and they flee to Sparta, where they each marry one of the king's daughters, Agamemnon choosing Clytemnestra and Menelaus Helen. Agamemnon and Clytemnestra have one son, Orestes, and three daughters, Iphigenia, Electra, and Chrysothemis. Tyndareos, king of Sparta, makes Menelaus his heir and helps Agamemnon recover his kingdom.

Before her marriage, Helen of Sparta is courted by all the kings of Greece, and it takes some pressure from Agamemnon to ensure that she becomes the bride of his brother Menelaus. To prevent any subsequent dissension, he persuades all the suitors to swear an oath to defend the rights of whoever succeeds in winning her. Thus when Paris of Troy steals Helen, the kings of Greece are bound by their oath to recover her, and Agamemnon, as commander-in-chief, supplies 100 ships, the largest single contingent. The avenging fleet is becalmed at Aulis, however, and an oracle informs Agamemnon that he has offended Artemis by killing her favorite stag, and the winds will only turn favorable if he sacrifices his daughter Iphigenia to the goddess. At first he is reluctant, and tells the assembled Greeks to return home and abandon their quest, but under pressure from Odysseus and the other generals, he summons Iphigenia on the pretext of marriage with Achilles, and is about to sacrifice her when her place is miraculously taken by a stag.

The Trojan campaign lasts many years, and just as the Greeks have the Trojans penned within their city, Agamemnon has a disastrous quarrel with the principal Greek hero, Achilles, whose mistress Briseis he commandeers by virtue of his superior rank. Achilles refuses to fight, and the Greeks almost lose the war until the intervention and death of Patroclus brings Achilles back into the fray. On the fall of Troy, Agamemnon takes the Trojan king Priam's prophetess daughter Cassandra as his prize and brings her home to Mycenae. His wife Clytemnestra, bitter both about the fate of Iphigenia and the presence of Cassandra as her husband's lover, murders them both as they come from the bath, and is in turn murdered by her son Orestes, the final victim of the curses laid two and three generations earlier. See Atreus, Pelops.

Agave

Daughter of Cadmus, founder and king of Thebes, and Harmonia, daughter of Aphrodite. She marries Echeon, one of the soldiers who sprang from the dragon's teeth that her father sowed in the ground. When the young Dionysos, Greek god of wine and fertility and son of Agave's sister Semele, appears in Boeotia, she welcomes him and contributes to his education, for which she receives divine honors after her death. Her son Pentheus, however, refuses to allow the god into Thebes, and is torn to pieces by the Maenads, followers of Dionysos.

Aglaia

One of the three Graces, also sometimes called Pasiphae. They were the daughters of Zeus.

Ajax

Son of Telamon, king of Salamis, Ajax is the greatest after Achilles of all the Greeks who fight in the Trojan War. His parents are childless until Heracles prays that Telamon shall father a son with skin as tough as the hide of the Nemaean lion, which Heracles is then wearing. Zeus grants the petition, and when the child is born Heracles wraps him in the lion skin, which makes all but the hero's back (or neck in some versions) impenetrable. Ajax becomes a mighty and courageous warrior, although Homer in the *Iliad* shows him also to be unimaginative and dense. He fights with Hector in the course of the Trojan War, and exchanges arms with him afterward as a mark of respect for a worthy adversary. After the death of Achilles, he argues with Odysseus as to which of them is entitled to the arms of the dead hero. When the Greeks award them to Odysseus, Ajax is so enraged that he loses his reason,

slaughters a whole herd of sheep, supposing them to be the sons of Atreus who gave Odysseus the preference, and stabs himself. This is the account given in the play *Ajax* by Sophocles, but other versions have Ajax killed by Paris, the abductor of Helen, or even slain by the crafty Odysseus.

Ajax

Another Ajax figures in the Trojan War, the son of Oileus, king of Locris and one of the suitors of Helen before she chooses Menelaus. At the fall of Troy he tries to rape Cassandra, daughter of King Priam, who flees into the temple of Athena and invokes the goddess's support. On his return home, as a punishment for his impiety,

Left The heroic Ajax, statue by Antonio Canova (1757-1822).

Below Ajax the Lesser attacks the Trojan princess Cassandra at the fall of Troy.

Ajax's ship is destroyed in a storm. He swims to a rock and defies the vengeance of the gods, which so infuriates Poseidon that he strikes the rock with his trident and Ajax falls into the sea and is drowned. In Offenbach's light-hearted opera *La Belle Hélène*, Ajax A and Ajax B feature as the macho element in a delightfully camp reinterpretation of the Trojan War.

Alcestis

Daughter of Pelias, the usurping king of Iolcos who tries and fails to debar Jason as rightful heir. When Jason returns from his quest for the Golden Fleece, Medea, who accompanies him, convinces Pelias's daughters that she can rejuvenate him. Alcestis and her sisters put their father to death on the basis of Medea's promise, but she then refuses to perform, as revenge for Pelias's ill-treatment of Jason. Appalled at their own involuntary

Above This sixteenth-century Italian plate shows Medea inciting Alcestis and her sisters to kill their father.

patricide, the sisters flee to the court of Admetus in Thessaly, and Admetus falls in love with and marries Alcestis. In one version her brother Acastus pursues the sisters with an army and captures Admetus; in another Admetus is afflicted with an incurable disease; in both Alcestis offers her own life to save that of her husband, but is brought back from the underworld by Heracles as a reward for her conjugal devotion. The theme inspired a play by Euripides, who casts some doubt on Admetus's character as a husband; an opera by Gluck, in which Alcestis is rescued by Apollo; and T. S. Eliot's play *The Cocktail Party* in which Celia/Alcestis prefers death, as the greater reality.

Alcinous

King of Phaeacia or Corcyra (Corfu) and father of Nausicaa, who entertains Odysseus in the course of his wanderings and listens to the story of his adventures; the phrase "stories of Alcinous" comes to mean wild traveler's tales in classical usage. He also receives the Argonauts on their return from Colchis, and protects the sorceress Medea from the anger of her father Aeetes, king of Colchis.

Alcithoe

A Theban woman who makes mock of the Greek wine-god Dionysos when he arrives in Boeotia. As punishment she is changed into a bat, and the spindle and yarn with which she is spinning becomes a vine and ivy.

Alcmaeon

One of the heroes of the Theban cycle of early Greek epics, regarded as the ancestor of the Athenian general and statesman Pericles. Alcmaeon is the son of the prophet Amphiarus and Eriphyle. When Eriphyle's brother, Adrastus, king of Argos, declares war on Thebes, Amphiarus tries to avoid accompanying him because he foresees his own death. Betrayed by Eriphyle, he commands Alcmaeon to kill his mother in revenge as soon as he hears the news of his father's death, which Alcmaeon dutifully does. He has served gloriously in the war and led the troops that captured Thebes, but is pursued by the Furies for the murder of his mother, and forbidden to live in the country where this outrage took place. He finally settles on the new alluvial soil at the mouth of the River Phlegeus, and marries the river-god's daughter, Alphesiboea. He gives her the fateful necklace, originally the marriage gift of Harmonia, with which his mother was bribed to betray his father. Still pursued by his mother's ghost, he leaves his wife by order of the oracle to seek further expiation. This time he settles near the River Achelous, and has two sons by the river-god's daughter Callirhoe, to whom he rashly promises the necklace. When he tries to recover it from Alphesiboea, her brothers murder him, and are in turn murdered by Callirhoe's children.

Alcmene

Princess of Argos and mother of Heracles by Zeus. Her father Electryon, king of Argos, promises her in marriage to the Theban prince Amphitryon on condition that he first wages war against the people of Aetolia, who have killed all Electryon's sons. While Amphitryon is away on campaign, Zeus falls for Alcmene, assumes the likeness of Amphitryon, and insinuates himself into Alcmene's bed. To delay the true husband's return and prolong his own pleasure, he orders his messenger, Hermes, to prevent the rising of the sun-god Phoebus for three consecutive days. When Amphitryon returns triumphant, Alcmene realizes she has been deceived and shows him a cup given her by her lover, which Amphitryon recognizes as coming from his booty. Baffled, he consults the prophet Tiresias, who explains what has happened, and Amphitryon is proud to have such a rival, particularly when Alcmene finds she is pregnant.

When Alcmene goes into labor, however, Zeus boasts that he will give absolute power over his neighbors to the child to be born that day. Hera, jealous and infuriated, prolongs the unfortunate Alcmene's labor for three days, the period that Zeus had spent with her, and ensures that the wife of the king of Argos bears a son, Eurystheus, first, two months prematurely. Alcmene finally bears twins, Heracles by Zeus and Iphicles by Amphitryon, but because Eurystheus is the first-born, Heracles is subject to his power and has to perform the Twelve Labors before he can earn his freedom.

Alcyone

Daughter of the wind-god Aeolus, she marries Ceyx, legendary king of Trachis. They are devoted to each other, but Ceyx is drowned as he goes to consult the oracle in Claros. The gods send Alcyone a dream to tell her of her husband's fate, and when she finds his body on the shore in the morning, she throws herself into the sea. They are both changed into birds, who keep the waters of the Aegean sea calm while they build their nests and hatch their chicks, a period of seven, 11 or 14 days, hence the sailors' phrase "halcyon days."

Alecto

One of the Furies, who administer the vengeance of the gods on those who have offended them in Greek myth. Alecto's head is covered with serpents, she holds flaming torches, and she breathes war and plague on those whom the gods condemn.

Alectryon

Servant of Ares, who is stationed at the door as guard while Ares and Aphrodite make love. He falls asleep, however, and the sun-god Apollo discovers the errant lovers in each other's arms and exposes them to the lame god Hephaestus, Aphrodite's husband, and the other gods. In punishment, Ares turns Alectryon into a cock, which must always announce the first crack of dawn.

Below Alcmene in labor with Heracles.

Alope

Daughter of Cercyon, king of Eleusis, she is loved by Poseidon, Greek king of the sea, and has a child by him. Not daring to tell her father, she abandons the baby in the woods, swaddled in a piece of her dress. The boy, Hippothoon, is discovered and fed by mares, and taken by shepherds to Cercyon, who recognizes the garment and condemns his daughter to death. Poseidon is unable to save his lover, but causes her to be transformed into a fountain. Hippothoon grows to manhood and, with the help of Theseus, inherits his grandfather's throne.

Alpheus

God of the famous river of the Peloponnesus, in mainland Greece. Alpheus falls in love with a nymph, Arethusa, and pursues her, but Artemis takes pity on her and changes her into a fountain on Ortygia, a small island off the coast of Sicily. Alpheus is so besotted with her, however, that he plunges under the sea and, without mingling with the salt waters, rises again in Ortygia and joins Arethusa.

Althea

Princess of Pleuron who marries Oeneus, king of Calydon, by whom she has the hero Meleager. At his birth the Fates predict, among other things, that he will live as long as the log then burning on the fire. Althea snatches the log from the fire and carefully guards it, to preserve her son's life. When Artemis sends the Calydonian boar to ravage Oeneus's lands, Meleager is one of the leaders of the great hunt of the Calydonian boar, and kills the creature himself. He gives the skin to Atalanta, however, which makes his uncles, Althea's brothers, jealous, and they plot to steal it from Atalanta. When Meleager learns of their guile, he kills them both. Althea meets their funeral train as she goes to the temple to give thanks for her son's victory, and is so appalled that she immediately throws the log onto the center of the fire, where it is at once consumed, and Meleager dies at the same instant.

Amalthea

Daughter of Melissos, king of Crete, she shelters the infant Zeus when he is

hidden by his mother from the fury of his father, Cronos, who is determined to destroy his children. She sustains the baby god with goat's milk, and is sometimes represented in classical art as a goat. As a reward for her kindness, Zeus places her in the heavens as a constellation, and gives one of her goat's horns to the nymphs. This becomes the cornucopia, the horn of plenty, with the power to give the nymphs their hearts' desire.

Amazons

A race of mythical female warriors supposedly living in south-west Asia, who devote their entire existence to sport and war. They avoid the company of men altogether, only visiting neighboring countries for a few days in order to get pregnant, and returning any male babies to their fathers or, in one gruesome version, strangling them at birth. Classical writers, who regarded the Amazons as representative of the barbarian peoples whom the Greeks defeated or civilized, interpreted their name as meaning that they cut off their right breast (Greek *mazos*) in order to throw the javelin and draw the bow more conveniently. They feature in a number of Greek myths. Heracles makes war on them in order to capture the girdle of their queen, Hippolyta, as one of his Twelve Labors, and Theseus subsequently marries her, for which unforgivable offense the Amazons invade Attica. They also battle with the

Above Amalthea feeds the infant Zeus on goat's milk and honey in his hiding-place on Crete. Nineteenth-century etching.

Trojan king Priam and the hero Bellerophon, but come to the aid of Troy after the death of Hector, and their queen, Penthesilea, is killed by the Greek warrior Achilles, who falls in love with her even as he strikes the fatal blow.

Ammon

The name by which Jupiter, chief of the Roman gods, was worshipped in Libya, a conflation with the Egyptian god Amun. Bacchus supposedly leads an army into the deserts of Africa, where they are threatened with death by drought until Jupiter appears to his son and shows him a fountain. In gratitude Bacchus builds a temple to Jupiter Ammon, and representations of the god show him with the horns of a ram. The temple, nine days' journey from Alexandria, contained a famous oracle which was consulted by many heroes, including Heracles and Perseus, but when it pronounced Alexander the Great to be the son of Jupiter, its credibility was destroyed, for he was well known to be the son of Philip of Macedon, and the site was gradually abandoned.

Amor

See Cupid, Eros.

Amphiarus

A famed Theban prophet, who is at the hunt of the Calydonian boar (see Meleager) and accompanies the Argonauts on their expedition to recover the Golden Fleece. For his knowledge of the future, he is sometimes acclaimed the son of Apollo. He marries Eriphyle, sister of Adrastus, king of Argos, and they have two sons, Alcmaeon and Amphilocus. When Adrastus, urged on by Oedipus's displaced son Polynices, declares war on Oedipus's kingdom of Thebes, Amphiarus foresees that they will lose and he will meet his death, and he tries to hide. But his wife is bribed by Polynices to betray him; Amphiarus has undertaken to abide by her decision in any dispute with Adrastus. Amphiarus therefore goes reluctantly to war, charging his son Alcmaeon to kill his mother when he gets news of his father's death. Amphiarus in his chariot is swallowed up by the earth, on the order of Zeus, as he tries to escape. A shrine and oracle is established at the spot where he vanishes; supplicants have to give up food for a day and wine for three days, purify themselves in a nearby fountain, sacrifice a ram and then sleep on its skin, and they will receive in a dream the oracle's answer to their quest.

Below Jupiter Ammon, a Romanized version of the Egyptian Amun.

Amphion

Son of Zeus and the Theban princess Antiope, who gives birth to Amphion and his brother Zetus on the slopes of Mount Citheron, where she has fled to avoid her father's anger. The twins are saved and brought up by a shepherd, and Amphion proves to have such an extraordinary musical talent that Hermes himself teaches him and gives him the first lyre. His mother is cruelly treated by her husband Lycus's first wife, Dirce, and the twins in vengeance besiege Thebes, put Lycus to death, and tie Dirce to the tail of a wild bull, which drags her through the wilderness until she dies. Amphion plays so exquisitely on his lyre that the very stones move, and rise to form a wall round Thebes, which he then rules peacefully.

Amphitrite

Greek sea-goddess, with whom Poseidon falls in love when he sees her dancing on the island of Naxos. She resists his advances and flees to Atlas for protection, but Poseidon sends all his sea creatures to look for her. At last a dolphin finds her, and pleads Poseidon's cause so eloquently that she agrees to marry him. The triumph of Amphitrite, riding in a dolphin-drawn carriage, is a frequent subject of Roman mosaics.

Below The music of Amphion raises the walls of Thebes, although his lyre is shown as a violin.

sequently identified with the Greek god Zeus and the Roman Jupiter, as Jupiter Ammon.

Ancaeus

A son of Poseidon, he is one of the Argonauts who sail to recover the Golden Fleece, and serves as pilot of the ship *Argo*. He subsequently establishes a kingdom in Ionia, where he is known for the hard labor he demands in his vineyards. One of his servants tells him that he will never taste of his own produce; he is holding a wine cup at the time, and challenges the speaker to prove his point. At that moment a wild boar enters his vineyard and begins to trample the vines, and Ancaeus is killed trying to drive it away.

Anchises

A Trojan prince, beloved of Aphrodite, who takes the form of a nymph in order to enjoy a relationship with him on the slopes of Mount Ida. When she becomes pregnant, she forbids Anchises ever to reveal the truth, on pain of death by thunderbolt, and the child, the future hero Aeneas, is brought up by shepherds and then entrusted to the centaur Chiron. Anchises, curiously, then vanishes

Left Andromeda rescued from the sea serpent by Perseus. Roman wall-painting.

Below The parting of Andromache and Hector.

Amphitryon

King of Thebes, whose wife Alcmene loses her virginity to Zeus in the guise of Amphitryon, and bears twin sons, Heracles, son of Zeus, and Iphicles, son of Amphitryon. Sensibly, on having the situation explained to him by a helpful oracle, Amphitryon is flattered rather than appalled, and raises both children as his own. The comic possibilities of the situation, with the willing lady and the two lovers, have inspired many dramatists.

Amun

Egyptian ram-headed god, often shown as a bearded man wearing a cap with two plumes. A sky-god, Amun is regarded as one of the creators of the universe, and is sub-

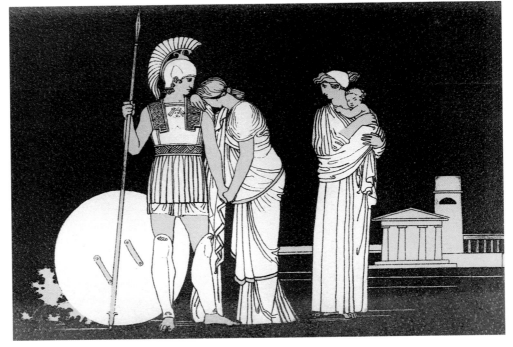

Andromache

The devoted wife of the Trojan hero Hector, who is so fond of her husband that she feeds his horses with her own hand. In the *Iliad* she is shown as the archetype of all women who passively suffer the horrors of war. Her farewell scene with Hector, before he is killed in battle by the Greek warrior Achilles, is one of the most tender and touching in the whole epic. As Troy burns, she manages to save her only son, Astyanax, from the flames, only to see him thrown from the walls by Achilles. After the sack of Troy, when the unfortunate women are shared out by the conquerors as the spoils of war, Andromache falls to the lot of Neoptolemus, son of Achilles, who takes her home to Epirus. His wife Hermione becomes jealous of the foreign princess (who in some versions has a son by Neoptolemus) and plots to kill her while Neoptolemus is away; this is the subject of the tragedy *Andromaque* by the seventeenth-century playwright Racine. Andromache survives, however, and after Neoptolemus's death she marries Helenus, one of Hector's brothers. Virgil has Aeneas meeting Andromache and Helenus during his prolonged voyage to Italy.

Andromeda

Ethiopian princess, whose mother Cassiopia rashly boasts that her daughter is more beautiful than Poseidon's daughters the Nereids, at which a furious Poseidon sends a sea monster to ravage the country. Her father is told that the monster will only be placated by the sacrifice of Andromeda, and so she is tied naked to a rock and left to be devoured. Fortunately Perseus, wearing the winged shoes of Hermes, flies past in the nick of time, on his way home from killing the Gorgon, and falls in love with Andromeda. He promises to rescue her and destroy the monster in return for her hand in marriage, and turns the monster to stone by showing it the head of the Gorgon. The damsel in distress theme has been popular with painters for centuries. Two Roman wall-paintings from Pompeii, dating from the first century AD, show Andromeda as umistakably black, whereas paintings by Renaissance and later masters, such as Titian and Ingres, represent her as the archetypal fair-haired, blue-eyed heroine of a fairy tale.

A. Dieperbeck fig.

Andromede .

— κεφαλὼ ὃ λιθογλώοιο Μεδούσης
Κυφίζων, πεἵμεβρν ὅλον πετρώσαΐξ κῆτος.
Δεσμοις δ' Ανδρομέδης δὲελύσατο. —

Nonnus lib. 47.

Above Unusually, this seventeenth-century engraving shows the Ethiopian princess Andromeda as black.

from the story of Troy until the end, by which time he is so old and frail that the devoted Aeneas has to carry him from the burning city. He accompanies Aeneas on the first part of his voyage, retold by Virgil in the *Aeneid*, and dies in Sicily, having forgotten Aphrodite's prohibition and finally boasted of his conquest.

Androgeos

Son of King Minos of Crete and Pasiphae. A famous wrestler, he attends the games at Athens and overcomes every opponent. He becomes such a favorite of the people that the Athenian king, Aegeus, grows jealous and distrustful, and has him assassinated on his way to Thebes. Minos declares war on Athens in revenge, and peace is concluded only after a debilitating seven-year war, and on condition that Athens send an annual tribute of seven boys and seven girls, all virgins, as prey for the Minotaur, the monstrous half man, half bull. When Theseus arrives in Athens and is revealed as the son of Aegeus, he volunteers to be one of the victims, and succeeds in killing the Minotaur.

Anius

Son of the sun-god Apollo and the earth-goddess Rhea, he is king of the sacred island of Delos. He has three daughters, to whom the fertility-god Dionysos gives the power of changing whatever they please into wine, corn, and oil. When Agamemnon leads the united Greek armies to the Trojan War, he wants to take Anius's daughters to keep the Greeks supplied, but they supplicate Dionysos to be spared this doubtful privilege, and he changes them into doves.

Anna

Roman goddess, the sister of Dido, queen of Carthage, who flees to Italy after Dido's death and the fall of Carthage. She meets Aeneas, who has loved and abandoned Dido, and he gives her an honorable reception, but his wife Lavinia becomes jealous and plots against Anna. Warned by Dido in a dream, Anna takes refuge with the River Numicius and becomes a river-goddess, ordering the inhabitants of the region to call her Anna Perenna, because she will remain for ever under water. The Romans celebrated her festival on 15th March, and sacrificed to her to obtain a long life.

Antaeus

A giant, son of Poseidon and Ge (the earth). He lives in Libya and challenges all comers to a wrestling match, boasting that he will build a temple to his father with the skulls of the defeated. Every time he is thrown to the ground, he is given renewed strength by this contact with his mother, and is only finally defeated by Heracles, on his way to the Garden of the Hesperides, who lifts him from the earth and squeezes him to death.

Antenor

Trojan prince, who advises Priam to return the Greek queen Helen when she is brought to Troy by her lover, Paris. He also entertains Odysseus and Menelaus, when they come as envoys requesting Helen's return, and may have secretly communicated with the

Left The giant Antaeus, invincible as long as he remains in contact with his mother, the earth.

Greeks during the ten-year war that follows. Certainly when Troy is sacked, Antenor's life and property are protected by the victorious Greeks.

Anteros

Son of Aphrodite and Ares, younger brother of Eros, and the god of mutual love. Aphrodite complains to Themis that her son Eros always remains a child, and is told that if he has a brother he will grow up rapidly. As soon as Anteros is born, Eros's strength grows and his wings enlarge, but when his brother is at a distance, his strength decreases again, implying that passion thrives on requited love.

Above Antigone's sister Ismene tries to dissuade her from her course.

Anticlea

Daughter of the famous robber Autolycus, who is seduced by the crafty prince Sisyphus in revenge for her father's theft of some cattle. She marries Laertes, king of Ithaca, but is already pregnant with the hero Odysseus, who becomes Laertes' heir.

Antigone

Daughter of Oedipus, king of Thebes, by his own mother Jocasta. After Oedipus has blinded himself on discovering his sin, and his sons Polynices and Eteocles have seized the throne, Antigone acts as her father's guide in his wanderings, although already betrothed to Haemon, son of Jocasta's brother Creon. When at last Oedipus dies, Antigone returns to Thebes, where Polynices and Eteocles have quarreled and killed each other. Creon, now king, buries Eteocles with full honors, but Polynices has led an army against his city and is condemned to rot unburied. Antigone insists on burying his body, and is in turn condemned to be buried alive, but kills herself before the sentence can be carried out. Haemon stabs himself on her tomb. Antigone did not play a significant role in the Theban saga until Sophocles wrote his Theban trilogy, devoting *Antigone* to her story, and the conflict she feels between conscience and family loyalty on the one hand and the dictates of the law on the other.

Antiope

Princess of Thebes, whom Zeus seduces in satyr form. She bears him twin sons, Amphion and Zetus, but is forced by her father to abandon them on the mountainside, where they are rescued by shepherds. She flees to Sicyon and marries the king, Epopeus, but is pursued by her father and her uncle, Lycus, who inherits the crown of Thebes, defeats and kills Epopeus, and forces Antiope to marry him. Antiope is imprisoned and tormented by Lycus's first wife, Dirce, but finally escapes to her sons, who avenge her. The subject

Below Zeus seduces Antiope in the form of a satyr.

Above Anubis weighs the heart of the deceased against Maat's feather of truth.

of the princess and the satyr, like that of Leda and the swan, appealed to painters; there are versions by Titian, Coreggio and Watteau, among others.

Anubis

Jackal-headed funerary god of Egypt, who is considered the chief god of the dead before Osiris rises to prominence, and continues to be the patron of embalming and guardian of the tomb.

Aphaia

Greek goddess worshipped in the Mediterranean island of Aegina, and identified with Artemis and the Cretan goddess Britomart. The great temple dedicated to her still stands in ruins on the summit of Aegina; the pediment contained some of the most masterly sculpture of the archaic period, illustrating the Trojan War.

Aphrodite

Greek goddess of beauty, love, laughter, and reproduction, the source of all graces and pleasures and the patroness of prostitutes. She was later identified with the Roman Venus, and was worshipped particularly at Paphos in Cyprus, Cythera, Corinth, and on Mount Eryx in Sicily. There are various versions of her birth, the most famous being that she is born from the sea foam after Cronos has castrated his father Uranus and thrown his genitals into the sea. She is wafted ashore on Cyprus by the zephyrs, wind-gods, and received there by the seasons, daughters of Zeus and Themis, a scene most memorably represented by Botticelli in *The Birth of Venus*. A more prosaic story has it that she is the daughter of Zeus and the nymph Dione.

When she arrives on Mount Olympus, all the gods vie for her favors, and she is married to the lame god Hephaestus in punishment for refusing Zeus himself. Goddess of sexual love rather than matrimonial loyalty (the province of Hera), she is anything but faithful to Hephaestus, and in early Greek mythology is depicted as wholly irresponsible in her amours. She is mother of Eros, Anteros, and Hermione

Above Venus and Cupid by the French painter François Boucher.

Left Aphrodite of Melos or the *Venus de Milo*, late second century BC.

by Ares; Hermaphrodite by Hermes; Priapus by Dionysos; and Eryx by Poseidon. Hephaestus is so infuriated by her blatant affair with Ares that he entraps them naked in a net on his own bed, and exposes them to the ridicule of the other gods. Zeus makes her fall in love with the Trojan Anchises in punishment for her mockery of the gods, and she bears him a son, Aeneas, whose interests she protects throughout the Trojan War. Other humans who benefit from her interest include Jason, whom she assists in the quest for the Golden Fleece, and Paris, who awards her the golden apple designated "for the fairest," over which she, Hera, and Athena dispute (see Paris).

While generous to her favorites, the Greek goddess of love is inevitably cruel and capricious (she becomes more serious, romantic, and benevolent in her Roman guise; see Venus), and particularly vengeful and unforgiving to both gods and mortals who offend her. She makes Myrrha fall in love with her father; Pasiphae, queen of Crete, falls in love with a bull and conceives the Minotaur; Theseus's son Hippolytus, who believes himself above the power of love, is falsely accused by his stepmother and cursed by his father. When the women of Lemnos neglect the rites of Aphrodite, she makes them smell so foul that their husbands abandon them, and is only persuaded to relent when the Argonauts arrive and Hephaestus intercedes with her. The Muse Calliope, who adjudicates in the dispute between Aphrodite and Persephone over their rival claims to Adonis, is punished by the death of her son Orpheus. The goddess of the dawn, Eos or Aurora, who has a fling with Aphrodite's lover Ares, is made to fall in love with two mortals, Cephalus and Tithonus.

The power of Aphrodite over the heart is reinforced by a celebrated belt or girdle, which gives beauty, grace, and elegance even to the most deformed, exciting and renewing love. Even Hera is reduced to borrowing the girdle of Aphrodite to regain her power to attract Zeus, while Aphrodite herself, however appalling her infidelities, can always reduce her husband Hephaestus to pathetic surrender when wearing it.

Among the Greeks she was a favored and much lauded deity; the most famous work of the celebrated Greek sculptor Praxiteles was the *Aphrodite of Knidos*, now only known from Roman copies. The *Venus de Milo* is based on Praxiteles' work, while the various Roman works showing a *Crouching Aphrodite* by her bath are also based on a classical Greek original.

Apollo

One of the 12 Olympian gods, Apollo is known, unusually, by the same name to both Greeks and Romans. He is the god of light and the sun, and is given the epithet Phoebus (shining). He is also god of prophecy and divination,

Below The *Apollo Belvedere*, Roman copy of a Greek statue showing Apollo as an archer.

having received from his father Zeus the power of seeing into the future, as well as of flocks and herdsmen, archery, medicine, oratory, and all the arts, above all music, and he rules directly over the nine Muses. His mother, the Titan Leto, one of Zeus's many amours, is pursued by the wrath of Hera and unable to find anywhere to give birth, finally taking shelter on the floating island of Delos, where she bears Apollo and his twin sister Artemis (Diana to the Romans).

Delos remains sacred to Apollo, but he soon leaves the island in search of a place to establish his own oracular shrine, having miraculously grown to his full stature in a few days on the diet of nectar and ambrosia fed him by the goddess Themis. He comes to Delphi, where he first has to overcome the Python, a huge serpent with prophesying powers, who is the daughter of Ge, the earth-goddess (the name Python is also sometimes given to the serpent sent by Hera to pursue Leto). Apollo kills the Python, earning the title Pythian Apollo, and the oracle at Delphi becomes the most important in the Greek world, renowned for its gnomic and ambiguous utterances.

Apollo, however, has to do penance for his killing of the Python, as she was the daughter of a goddess, and is banished to the Vale of Tempe, where the Delphians send envoys to him every eighth year. He is also condemned by Zeus on another occasion to spend a long period in the world of humanity, in punishment for his killing of the Cyclops, who in turn had made the thunderbolts with which Zeus killed Apollo's son Asclepius. At first Zeus is so enraged that he threatens to cast Apollo into Tartarus. He then relents, and condemns Apollo simply to a year's servitude. Apollo works as a herdsman for Admetus, king of Thessaly, and rewards him for his gentle treatment by giving all his cows twins and promising him eternal life.

When Heracles kills his friend Iphitus in an attack of madness, it is to Delphi that he goes to be cured and purified. At first the priestess refuses to help him, as the crime is so heinous. Heracles, enraged, seizes the sacred tripod which stands at the shrine, and Apollo appears to protect it. The two gods struggle until Zeus separates his warring sons with a thunderbolt. Apollo advises Heracles that he can be cured of his madness and salved of his sin by being thrown into slavery for three years. Since Apollo himself has already endured a period of servitude, Heracles is prepared to accept this verdict, and in gratitude spreads the worship of Apollo.

In helping Poseidon to build the walls of Troy for the Trojan king Laomedan, Apollo undertakes a voluntary act of service for a mortal. There is a fee involved, however, which Laomedan refuses to pay, bringing on his newly created city a plague sent by Apollo and a sea serpent sent by Poseidon (see Hesione). Despite this bad faith, Apollo continues to champion the Trojans, perhaps reflecting his own eastern origins, and gives the gift of pro-

Above Apollo with his lyre, pouring a libation. Fifth-century BC Greek dish.

He is more effective as an instrument of vengeance. The curse he lays on Cassandra resonates throughout the Trojan War. When the Greeks carry off Chryseis, the daughter of his priest Chryses, he punishes them with a plague, and it is he who kills the Greek hero Achilles with an arrow shot from the bow of the Trojan prince Paris. He orders Orestes to kill his mother Clytemnestra for the murder of her own husband, but is constant in his favorites, for when Orestes comes to trial before the court of the Areopagus at Athens, Apollo himself appears to defend him against the charges of the Furies and Clytemnestra's ghost.

One of the few classical gods to be represented in medieval manuscripts, Apollo usually appears as a doctor or scholar, but from the Renaissance onward he is represented either in his function as a god of the arts, surrounded by the Muses on Mount Parnassus, or as a lover. Louis XIV of France termed himself *Le Roi Soleil*, taking Apollo as his emblem and instructing the artist Lebrun to decorate the Galerie d'Apollon in the Louvre Palace on the same theme.

phecy to Laomedan's granddaughter Cassandra, though when she still refuses him her bed, he ordains that she will never be believed.

Despite his identification with light, healing, and the arts, Apollo seems to have been notably unlucky in love. The mother of Asclepius, Coronis, marries a mortal while she is pregnant with the sun-god's child. Apollo cannot bear to punish her himself, but asks his sister Artemis to kill her, and snatches the unborn baby from her dead body. The nymph Daphne flees from him and is turned into a laurel tree in preference to accepting him as a lover; Marpessa, when given the choice between Apollo and the mortal Idas, prefers Idas; the nymph Sinope asks a favor before succumbing, and requests perpetual virginity. Only Cyrene, daughter of the king of the Lapiths (or, in some versions, a river-nymph) and renowned as a virgin huntress, seems to have proved co-operative; Apollo carries her off to Africa, where she bears him Aristaeus, god of cattle and fruit trees, and the prophet Idmon.

With men Apollo does not appear much more successful; the beautiful Hyathincus is killed by a discus and turns into the hyacinth flower, while Cyparissus is so distressed when he kills a tame stag that Apollo turns him into a cypress tree to give him peace.

Arachne

An expert weaver, daughter of Idmon the dyer, of Colophon in Lydia. She is so convinced of her skill that she chal-

Below Arachne transformed into a spider by Athena.

lenges Athena, mistress of the art, to a competition. Athena comes to her in the form of an old woman, warning her not to take on the gods, but Arachne persists. Athena resumes her own shape and weaves a tapestry showing the fate that befalls presumptuous mortals. Arachne responds by creating a weaving depicting the amours of Zeus with Europa, Antiope, Leda, Danae, Alcmene, etc. So masterly and pointed is this that Athena, daughter of Zeus, tears it apart and beats Arachne over the head with her shuttle. In despair, Arachne hangs herself and is transformed into a spider, retaining her skill as a weaver but losing her battle with the unreasonable gods.

Arcas

Son of Zeus and the nymph Callisto. Callisto is transformed into a bear, and Arcas is seized from her body and becomes king of Arcadia, where he teaches his people how to weave, grow corn, and make bread. He marries Erato, a dryad or tree-nymph, who asks his help in diverting a river away from the roots of the tree which is her lifeline. In one version of the story he sees a bear entering the temple of Zeus and kills it, only to find that it was his mother. In pity, Zeus turns Callisto into the constellation of the Great Bear, and Arcas into the Little Bear.

Archemorus

Son of the king of Nemaea, brought up by his nurse Hypsipyle. When the army of Adrastus marches against Thebes, they meet Hypsipyle and demand that she shows them a spring where they can drink. To do so she places the infant Archemorus on the ground, and when she returns she finds him dead of a serpent bite, portending the disastrous outcome of the attack on Thebes (see Adrastus). The Greeks were so struck by the tragedy that they instituted the Nemaean games in honor of the dead prince.

Ares

The Greek god of war, later equated with the Roman god Mars and never very popular in myth. The only son of Zeus by his lawful consort Hera, he has a long-standing liaison with Aphrodite, by whom he fathers Harmonia and the twins Phobos (panic) and Deimos (fear), and is caught in her bed by her husband Hephaestus (see Aphrodite), much to the amusement of the other gods. He also has a daughter, Alcippe, with the mortal Aglaurus, of whom he is sufficiently fond, or possessive, to strike instantly dead Halirrhothius, son of Poseidon, when he rapes her near the Acropolis in Athens. Poseidon summons Ares to trial for murder before the council of the gods. The trial is conducted at the same spot, henceforth called the Areopagus, or Ares' hill, and Ares is acquitted.

His main interest is warfare, and he is shown as boastful and impulsive, easily outwitted by Athena, the goddess of strategy and courage. During the wars between the Olympian gods and the Titans, Ares is imprisoned in a bronze jar by the giants for 15 months, until Hermes discovers his plight and releases him. In the Trojan War he supports the Trojans, but is wounded by the Greek Diomedes, with the aid of Athena, and complains bitterly to Zeus. He tries to join the battle after Zeus has forbidden any further intervention, and is forcibly restrained by Athena. He hurls his spear at her, but it bounces harmlessly off her shield, and she knocks him down with a stone. To the Greeks he is always a slightly ridiculous figure, bombastic and irrational; the Romans accorded much greater dignity and veneration to Mars.

Arethusa

Greek wood-nymph, who bathes in the River Alpheus and excites the passion of the river-god. He pursues her to the sea, where Artemis opens a passage for her to Sicily and transforms her into a fountain.

Argonauts

Warriors who sail with Jason in the *Argo* to Colchis on the Black Sea, to recover the Golden Fleece. The story is one of the oldest Greek legends, known from several sources, and may commemorate a real prehistoric journey. The *Argo* is the first longship, with 50 oars and a prow made from a tree felled by Athena in the sacred grove of Dodona, which has the gift of prophesy. As freemen, the Argonauts each man an oar, a custom continued in the historical Athenian navy.

Ariadne

Daughter of Minos, king of Crete, she falls in love with Theseus when he comes to Crete to kill the Minotaur, and guides him out of the Labyrinth with a ball of thread. He promises to marry

Right The Argonauts pass through the Symplegades, or clashing rocks.

Below Ariadne abandoned on Naxos by Theseus. Roman wall-painting.

her and they flee together, but he abandons her on the island of Dia (Naxos), and she is rescued by the wine-god Dionysos. He gives her a garland of seven stars, which becomes the Corona Borealis.

Aristaeus

Greek shepherd and bee-keeper, the son of Apollo and Cyrene, who lives an idyllic rustic life with his wife Autonoe and son Actaeon, until one day he sees

Below Classical Greek statue of Artemis, the hunter-goddess.

and pursues a beautiful woman. This is Eurydice, wife of the great singer and musician Orpheus; as Eurydice runs from him, she is bitten by a snake and dies. Soon after, Aristaeus's bees begin to die, and he cannot understand why. His mother advises him to capture the sea-god Proteus, who has the power of prophecy, and Proteus explains that he must appease the shade of Eurydice by sacrificing four bulls and four heifers. As soon as this is done, the bees recover. After the death of Actaeon, however, the inconsolable Aristaeus travels through Greece teaching the skills of husbandry, com-

petes with Dionysos to see whether men prefer wine or mead, and lives riotously with the wine-god in Thrace, receiving diving honors on his death.

Artemis

Greek virgin-goddess of hunting and archery, one of the 12 Olympian gods and the twin sister of Apollo, Artemis seems to derive from an earlier earth-goddess cult. The great Artemisium, or temple of Artemis, at Ephesus contained a multi-breasted statue of the goddess as a fertility figure, and she is also the defender of the new-born. In Greek mythology, however, she is irrevocably chaste and punishes any attempt to seduce herself or her followers, transforming Callisto into a bear after she succumbs to Zeus. Most of the stories told about Artemis relate to hunting; she causes the deaths of the huntsmen Actaeon and Orion, and sends the wild boar of Calydon as a punishment for neglected rites, leading to the death of Meleager.

Artemis and Apollo are the children of the nymph Leto, who is pursued by the vengeful Hera and can find no place to give birth. Artemis is finally born either with Apollo on the floating island of Delos, or before him on Ortygia. Both gods remain devotedly loyal to their mother and implacable to her enemies; see Niobe, Tityus. The jealousy of Hera pursues them both; in the *Iliad*, Hera is shown insulting Artemis, spilling her arrows and boxing her ears, whereupon Artemis rushes to Zeus and sits weeping on his knee. She is held to bring natural death to women, just as Apollo does to men, and becomes associated with the witch-goddess Hecate. She is also identified with the moon, as Apollo with the sun, and takes on attributes of the moon-goddess Selene.

Ascanius

Son of the Trojan hero Aeneas by his first wife Creusa. Ascanius is a child when Troy falls, and accompanies his father on the lengthy voyage that ends in Italy. Latin writers also called him Julius, and the Julian family claimed descent through him from Aphrodite.

Asclepius

Greek god of medicine, son of Apollo by Coronis, adopted by the Romans as

Aesculapius. Asclepius is removed from his mother's womb after she has been killed by Artemis, and given to the centaur Chiron to raise; alternatively he is abandoned by his mother near Epidaurus and found by a goatherd, who recognizes him as a god by the rays of light emanating from his head. He accompanies the Argonauts on their voyage, and restores so many men to life with his medical skill that Hades, god of the underworld, complains to Zeus, who strikes Asclepius dead with a thunderbolt. He receives divine honors after his death, and his chief shrines are established at Epidaurus and Kos. His cult was widespread in Greece, and each shrine had baths and a gymnasium for treatment, but the most important part of the ritual was to pass the night in the temple, awaiting a message from the god. The serpent is sacred to him as a symbol of prudence and foresight, and he is usually represented in Greek art as bearded, holding in one hand a staff round which is wreathed a serpent, and with the other resting on a serpent.

Astarte

Syrian mother-goddess, the consort and sister of Baal and identified by the Egyptians with Hathor and by the Romans with Venus. She is an aggressive deity, portrayed with helmet, battle-ax and spear, wading in the blood of her human victims.

Asterius

King of Crete, who marries Europa when she comes to the island after being carried off by Zeus, and adopts her three sons, Minos, Rhadamanthys, and Sarpedon, as his own. He has one daughter, Crete, with Europa, and is succeeded by Minos.

Astraea

Greek goddess of justice, variously described as daughter of Saturn's brother Titan and Eos, or of Zeus and Themis. In the mythical golden age of the heroes, she lives on earth, but is driven to Olympus by the wickedness of the succeeding ages, and is placed among the stars as the constellation Virgo. She is represented as a stern and majestic figure, holding a sword and a pair of scales.

Above Asclepius, Greek god of medicine, with the serpent sacred to him.

Astyanax

The son of Hector and Andromache, a child at the time of the Trojan War, shown in the *Iliad* as being afraid of the horsehair plume on his father's helmet. When Troy falls he is flung to his death from the walls, because Odysseus has warned that no male descendant of the Trojan king Priam should be spared.

Astydamia

Wife of Acastus, king of Iolcos, she falls in love with Peleus when he visits their court. When he refuses her, she falsely accuses him of rape, causing her husband to leave him for dead in the mountains. He survives to dethrone Acastus and kill Astydamia.

Atalanta

One of the few genuine heroines in Greek mythology, born in Arcadia but abandoned by her father, who wanted a son. She is suckled by a bear and grows up to be a famous huntress, pledged to virginity. When two cen-

Above Atalanta joins the hunt of the Calydonian boar, on this Roman mosaic from Tunisia.

taurs try to rape her, she kills them with her arrows, and begs to be allowed to accompany the Argonauts on their quest, but Jason refuses her on the grounds that her presence will cause jealousies in the all-male crew. She does, however, join in the hunt for the Calydonian boar (see Meleager), despite the protests of some of the participants, and draws first blood. Meleager, who loves her, kills the boar and gives the hide to her, but his mother's brothers try to take it from her. Meleager kills them, and is in turn killed by Althaea, his mother.

Atalanta's fame grows until her father, variously described as king of Arcadia and of Boeotia, recognizes and acknowledges her. He, however, insists that she marry, and to avoid this undesirable fate she stipulates that she will only marry the man who can run faster than her, and if he is slower he must die. Despite this hazard, many men are inspired by her beauty to try, and all fail, even though she runs clothed and armed and they run naked. Finally Hippomenes, aided by Aphrodite, beats her by rolling the three apples of the Hesperides that the goddess has given him across Atalanta's path. She is distracted by the divine fruit, stops to pick them up, and is overtaken. The union is a happy one; so happy, in fact, that the lovers consummate it within the precinct of the temple of Cybele, which so offends the goddess that she turns them into lions.

Ate

In later Greek mythology, Ate is the personification of evil and stupidity, the daughter of Zeus and Eris (Strife). It is through her machinations that Zeus's son Heracles has to perform his Twelve Labors for Eurystheus. This makes Zeus so angry that he casts her out of Olympus, and she instead lives on earth, spreading discord among mankind.

Athamas

Son of the wind-god Aeolus and king of Boeotia, he marries the nymph Nephele and their children are Phrixus and Helle. Presently he abandons Nephele and marries Ino, sister of Semele, who has two sons by Athamas and becomes jealous of his children from the earlier marriage. When Athamas sends to the Delphic oracle to discover why the harvest has failed, Ino bribes the returning messengers to tell him that Phrixus must be sacrificed to avert a famine. This the credulous father is about to do when Zeus, who abhors human sacrifice, sends a golden-fleeced ram to rescue both Phrixus and his sister Helle.

Subsequently Ino and Athamas foster Dionysos, Semele's son by Zeus, which brings down the vengeance of Zeus's consort Hera upon them and she drives them mad. Athamas kills one son with an arrow, while Ino leaps into the sea holding the other son, and they both drown. Athamas has thus lost two families, and is banished from his kingdom. He consults the oracle at Delphi, this time in person, and is told he may settle where wild animals invite him to share their food. Wandering through Thessaly, he comes across a pack of wolves devouring a lamb. They run away at his approach, and so he settles there. When he is very old, his grandson Cytissorus, son of Phrixus, returns with the Argonauts, and becomes his heir.

Athena

Greek virgin warrior-goddess, the personification of wisdom and patron of arts and crafts, one of the 12 Olympian gods. She is the daughter of Zeus by his first wife, the Titan Metis. While Metis is pregnant with Athena, Zeus is warned that the next child will be mightier than himself, and so he swallows Metis. Some time later he develops such an agonizing headache that he commands Hephaestus to split his head open with an axe, and Athena springs out, already fully armed and ready for battle. She plays an essential role in the battle between the gods and giants (see Giants), killing Pallas and immobilizing Enceladus by throwing

the island of Sicily on top of him. While the war-god Ares represents mindless violence, Athena is the patron of military strategy and cunning.

As a deity of war and warriors, she lends her support to many courageous adventurers, including Perseus, who gives her the Gorgon's head to wear on her shield, Bellerophon, Heracles, and Jason. Offended by the Judgment of Paris (see Paris), she supports the Greeks in the Trojan War, but is outraged by Ajax's rape of Cassandra in her own temple during the sack of Troy and withdraws her favor from the Greeks. As they return to their homes, she sends a savage storm which scatters their ships and drowns many of them. Only Odysseus continues to receive her protection, and she ensures that he finally reaches home despite the intense hostility of Poseidon.

Athena also competes with Poseidon for possession of Attica, in mainland Greece. Each gives the land the most precious gift at their disposal; Poseidon points his trident at the Acropolis, the local defensible high point, and a salt-water spring appears, while Athena plants the first olive tree. The tribunal appointed by Zeus to mediate decides in favor of Athena and she becomes the patroness of the city,

Left Athena, represented on a Greek wine-vase or amphora.

Below Athena Lemnia. Roman copy of an original by the Greek sculptor Phidias.

which henceforth is called Athens. The great temple of the Parthenon is built in her honor (*parthenos*, virgin), and inside it is placed the gold and ivory statue by the fifth-century BC sculptor Phidias, known only from copies. Ericthonius, the first king of Athens, is fostered by Athena after Hephaestus, having failed to persuade the goddess to sleep with him, instead fathers Ericthonius on Ge, the earth.

Above The giant Atlas weighed down by the weight of the world.

Atlas

One of the Titans, originally thought of as the guardian of the pillars of heaven, and later believed to hold the sky up on his own shoulders. In one early legend, he is king of Mauritania and is visited by Perseus, returning from slaying the

Above The entrance to the "treasury of Atreus," actually a tholos tomb on the acropolis of Mycenae.

Gorgon. Atlas has been warned by an oracle that he will be dethroned by a son of Zeus, and so refuses Perseus hospitality. Perseus holds up the dead Gorgon's head and Atlas is turned to stone and identified with Mount Atlas. In the story of Heracles, however, he is a real giant, who agrees to fetch the apples of the Hesperides for Heracles if the hero will take his place supporting the sky for a while. When he returns with the apples, he plans to leave Heracles forever in his place, but is tricked into resuming his burden.

Atreus

King of Mycenae, whose father Pelops is cursed for the murder of Myrtilus, and who in turn brings another curse upon himself and his family. The troubled house of Atreus is at the heart of many of the most famous Greek myths.

Atreus and his brother Thyestes are persuaded by their mother to murder their half-brother Chrysippus, for which they are banished from Mycenae and flee to Argos. Atreus marries Aerope and their sons are Agamemnon and Menelaus, but Aerope then falls in love with her brother-in-law Thyestes and bears him twins. In revenge, Atreus serves the bodies of these boys to Thyestes at a feast, telling him the truth only after he has devoured the flesh of his own children. The sun turns back in its course in horror at such an unnatural deed, and Thyestes curses the whole family of Atreus.

The evil complications have only just begun, however, for Atreus, having renounced Aerope, subsequently marries Thyestes' daughter Pelopea, who is already pregnant, raped, although she does not know it, by her own father. She bears a son, Aegisthus, who is brought up by Atreus. Atreus's sons by Aerope, Agamemnon, and Menelaus, capture Thyestes at Delphi and bring him back to Mycenae, where Atreus imprisons him and sends Aegisthus to kill him. Thyestes recognizes his son by the sword which he gave Pelopea, however, and reveals himself as Aegisthus's father, where-upon Aegisthus returns to Atreus and kills him. The horrendous curse continues to work through subsequent generations. See Agamemnon, Clytemnestra, Orestes.

Attis

Shepherd loved by the Phrygian mother-goddess Cybele in a version of the ubiquitous death and regeneration myth which became popular among the Romans. There are a number of variants on the story of Attis and Cybele. In the oldest, the other gods castrate the hermaphrodite deity Agdistis, whose genitals land in the earth and grow into an almond tree. The fruit of this tree falls into the lap of the nymph Nana, who conceives and bears a son, Attis. Attis is abandoned, reared by goats, and found among the reeds by Cybele, who is Agdistis in female form. She becomes so passionately enamored of him that she cannot bear the possibility of his being unfaithful (alternatively, having promised to be true to Cybele, he falls in love with the nymph Sagaritis and is duly punished). Whatever her motivation, the goddess makes Attis insane, and in his madness he castrates himself and dies of the wound. Overcome with grief, Cybele turns him into a pine tree, or in some versions raises him from the dead for a part of the year.

Auge

Lover of Heracles, she bears a son, Telephus, by him and hides him in the temple. Hera, jealous of Zeus's love children, sends a plague to devastate the land, and so Auge's father Aleus, king of Arcadia, learns the truth. Furious, he exposes the child on a hillside and sends his daughter to Nauplius, one of the Argonauts, king of Nauplia and a slave trader, with instructions either to drown her or to sell her into slavery. Nauplius instead passes her on to Teuthras, king of Mysia, who adopts her as a daughter. Some time after, Teuthras's lands are invaded, and he offers Auge as a reward to whomever will rid him of his enemy. It is Telephus who wins the prize, but Auge instinctively shrinks from him, takes a sword to bed, and tries to stab him, but is prevented by a large snake (a creature sacred to Heracles). When Telephus in turn threatens to kill her, she calls on her lover Heracles for help, and Telephus recognizes her as his mother. They return gladly together to Auge's homeland.

Augeas

One of the Argonauts, who afterward becomes king of Elis. He owns a huge herd of cattle and horses, whose dung fills his stables. Heracles is ordered to cleanse these proverbial stables as his fifth labor, which he does by diverting the River Alpheus through them. When Augeas fails to pay the agreed price of one-tenth of the cattle, Heracles invades Elis and kills Augeas.

Aurora

The Roman goddess of dawn, identified with the Greek Eos. Driving across the sky with her chariot and horses, she is a favorite subject of baroque ceiling painters.

Auster

In Greek mythology, a wind from the south, whose blast brings death to flowers and disease to man. He is the father of rain.

Autolycus

A famous thief, son of Hermes and Chione, and one of the Argonauts. He lives near Mount Parnassus, in central Greece, and plagues his neighbors by stealing their cattle. Sisyphus, however, marks the hooves of his animals and is able to prove Autolycus the thief, which so delights the villain that he welcomes Sisyphus as a friend and encourages him to seduce Autolycus's daughter Anticlea, who becomes pregnant with Odysseus, another noted thief.

Autonoe

Daughter of King Cadmus of Thebes and Harmonia, she marries the shepherd-god Aristaeus. When Zeus carries off her sister Semele, who becomes the mother of the wine-god Dionysos, Autonoe and her sisters, except for Ino, deplore Semele's actions, and are punished by Dionysos, who drives them to murder Pentheus in a bacchic frenzy. After the death of her son Actaeon at the hand of Artemis, Autonoe leaves Aristaeus and settles near Megara.

Below Aurora, goddess of dawn, admires the sleeping Endymion.

B

Bacchus

Latin name for the wine-god Dionysos, originally a pre-Greek deity. While Dionysos becomes one of the most important and popular gods in later Greek mythology, Bacchus is usually shown as a debauched and slightly ridiculous character, befuddled rather than empowered by the effects of wine.

Below Michelangelo's decadent, precarious *Bacchus* subverts the dignity of the classical nude.

Bastet

Egyptian cat-headed goddess, probably originally associated with the lion rather than the domestic cat. The daughter of Re, the sun-god, she is a royal protectress. Sacred cats were kept near her temple at Bubastis.

Baucis

Baucis and her husband Philemon are the Greek equivalent of Noah and his family. The Greek gods become disen-

Above Egyptian bronze cat sacred to the goddess Bastet.

chanted with mankind and decide to cleanse the world with a flood. Zeus and Hera first travel across the earth in disguise, to test whether anyone is worthy to be saved. Baucis and Philemon, although old and poor, receive them hospitably and prepare to kill their only remaining goose to feed their guests. The gods reveal themselves and, pleased to find some goodwill in the world, preserve the couple's cottage from the flood. This is then transformed into a magnificent temple, where Baucis and Philemon serve the rest of their lives as priests, their only request being that they should die at the same moment.

Bellerophon

Greek hero, son of the king of Corinth, who is exiled for accidentally killing his brother (or, in one version, a tyrant named Bellerus, hence his name). At the court of Proetus, king of Argos, he repels the advances of the queen, who denounces him to her husband. Proetus is unwilling to breach the laws of hospitality by killing Bellerophon himself, and instead sends him on to the

Below Bellerophon, mounted on the winged horse Pegasus, battles with the Chimera.

king of Lycia with a sealed letter demanding Bellerophon's death. He is set three impossible tasks, each of which is intended to kill him, and each of which, with the help of the goddess Athena, he successfully accomplishes. The first is to overcome the Chimera, a fire-breathing monster with the head of a lion, the body of a goat, and the tail of a serpent.

Athena advises him to break in the wild winged horse Pegasus to help him in this quest. At first Bellerophon is unable even to approach Pegasus, and enlists the aid of the seer Polyidus, who tells him to lie for a night on the altar of Athena. There he dreams that the goddess gives him a golden bridle and tells him to sacrifice to Poseidon the horse-tamer, supposedly Pegasus's father. When Bellerophon awakes, he finds the golden bridle

beside him, performs the sacrifice, and is permitted by a now tame Pegasus to ride him. Together they fall upon the Chimera from above, and Bellerophon kills it with arrows from his bow.

Still his original sin is not expiated, however, and he is sent first to fight single-handed against the Solymi, enemies of Lycia, and then against the Amazons. Each time he triumphs, and the Lycian king finally relents, marries him to his daughter Philonoe, and makes him his heir. In one story, Bellerophon returns to Argos and punishes the false queen by pretending that he loves her, inviting her to ride with him on Pegasus, and casting her into the sea. Subsequently his pride becomes too great and he decides to challenge the gods themselves, riding Pegasus up to Mount Olympus. Zeus contemptuously sends a gadfly to sting the horse; Bellerophon is thrown ignominiously back to earth, and forced to spend the rest of his life wandering the earth, lame and unknown.

Bellona

Roman goddess of war, identified with the Greek Enyo. She is an important cult figure among the Romans, and her temple near the Porta Carmentalis was where they received foreign ambassadors and generals returning from war. Bellona prepares the chariot of Mars for battle, and accompanies him armed with a whip to goad the combatants.

Beroe

Nurse to Semele. When Zeus falls in love with Semele, the jealous Hera borrows the girdle of Ate and assumes the form of Beroe, in order to entrap Semele into destroying herself. She persuades the gullible young woman to demand that Zeus prove his divinity by coming to her not in his usual disguise, but in his immortal form. Bound by a rash oath, he is forced to do so, and Semele is consumed by fire.

Bes

Egyptian household-god, usually represented as a bearded, long-armed dwarf with a tail. Unlike other Egyptian gods, who are invariably shown in profile, Bes appears full face, perhaps because he is a benign and genial figure, associated with fertility, childbirth, and domestic harmony.

Bias

King of Argos, who falls in love with Pero, princess of Pylos. Her father will only give her in marriage in exchange for the oxen of Phylacus, and Bias prevails upon his seer brother Melampus to steal them. Melampus is caught in the act and imprisoned in a chest, but amazes Phylacus by surviving and is given the oxen as a reward, and so Bias wins Pero.

Biton

See Cleobis.

Boreas

Greek god of the north wind, son of the sky deities Astraeus and Eos (stars and dawn). A violent, unpredictable deity, he is sometimes represented as a horse, like all the wind-gods, because the Greeks believed that the wind could impregnate mares. He courts Orithyia, an Athenian princess, but she resists him. When he finds her dancing in the meadows by the River

Below An irreverent view of the trials of Odysseus at the mercy of the unpredictable wind-god Boreas.

Ilissus, he wraps her in a cloud and carries her off to Thrace, where she bears him two winged sons, Zetes and Calais, and a daughter Chione. The Athenians regarded him as their particular patron; on the Tower of the Winds in Athens he is represented as a scowling, bearded, old man.

Briareos

A monster with 100 hands and 50 heads, born of Ge (earth) and Uranus (sky). When Hera, Poseidon, and Athena conspire against Zeus, Briareos ascends to Olympus and seats himself next to the father of the gods, so terrifying the plotters that they abandon their schemes. When Poseidon and Apollo dispute the ownership of the isthmus of Corinth, which is both land and sea, he arbitrates, giving Acrocorinth, the high hill on which the citadel stands, to Apollo, and the low-lying lands to Poseidon. In some accounts he sides with the Titans in their war against the gods, and is imprisoned under Mount Etna, causing the volcano to erupt when he struggles against his bonds. Other stories make him the jailer of the defeated Titans in Tartarus, the lowest section of the underworld.

Briseis

A Trojan woman taken prisoner by Achilles during the siege of Troy, and the cause of the festering quarrel between Achilles and Agamemnon which almost loses the Greeks the war. At the same time that Achilles takes Briseis as his mistress, Agamemnon seizes Chryseis, daughter of the priest of Apollo. The god is offended and sends a plague to curse the Greeks. Agamemnon finally agrees to return Chryseis, but takes Briseis from Achilles instead, who in turn is mortally offended, and refuses to fight until the death of his friend Patroclus spurs him to revenge.

Britomartis

Cretan nymph or goddess, mistress of wild animals and associated with Artemis. She is pursued by Minos, king of Crete, but throws herself off the cliffs rather than yield to him, and is transported by Artemis to Aegina. Minos follows her there, but she vanishes in the sacred grove of Artemis and is worshipped by the islanders as Aphaia, "the invisible." In Spenser's *The Faerie Queen*, Britomart is a female knight, the embodiment of chastity.

C

Cacus

A fire-breathing, three-headed monster, son of Vulcan and Medusa, who lives in a cave in Italy, devouring human flesh and plundering the surrounding countryside. When Heracles is on his way back to Greece with the cattle of Geryon, his ninth labor, Cacus steals four bulls and four heifers while Heracles sleeps, and drags them backward into his cave to prevent discovery. Their lowing alerts Heracles to his loss, and he tears off the top of the mountain so that he can see into the cave, and kills the monster with his arrows.

Cadmus

Legendary founder of the Greek city of Thebes. He is the son of Agenor, king of Tyre, and is ordered by his father to go in search of his sister Europa after she has been carried off by Zeus. Finding no trace of her, he consults the oracle at Delphi, and is told to abandon his search and instead to follow a cow marked with a crescent and to found a city where the cow lies down. This he does, and prepares to sacrifice the cow to Athena. Needing water, he sends his companions to fetch some from a nearby spring, but the spring is sacred to Ares and is guarded by a dragon which kills all his men. With the aid of Athena, Cadmus overcomes the dragon and, on her advice, sows its teeth in the ground. From this unusual crop springs an army of soldiers, who fight until only five, the boldest and strongest, are left. These are the first citizens of Thebes and regarded as the ancestors of the Theban nobility.

Because he has killed Ares's dragon, Cadmus has to serve the god for eight years. At the end of this time he becomes king of Thebes and marries Harmonia, daughter of Ares and Aphrodite. The gods attend the wedding in person – the only other mortal to be so honored is Peleus – and bring magnificent gifts. Hermes gives Cadmus a lyre (according to one legend, the walls of Thebes rise to the sound of Amphion's music), and Demeter gives him grain, but the necklace made for Harmonia by Hephaestus is destined to bring grief to those who own it (see Alcmaeon). Of the children of Cadmus

Above The marriage of Cadmus and Harmonia, by the classical Greek vase-painter Exekias.

and Harmonia, only Polydorus thrives and succeeds his father on the throne. Their daughter Semele gives birth to the wine-god Dionysos, fathered by Zeus, but dies when she charges her lover to cast off his disguise; Semele's sister Ino, who shelters Dionysos, is driven mad; Autonoe marries Aristaeus, but loses her son Actaeon to the hounds of Artemis; and Agave joins the Maenads, wild women of Dionysos, and tears her own son Pentheus to pieces. Cadmus and Harmonia leave Thebes and settle in Illyria to mourn their losses, and Ares finally takes pity on them and turns them into serpents, which are revered by the Greeks as containing the spirits of dead heroes.

Caeculus

Roman hero, founder of the city of Praeneste. His mother conceives him when a spark flies into her lap from the fire, and so his father is held to be Vulcan, god of fire. He is abandoned at birth and brought up by peasants, whom he urges to become citizens of his new city. When they prove reluctant, he calls on Vulcan for help, who circles the site of the city with fire, convincing the locals that they should hail Caeculus as their leader.

Calchas

Seer who accompanies the Greek army to the Trojan War. He receives the power of divination from Apollo, and correctly foretells many of the events of the war. When Achilles is nine years old, Calchas proclaims that without his help, and that of Philoctetes, the war will not be won. When the fleet is becalmed at Aulis, he sees a snake devour a sparrow and eight fledglings, and predicts that the war will last nine years. He also commands the sacrifice of Iphigenia to appease the anger of Artemis and ensure favorable winds. As the war progresses, he explains the plague that afflicts the Greeks as due to Agamemnon's seizure of Chryseis, daughter of a priest of Apollo, and is instrumental in the building of the Wooden Horse which effects the final fall of Troy. At his birth it is foretold that he will die when he meets a better prophet than himself; when, long after the fall of Troy, Mopsus wins a contest with Calchas, the old seer dies of grief.

Calliope

Muse of eloquence and heroic poetry, and mother of the musician Orpheus by Apollo. She is represented holding a trumpet in one hand and books in the other, and crowned with laurels.

Callirhoe

Second wife of Alcmaeon, son of the prophet Amphiarus. Alcmaeon's mother, bribed with the gift of the divine necklace bestowed by the gods on Harmonia when she marries Cadmus, betrays his father and is in turn killed by her son. He gives the necklace to his first wife Alphesiboea, but when he abandons her he tries to retrieve it to give to Callirhoe. Alphesiboea's brothers resent the loss of the necklace rather more than their sister's ill-treatment, and kill Alcmaeon, whereupon Callirhoe prays to Zeus that her infant children shall avenge her husband. Zeus causes them to grow to manhood in a day, and they kill their father's murderers.

Callisto

Variously a princess of Arcadia and a nymph, she is a follower of Artemis and vows eternal chastity. Zeus falls for her, however, and seduces her in the guise of Artemis. She bears a son, Arcas, but is turned into a bear either by Hera in jealousy, or by Artemis for breaking her vow. Zeus then transforms her into the Great Bear constellation, and Arcas into the star Arcturus.

Calydonian Boar

A wild boar sent by Artemis to ravage the kingdom of Calydon because the king, Oeneus, has not properly observed her rites. All the Greek princes assemble to hunt the magic creature; it is wounded by the huntress Atalanta and killed by Meleager.

Below The Muse Calliope courted by Apollo, who becomes the father of her son Orpheus. Nineteenth-century lithograph.

Calypso

Minor Greek goddess of silence and death, daughter of the giant Atlas, she offers the hero Odysseus immortality in exchange for marriage when he is wrecked on her island of Ortygia on his prolonged journey home from Troy. He refuses, but she keeps him with her for seven years, until Zeus takes pity on him and sends Hermes to release him.

Camilla

Roman heroine, a princess of the Volsci, whose father is driven out by his people when she is a baby and flees with her. He comes to a deep river and, not knowing how to get her safely across, ties her to his spear, prays fervently to Diana, Italian woodland-goddess and patroness of women, and hurls her across. When he has swum over himself, he finds Camilla unharmed and dedicates her to the service of Diana, bringing her up in the hills and teaching her to hunt and fight. She joins Turnus in his war against the invader Aeneas, leading a band of warrior maidens, but is finally killed by the Etruscan Arruns, helped by Apollo.

Canens

Italian wood-nymph, daughter of the two-headed god Janus. The sorceress Circe tries to seduce her lover Picus, and is so incensed when he refuses her that she turns him into a woodpecker. Canens vainly searches for him and pines away until only her voice is left; "canens" means singing.

Capaneus

One of the seven champions who fight for Polynices against Thebes. He swears that, even if Zeus forbids it, he will take the city by storm; as he scales the walls, he is struck down by a divine thunderbolt. His wife Evadne is so desolate that she throws herself onto his funeral pyre.

Carna

Roman virgin-goddess, who tricks potential lovers into entering a cave, promising to follow them but then vanishing. Janus sees through her ruse and succeeds in making love to her, in return giving her power over homes and doorways.

Cassandra

Princess of Troy, the daughter of Priam. Her beauty is renowned, and the god Apollo gives her the gift of prophecy in the belief that she will become his lover, but she refuses him. He cannot countermand his gift, but condemns her never to be believed. Another story has it that she and her brother Helenus acquire the ability to foretell the future when they are playing in the temple as children and are licked on the ears and mouth by the sacred serpents. Several of Priam's allies in the Trojan War fight in the hope of winning Cassandra, but none survive to claim her. The Trojans themselves believe her to be mad and ignore her, even though she recognizes Paris when he enters Troy a stranger, and predicts the devastation he will cause by going to Sparta (where he steals Helen). She warns the Trojans that the Wooden Horse is a trick

Above Cassandra warns the disbelieving Trojans against the Greeks' Wooden Horse.

(see Odysseus). When, as a direct result, Troy falls, she is brutally raped by Ajax in the temple of Athena where she has taken refuge, causing the statue of the goddess to turn up its eyes in horror. The Greeks impose no penalty on Ajax for this outrage, and Athena therefore kills many of them on their homeward journey. Cassandra is given to Agamemnon as part of the spoils of war and has two sons by him, Teledamus and Pelops. When he takes her back to Mycenae, she foretells her own death and that of Agamemnon at the hands of his jealous wife Clytemnestra and her lover.

Cassiopia

Queen of Ethiopia and mother of Andromeda, who causes Poseidon to send a sea serpent to devastate the

Above Castor and Pollux Carry off the Daughters of Leucippus, by Peter Paul Rubens (1577-1640).

land when she boasts that Andromeda is more beautiful than the Nereids, or sea-nymphs.

Castor and Polydeuces

Greek heroes who become important Roman gods; Polydeuces is more commonly known by his Roman name, Pollux. Often called the Dioscuri, they are the twin brothers of the beautiful Helen of Sparta and of Clytemnestra. Their mother is Leda, wife of Tyndareos, king of Sparta, but there is some disagreement as to whether one or both of them are, like Helen, the children of Zeus. They accompany Jason and the Argonauts on the quest for the Golden Fleece, and when a storm threatens the expedition, flames are seen to play around their heads and the sea at once becomes calm. They

thus become the patrons of sailors and of navigation. They also take part in the Calydonian boar hunt, and when Theseus and Pirithous carry Helen off to Attica before her marriage to Menelaus, they rescue her and in return seize Theseus's mother Aethra.

When invited by their uncle Leucippus to a feast to celebrate the marriage of his daughters Phoebe and Talaira, however, they fall in love with the girls themselves and try to carry them off. This not unnaturally enrages their prospective husbands, Lynceus and Idas, and battle breaks out. Castor kills Lynceus, but is killed by Idas. In this story, it is Pollux alone who is the son of Zeus and therefore immortal, but he cannot bear to live without his twin, and begs Zeus either that Castor shall be restored to life or that he himself shall lose his immortality. Zeus allows them to share Pollux's immortality, so that each of them spends alternate days with the gods on Olympus and in Hades, and subsequently places them in the sky as the constellation Gemini or The Twins.

Cecrops

Mythical first king of Athens, believed to be a serpent below his waist. He arbitrates between Athena and Poseidon when they dispute the ownership of Attica. Each gives a gift to the land, Athena the olive tree and Poseidon a spring, and Cecrops awards the title to Athena, who becomes the patron of the city named for her.

Celeno

One of the harpies, winged monsters with the heads of women and the bodies of vultures. See Harpies.

Centaurs

Wild creatures with the head, arms, and torso of men and the body and legs of horses, fathered by the Lapith king Ixion on a cloud which he thinks is Hera. The centaurs feature in the earliest pre-Homeric Greek myths, representing primitive and unbridled desires and appetites. The battle between the centaurs and the Lapiths is a popular subject on Greek vases and in sculpture. The centaurs are invited to the wedding feast of the Lapith king Pirithous, get roaring drunk, and try to carry off the Lapith women; the scene features in the architectural sculpture both of the Parthenon and of the temple of Zeus at Olympia. The centaur

Below Nineteenth-century engraving from Botticelli's *Pallas and the Centaur.*

Above One of a series of sculptures on the Parthenon showing the battle of the centaurs and Lapiths.

Chiron, however, is both wise and learned, and acts as tutor to a number of Greek heroes, including Achilles.

The centaurs also feature in the Labors of Heracles. He is entertained by the centaur Pholus during his pursuit of the Erymanthian boar, and they open a jar of wine given by Dionysos. Again the centaurs become drunk, and Heracles has to kill many of them with the arrows he has dipped in the poisonous blood of the Hydra, including, accidentally, both Pholus and Chiron. Nessus, a survivor, revenges himself on Heracles by giving his wife Deianira a poisoned robe, which she believes will restore her husband's love, but which kills him when he puts it on.

Cephalus

Greek hero, passionately in love with his wife Procris, but carried off by Eos, goddess of the dawn. She finally releases him, although in some stories she first has a son, Phaethon, by him. To try the fidelity of his wife on his return home, Eos persuades Cephalus to disguise himself and try to seduce her.

Procris at first refuses him, but finally succumbs to the offer of a fortune in gold. Cephalus at once reveals himself, and Procris flees from him in shame and horror, taking shelter in the mountains with the hunter-goddess Artemis, who presents her with an arrow that never misses its mark. Presently Procris decides to play the same trick on Cephalus that he has on her, and presents herself before him, offering the magic arrow in return for a night with him. She too reveals herself once he has surrendered, the two are reconciled, and are even more devoted than before. Cephalus continues to be a keen huntsman, however, and Procris becomes jealous of the time he spends away from her. Following him to the woods one day, she hears him praying for "Aura," a breeze, and thinks he is addressing a lover; he, hearing her movements in the bushes, thinks she is a wild beast, and fires at her the arrow that never misses. She dies in his arms, and he spends the rest of his life in miserable exile.

Cerberus

Monstrous dog who guards the entrance to Hades, the underworld, in Greek myth. Brother of the Hydra and the Chimera, he is described by Homer as having 50 heads, but in classical art he usually has three. His role is to prevent the dead escaping from and the living entering the underworld. He is chained at the gate, and dead souls are confronted by him once they have been ferried by Charon across the Styx. One of the Labors of Heracles is to bring Cerberus up from the underworld. Orpheus charms Cerberus to sleep with his lyre when he comes seeking Eurydice, while Aeneas is told to drug him with a wine-soaked cake when he visits the underworld, hence the expression "a sop to Cerberus."

Below *The Death of Procris*, mourned by Cephalus, by George Apperley (1884-1960).

Above Ceres, Italian corn-goddess, in a sixteenth-century woodcut.

Cercyon

King of Eleusis and champion wrestler, who challenges all travelers to a contest, defeating them all until he is himself overcome by Theseus, who is on his way to Athens to claim his heritage.

Ceres

Italian corn-goddess, whose temple was on the Aventine hill in Rome and whose spring festival, the Cerialia, was enthusiastically observed by the Romans. She is usually identified with the Greek goddess Demeter, and her daughter Proserpina with Persephone.

Chalciope

Princess of Colchis and daughter of Aeetes, she marries Phrixus when he flees to her father's court on the back of a golden ram. Aeetes, a cruel and barbarous king, kills Phrixus to acquire the Golden Fleece of the magic ram and threatens Chalciope's four children. When Jason comes in search of the fleece, it is Chalciope who persuades her sorceress sister Medea to help him.

Chaos

The shapeless mass of matter from which classical writers supposed Ge, the earth; Tartarus, the underworld; and Nyx, the night, had sprung. Chaos is sometimes called the oldest of the gods.

Charis

Greek goddess of grace and pleasure, sometimes identified as the wife of Hephaestus.

Charon

Ferryman, son of the primitive deities Erebus (darkness) and Nyx (night). In Greek myth he conveys the dead across the River Styx to Hades, as long as the funeral rites have been properly observed and a gold coin (obol) placed in the dead person's mouth as the ferryman's fee. If there has been no funeral, the dead soul has to wander the bank of the Styx for 100 years before qualifying to cross to the underworld. Only Heracles forces Charon against his will to convey him to the other side, for which lapse Charon is imprisoned for a year.

Charybdis

Lethal whirlpool in the straits of Messina off Sicily, identified in the *Odyssey* as a monstrous daughter of Poseidon, who sucks the water in and spews it out three times a day. On the other side of the strait is Scylla, a six-headed sea monster; when Odysseus passes, he risks Scylla rather than Charybdis.

Chimera

Fire-breathing monster with the head of a lion, the body of a goat, and the hindquarters of a dragon or serpent, killed by the Greek hero Bellerophon with the help of the winged horse Pegasus. Later classical writers rationalized the Chimera by explaining it as a fire-spouting volcano, whose upper reaches were the desolate resort of lions, its fruitful middle slopes the home of goats, and its marshy foot infested with serpents.

Chione

Greek princess renowned for her beauty (her name means snow-white), who counts among her suitors the gods Apollo and Hermes. Neither god approaches her directly, however; Hermes lulls her to sleep with his *caduceus*, or snake-entwined staff, while Apollo comes to her in the guise of an old woman. She bears twins, the thief Autolycus to Hermes, and the musician Philammon to Apollo, and becomes so proud of having two gods for lovers that she boasts herself more beautiful than Artemis, and in punishment is turned into a hawk.

Chiron

Centaur, half man and half horse and the son of Cronos. Cronos disguises himself as a horse in order to gratify his passion for Philyra without his wife Rhea finding out. This explains why, unlike the other centaurs, who are descended from Ixion, Chiron is wise, gentle, and learned. He figures as tutor

Right Charon, ferryman of Hades. Woodcut by Gustave Doré (1832-83).

Above The centaur Chiron tutors the young Achilles. Nineteenth-century engraving.

to most of the famous Greek heroes, including Achilles, Asclepius, Heracles, Jason, Aeneas, and Peleus, whose grandfather he is. As the son of a god he is immortal, but Heracles accidentally wounds him with a poisoned arrow when fighting the other centaurs, and Zeus yields to his plea to be relieved from the unrelenting pain of the wound, transforming him into the constellation Sagittarius.

Chryseis

Daughter of Chryses, the Trojan priest of Apollo, she is captured during the Trojan War and given to Agamemnon. In punishment, Apollo sends a plague

to devastate the Greek army, and Agamemnon finally agrees to return her, but instead seizes Achilles' mistress, Briseis, precipitating the quarrel that almost loses the Greeks the war. Only in medieval literature does the Trojan prince Troilus figure as the lover of Chryseis (Chaucer's Criseyde and Shakespeare's Cressida), who rejects him for the Greek warrior Diomedes.

Chrysippus

A beautiful youth, the son of Pelops by a nymph. He is abducted by Laius, king of Thebes, who has fallen in love with him. Pelops rescues his son and ritually curses Laius, whose children suffer for their father's evil-doing (see Oedipus). Pelops' legitimate sons, Atreus and Thyestes, murder Chrysippus on the order of their mother, Hippodamia, and are banished by their father. Pelops too is under a curse, which works its way through succeeding generations. See Atreus, Thyestes, Agamemnon.

Cinyras

King of Cyprus, whose daughter Myrrha falls in love with him and deceives him into sleeping with him. When Cinyras learns the truth, he tries to kill her, but she escapes and gives birth to Adonis, the mortal youth beloved by the goddess Aphrodite.

Below A domestic view of the sorceress Circe enchanting Odysseus on a fifth-century BC Theban vase.

Circe

Greek sorceress, sister of Aeetes, king of Colchis, and Pasiphae, queen of Crete, and the child of the sun-god Helios and a sea-nymph. She lives on a magic island which is guarded by tame lions and wolves, human victims of Circe's magic. Jason and Medea come to her to be cleansed of the murder of Medea's brother Absyrtus, and Odysseus visits her on his long voyage home to Ithaca after the fall of Troy. She turns his companions into pigs but Odysseus, advised by Hermes, carries the magic herb moly which helps him to resist her spells, and persuades her to swear not to harm him before he sleeps with her. He stays with her for a year and they part on good terms, with Circe giving him instructions about the rest of his voyage. In later legend she bears him a son, Telegonus, who accidentally kills his father and then marries Penelope, while Circe herself marries Penelope's son Telemachus and makes them both immortal.

Cleobis and Biton

Two young Greeks who come to the aid of their mother, a priestess of Hera, when no oxen can be found to pull her chariot to the temple, and pull it themselves. The priestess thanks Hera for her dutiful sons and prays that they may be given whatever is best for mortal man; they sleep that night in the temple and never wake again. The

Below Clio, Muse of history, with Urania, in an undated lithograph.

Greeks esteemed them as the happiest of men, and statues dedicated to them have been found at Delphi.

Clio

First of the Muses, she presides over history and is represented crowned with laurels and holding a book and a quill, in which she records the deeds of the heroes.

Clotho

Youngest of the three Fates or Moirae, daughters of Zeus and Themis. Clotho presides over the moment of birth, holding the distaff and spinning out the thread of life, which the second sister measures and the third cuts off.

Below Archaic statues of Cleobis and Biton, early sixth century BC, found at Delphi.

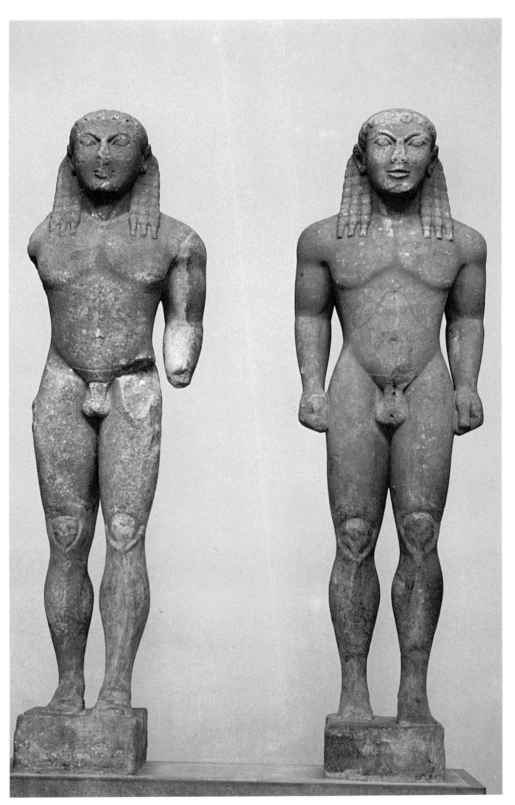

atropos   lachesis   Cloto

Clyte

Greek nymph, the daughter of Oceanus, she is loved by the sun-god Apollo, but abandoned by him in favor of Leucothoe. In revenge, she tells Leucothoe's father, and is turned by Apollo into a sunflower, which always turns its head to follow the sun.

Clytemnestra

Daughter of Tyndareos, king of Sparta, and Leda, the only one of Leda's children who is definitely human; she is sister of Helen, Castor, and Polydeuces. She and Helen marry the brothers Agamemnon, king of Mycenae, and Menelaus, who succeeds

Above Sixteenth-century Flemish tapestry of the three Fates: Clotho spins out the thread of life.

Tyndareos as king of Sparta. In one version of the story, Clytemnestra first marries Agamemnon's cousin Tantalus, son of Thyestes, who is killed by Agamemnon as part of the ongoing feud that results from the curse laid on his family (see Atreus). Clytemnestra has four children with Agamemnon, including Iphigenia and Orestes, and is finally turned against her husband when he sacrifices Iphigenia in order to gain a favorable wind for the Greek expedition to Troy to rescue Helen. She takes Aegisthus, brother of Tantalus, as her lover, and they overthrow Agamemnon on his return, killing both him and his Trojan captive Cassandra. For seven years they rule Mycenae, but Orestes then returns and murders them, for which he in turn is pursued by the Furies. In Homer, Clytemnestra is weak and easily led, but the Greek dramatists saw her as a decisive, vengeful figure.

Comus

Roman god of feasts and revelry, the son of Bacchus and Circe, and usually represented as a young drunkard, with a drooping garland on his head and a burning torch in his hand. During his festivals, men and women exchange dress. In Milton's masque *Comus*, a girl lost in the woods is invited to join Comus's revels and become his consort, but is rescued by Sabrina, goddess of the River Severn.

Concordia

Roman goddess of peace, whose temple in Rome was used by the magistrates for the transaction of public business.

Coronis

Greek princess, the lover of Apollo, by whom she becomes pregnant. When she marries Ischys, Apollo is so angry that he turns the white bird that brings him the news into the black crow, and persuades his sister Artemis to strike Coronis dead, rescuing from her funeral pyre her unborn baby, who becomes the medicine-god Asclepius.

Creon

A common name, which simply means ruler. One Creon is king of Corinth, to whose court Jason and Medea come. When Jason tires of Medea, Creon offers him his daughter Glauce and sends Medea into exile. Before she goes, Medea gives the new bride a poisoned wedding dress, which kills both her and her father.

The more famous Creon is the brother of Jocasta, wife of the Theban king Laius, and becomes regent when Laius is killed. A sphinx ravages the kingdom, and Creon offers the throne and the hand of Jocasta to whoever can solve the riddle it poses. When Oedipus achieves this, Creon resigns the throne to him; only when another plague afflicts the country is it revealed that Oedipus is Jocasta's son and their marriage is incestuous. Creon again becomes regent, but Polynices, Oedipus's son by Jocasta, tries to seize the kingdom, leading the Seven against Thebes in a vain attack on his uncle. He is killed in the attempt, and Creon decrees that his body shall remain unburied. Polynices' sister Antigone disobeys and buries her brother, and Creon in turn seals her alive in a tomb. He is finally killed by Theseus.

Creusa

Trojan princess who marries the hero Aeneas. In the confusion of the sack of Troy she becomes separated from her

Above Clytemnestra, urged on by Aegisthus, plans to murder the sleeping Agamemnon.

husband and lost, Cybele saves her and makes her appear in a vision to Aeneas, predicting his long journey and his final safe arrival in Italy.

Crocus

Greek youth who falls in love with the nymph Smilax, but she is slow to make up her mind and Crocus loses patience. He is changed into the swift-blooming crocus, and Smilax becomes the slow-growing yew tree.

Croesus

Last king of Lydia, in Asia Minor, renowned for his wealth. Aesop, the famous writer of fables, lives under his patronage. Threatened by the power of the Persian king Cyrus, he is told by the oracle that if he crosses the River Halys he will destroy a great empire; only when he is defeated by Cyrus does he realize that the empire destroyed is his own.

Above Cronos Devouring His Children by the Italian baroque painter Pietro della Vecchia.

Cronos

A primitive Greek god, one of the Titans, who are children of Uranus, sky, and Ge, earth. When his mother complains of the cruelty of his father Uranus, Cronos seizes a sickle and castrates Uranus when he next approaches Ge, throwing the severed genitals onto land and sea, where they become variously the Furies, the giants, the Cyclops, and the nymphs. Cronos marries his sister Rhea, but is warned that one of his children will do to him as he has done to his father, and so he swallows them all as they are born. After Hestia, Demeter, Hera, Hades, and Poseidon have all been disposed of in this way, Rhea finally rebels and conceals her sixth child, Zeus, in Crete. Zeus grows up in secret and takes as his first wife the Oceanid Metis, who gives Cronos an emetic which makes him vomit up his first five children. The six gods then make war on Cronos and depose him with the help of the giants and the Cyclops, imprisoning him in Tartarus.

Cupid

Roman god of love, a milder version of the Greek Eros. He is usually depicted as a winged child playing at love and aiming his arrows lightheartedly at mankind, rather than the tormenting spirit of earlier myth. His parents are Venus and Vulcan. In the myth of Psyche, the portrayal of Cupid comes closest to the overwhelming, destructive power of love that Eros represents.

Cybele

Phrygian mother-goddess, who becomes partially absorbed into Greek and Roman mythology and is usually identified with Rhea. The child of Zeus, she is supposed to have been born with both male and female genitals, but the potential of such a creature alarms the gods, who castrate it and it becomes Cybele. The severed genitals fall to the ground and grow into an almond tree, from which a river-nymph is impregnated and gives birth to Attis. Cybele falls in love with Attis, but he is unfaithful. She drives him mad, and in his frenzy he castrates himself and dies. Cybele is devastated and begs Zeus that Attis's body shall never decay; he becomes a god of vegetation and regeneration. The cult of Cybele and Attis involved orgiastic rites and ceremonies of purification, including a ritual bath in the blood of a sacred bull. Cybele's priests were originally eunuchs.

Cyclops

One-eyed giants, the children of Uranus and Ge, who in some stories live in a far-off land, preying on and devouring travelers, and in others are only three in number and work as skilled craftsmen in the forge of Hephaestus, the smith-god, making thunderbolts for Zeus. It is the former that Odysseus meets in his wanderings. See Polyphemus.

Cyparissus

A young Greek boy, much loved by Apollo. He has a tame stag which he leads each day out to graze, but one day he accidentally kills it with his spear. Distraught at his loss, he begs Apollo to be allowed to mourn forever and is transformed into the cypress tree, still a token of mourning.

Below Cybele in her lion-drawn chariot is attended by her son and lover Attis. Roman altar.

Above *Cupid and Psyche*, sculpture group from about the second century BC.

Cyrene

Virgin huntress, daughter of the River Peneus. Apollo sees her on Mount Pelion, wrestling with a lion and, dazzled by her beauty and bravery, seizes her up in his chariot and carries her off to Libya. There she bears him two sons, Aristaeus, the god of cattle and fruit trees, and the prophet Idmon. The city of Cyrene is named after her.

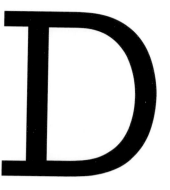

Daedalus

Athenian inventor and craftsman, renowned for his skill and supposedly responsible for the ax, the wedge, the level, and the sails of ships. His nephew is apprenticed to him and proves even more talented than his master, at which Daedalus is seized with jealousy and throws him off the Acropolis. He and his son Icarus take refuge in Crete, where Daedalus is employed by the Cretan king Minos to construct a vast labyrinth of winding underground passages from which no man can escape. He also, at the request of the queen, Pasiphae, constructs a wooden cow in which Pasiphae can gratify her unnatural passion for a bull.

Below Roman relief of Daedalus constructing wings for himself and his son, Icarus.

LCORNELIVS·SCIPIOOREITVS
V·CAVCVRTAVROBOLIVM

Above   Danae and the Shower of Gold by Titian (1485-1576).

The result of this curious union is the Minotaur, half man and half bull, which is penned inside the Labyrinth and fed on human flesh. Minos imprisons Daedalus for his part in this outrage, but he creates wings for himself and Icarus from feathers and wax, and they fly to freedom. Icarus, despite his father's warning, flies too close to the sun, which melts the wax and he falls into the sea. Daedalus, however, arrives safely in Sicily, at the court of Cocalus, who makes him welcome and for whom Daedalus constructs an impregnable city. Minos pursues Daedalus even to Sicily and besieges the new city, but Cocalus makes a show of friendship and invites the Cretan king to a feast, first offering him a ritual purifying bath. Daedalus, however, has equipped the bath with the first plumbing pipes, through which he pours boiling water, scalding Minos to death.

Danae

Princess of Argos, daughter of Acrisius. An oracle foretells that she will bear a son who will kill his grandfather, and so Acrisius confines his daughter in a bronze tower, permitting her to see no one but her old nurse. Zeus catches sight of her, however, and introduces himself into the tower in the form of a shower of gold. When Danae has a son, Perseus, Acrisius is amazed and furious, and puts both mother and baby to sea shut up in a box, assuming that they will drown. The wind, on the instructions of Zeus, drives them toward the island of Seriphus, where they are rescued and kindly treated by the fisherman Dictys, who educates Perseus in all the arts of a hero. Dictys's brother is the king, Polydectes, and he is determined to marry Danae despite her persistent refusals. He sends Perseus on what he believes to be an impossible quest, to fetch the Gorgon's head, and in his absence pressures Danae to succumb, but Perseus returns triumphant just in time to rescue his mother, and turns Polydectes to stone. Danae, with Perseus and his bride Andromeda, returns to Argos, where Perseus accidentally kills his grandfather Acrisius, thus fulfilling the oracle. The story of Danae, with its magical and erotic overtones, was very popular among Renaissance and later painters; there are four versions by Titian, and one of Rembrandt's rare nudes depicts Danae and the shower of gold.

Danaids

The 50 daughters of Danaus, who marry the 50 sons of Aegyptus but are forced by their suspicious father to murder their husbands on the wedding night. Only one, Hypermestra, spares her husband. All the others are punished in Tartarus by being permanently condemned to collect water in sieves.

Daphne

Mountain-nymph, with whom Apollo falls in love, having mocked the flimsy darts of Eros compared with his own skill at archery. Eros fires one arrow at him, making him fall passionately in love with Daphne, and another at her which renders her impervious to the god's persuasion. She flees from him, begging the gods to protect her from his advances, and they turn her into a laurel tree. As consolation, Apollo makes himself a laurel wreath, which becomes the winner's prize at the Pythian Games in honor of Apollo and a symbol of victory.

Daphnis

A Sicilian shepherd, the son of Hermes by a nymph, who is said to be the inventor of pastoral poetry. The god Pan teaches him to sing and gives him pipes to play. Daphnis boasts that he is

Right   Apollo and Daphne by Gianlorenzo Bernini (1598-1680).

Below   The Labour of the Danaids by the Pre-Raphaelite John Reinhard Weguelin.

impervious to love, and Eros and Aphrodite rise to this challenge by making him fall desperately in love with a river-nymph, Nais. She agrees to be his as long as he swears eternal faith, but a mortal woman, Xenia, tricks him into making love to her by getting him drunk, and Nais strikes him blind for his infidelity.

Deianira

Princess of Calydon, the sister of Meleager. She is renowned for her beauty and courted by many, but Meleager, after his death, meets the hero Heracles in Hades when Heracles descends there on one of his Twelve Labors, and begs Heracles to marry Deianira. Heracles' main rival is the

Left Daphnis and Nais. Undated woodcut.

Below Achilles on Scyros, in female disguise, by Nicholas Poussin (1594-1665).

river-god Achelous, whom he defeats in a wrestling match. After their marriage, Deianira and Heracles are traveling when they come to a river in flood. The centaur Nessus offers to carry Deianira across on his back while Heracles wades, but they are no sooner safely landed than he tries to rape her. Heracles, still on the far shore, shoots him with an arrow poisoned with the blood of the Hydra. Dying, Nessus tells Deianira in pretended remorse that if ever her husband's devotion should wane, she can win him back by giving him a shirt dipped in the centaur's blood. Many years later, after she has borne him three children, Deianira learns that Heracles has taken Iole as a lover. She follows Nessus's instructions, but instead of restoring Heracles to her, the shirt burns him agonizingly to death, whereupon she kills herself in despair.

Deidamia

Greek princess, whose father Lycomedes gives shelter to the young hero Achilles. In his efforts to avoid his predestined death in the Trojan War, Achilles disguises himself as a woman. Deidamia discovers the truth, falls in love with him, and bears him a son, Neoptolemus.

Deiphobus

Trojan prince, one of the many sons of Priam and Hecuba. After the death of Paris, the brothers Deiphobus and Helenus both claim Helen, and Deiphobus wins her. When the Wooden Horse arrives in Troy (see Odysseus), Deiphobus suspects, rightly, that it is a trick, and persuades Helen to imitate the voices of the Greek captains' wives in the hope that the hidden Greeks will give themselves away. She too suspects trickery, and hides Deiphobus's weapons in order to ingratiate herself with the Greeks. When the Greek warriors emerge from their hiding place in the Horse, it is Helen's first husband Menelaus who kills the unarmed Deiphobus.

Deiphon

Infant prince of Eleusis, whose father Celeus employs Demeter as his nurse in her wanderings in search of Persephone. In gratitude for this shelter, she begins to make him immortal, by plac-

ing him each evening on a bed of burning coals to purify him of his mortal parts. His mother Metanira is surprised by his rapid growth and spies on Demeter. When she sees her son in the fire, she tries to rescue him, disturbing the goddess's mysterious activities. Deiphon dies in the flames, and Demeter reveals herself and predicts that henceforth the sons of Eleusis will wage war on each other.

Demeter

Greek mother-goddess of the earth and fertility, identified with the Egyptian Isis, the Phrygian Cybele and the Roman Ceres. One of the 12 great Olympian gods, she is the daughter of Cronos and Rhea, and has a daughter Persephone by her brother Zeus. The

Above Demeter holds an ear of corn as a symbol of regeneration. Etruscan tomb painting.

disappearance of Persephone and the mourning Demeter's search for her is first told in the Homeric *Hymn to Demeter* and is one of the oldest Greek myths, personifying the seasonal cycle of death and regeneration. Hades asks Zeus for Persephone to be his wife. Zeus knows that Demeter will refuse and sanctions Persephone's abduction. While she is picking flowers in Sicily, the earth opens, Hades in his chariot rides out, seizes her, and vanishes again. Demeter hears her cries for help but cannot find her, and for a year wanders the earth in search of her lost daughter. At first she brings the gifts of agriculture to those who

DIANE D'EPHESE

Menetreius

Menetreius

Above Diana as the many-breasted fertility-goddess of Ephesus.

Deucalion

Son of the Titan Prometheus, he is warned by his father of the impending flood with which Zeus proposes to destroy mankind, and builds a boat for himself and his wife Pyrrha. They float on the flood for nine days and nine nights, and finally come to rest on Mount Parnassus when the waters subside. An oracle tells them to throw the bones of their mother over their shoulders; after some bafflement they realize this means their mother, the earth. The stones they throw become men and women and the earth is repopulated. Their son Hellen is regarded as the ancestor of the Greeks, who call themselves Hellenes and their country Hellas.

Diana

Italian goddess of woods, women, and childbirth, also associated with the moon and hunting through her identification with the Greek Artemis. Her oldest shrine was in a grove at Aricia on the shores of Lake Nemi. Her priest was always a runaway slave, who had to break a branch of the sacred tree, kill the current priest, and take his place. The temple of Diana at Ephesus was one of the seven wonders of the ancient world, and she was worshipped as a multi-breasted fertility figure akin to Cybele. The name Diana was more familiar than that of Artemis to Renaissance and later writers and artists, and it was to Diana that the seventeenth-century poet Ben Jonson addressed his appeal to the moon as "Queen and huntress, chaste and fair."

Dido

Queen of Carthage, who in Virgil's account falls in love with the Trojan hero Aeneas when he takes shelter at her court after the sack of Troy. She is daughter of the king of Tyre but flees her homeland when her brother Pygmalion becomes king and murders her husband. Landing in North Africa, she purchases from Iarbas, a local king, as much land as can be covered by a bull's hide; ingeniously, she cuts the hide into thin strips, enclosing an area large enough for a city. In one version of her story, she dies to escape marriage with Iarbas. According to Virgil, however, Aeneas stays with her long enough to rebuild his fleet, but is then instructed

receive her kindly in her wanderings, but after she has been prevented by Metanira from making Deiphon immortal, she commands Metanira's husband, the king of Eleusis, to build her a temple and takes refuge there, refusing the company of the gods and withdrawing her gifts from the earth.

Zeus realizes that if nothing is done to appease Demeter the earth will become barren, mankind will die out, and the gods will cease to receive their essential sacrifices. He finally agrees that, as long as Persephone has eaten nothing in Hades, she will be restored to her mother. Persephone, however, has eaten some pomegranate seeds and so she is only allowed to return for a part of the year, spending the winter and spring, when the grain is ripening in the ground, on earth with her mother, and the summer and fall, when the earth is dry and parched, in the underworld. In her happiness, Demeter once more bestows fertility on the earth, giving an ear of corn to Triptolemus with instructions to carry and propagate it throughout the world. Eleusis, where Persephone returns to earth, becomes the principal shrine of Demeter. The secret rites performed there, known as the Eleusinian Mysteries, celebrate the death and rebirth of the grain, and the purification and mystic rebirth of the celebrants.

by Zeus that he must fulfil his destiny and sail on to Italy. The deserted Dido throws herself on a funeral pyre.

Diomedes

One of the principal Greek heroes in the Trojan War, Diomedes also figures in Theban legend as one of the sons of the Seven against Thebes who march against the city to avenge their fathers. His mother is the daughter of Adrastus, king of Argos, who led the original Seven, and Diomedes in turn becomes king of Argos, marrying his cousin Aegiale. Previously he was a suitor to Helen of Sparta, and is therefore bound by oath to help her husband Menelaus to recover her when the Trojan prince Paris abducts her. Like his friend Odysseus, he enjoys the special protection of Athena and is successful in the war, fighting with Ares and wounding Aphrodite, and helping Odysseus to steal the Palladium, the sacred image of Athena on which the good fortune of Troy depends. In later legend, and in Chaucer and Shakespeare, he also wins Cressida (originally Chryseis) from Troilus. Aided by Athena, he is one of the few Greek warriors to have a safe and swift journey home, but Aphrodite has planned a long-term revenge for her wounding, and he finds that Aegiale has been unfaithful and his title to the throne of Argos is in dispute. He leaves Greece and finally settles in Italy.

Diomedes

Son of Ares, the Greek god of war, and the nymph Cyrene, and king of Thrace. He owns four savage mares which he keeps fastened to bronze troughs by

Below The betrayal of Dido by Aeneas, from a Roman mosaic in Somerset.

Above The Triumph of Dionysos, in his leopard-drawn chariot and surrounded by vines and dancing Maenads, from a Roman mosaic in Tunisia.

iron chains and halters and feeds them on human flesh. The eighth labor of Heracles is to steal these.

Dione

Earth-goddess and consort of Zeus, whose cult was confined to the ancient sanctuary of Dodona and is probably a variation on that of Hera.

Dionysos

Greek god of wine, fertility, and mystic ecstasy. The cult of Dionysos absorbed several similar cults from Asia Minor, which is reflected in his mythology; he is sometimes rejected for his "otherness" and the non-Greek abandonment of his orgiastic rites, and punishes such rejection severely. Son of Zeus and Semele, he is snatched at only seven months' gestation by Zeus from his mother's body as she is consumed by fire, and placed inside Zeus's own thigh until he reaches term. He is brought up first by Semele's sister Ino and then by nymphs in India, to keep him far from the vengeance of Hera, who brought about his mother's destruction. He is taught the use of the vine by Silenus and the satyrs, and returns across Asia to Greece, carrying his thyrsus, a staff entwined with vine and ivy, and leading his followers, the Maenads. His triumphal progress is a favorite subject in classical art, particularly in mosaic, while another legend, describing his crossing the sea by boat and making vine leaves spring from the mast, is exquisitely illustrated on a sixth-century BC Greek vase.

Among those who resist the powerfully irrational cult of Dionysos are Lycurgus, who persecutes him while he is still a child and is punished by death. Pentheus, king of Thebes, is horrified by the frenzied behavior of the Theban women under the god's influence and imprisons him, but the prison doors mysteriously open and free him, and Pentheus is torn apart by the Maenads, who include his own mother Agave. When the daughters of Proetus, king of Argos, refuse Dionysos his rites, they too are driven mad and roam the mountains imagining themselves to be cows. Dionysos can also be a benign deity, however, as in his rescue of Ariadne after she has been abandoned by Theseus; by gathering her up in his divine ecstasy he bestows a form of immortality on her.

The cult of Dionysos becomes established throughout Greece and he is accepted by Apollo at Delphi, where his rites continue in less frenzied form. He then descends into the underworld to restore the shade of his mother Semele to immortality, persuading Hades to release her in exchange for his favorite plant, the myrtle. Drama takes its origins from his cult, in which the spirits of the earth and fecundity were evoked by means of masks. The great Athenian dramatists wrote their plays as part of the spring festival of the Great Dionysia, and the release of powerful irrational impulses through controlled ritual continued to be considered a necessary catharsis or purge.

Dioscuri

See Castor and Polydeuces.

Dirce

Wife of the Theban king Lycus, who cruelly mistreats Zeus's lover Antiope because she is jealous of her beauty, finally planning to tie her to a bull and tear her to pieces. Antiope's sons by Zeus rescue her and punish Dirce with the death she has planned for Antiope. Dirce is a devotee of Dionysos, however, who avenges her death by driving Antiope mad.

Below Dionysos crosses the sea. Greek plate by the vase-painter Exekias.

Dis

Another name for the god of the underworld, Hades to the Greeks.

Discordia

Roman goddess of quarrels and dissension, identified with the Greek Eris.

Dolon

Trojan spy who is captured by Odysseus and Diomedes. He reveals the secrets of the Trojan defences in the hope of escaping with his life, but is killed by Diomedes for his treachery.

Dryads

Dryads and hamadryads are the Greek nymphs of trees, to whom offerings of milk, oil, and honey are made. Although long-lived, they are not immortal; dryads were believed to have an independent existence, whereas hamadryads were thought to live in a particular tree and die with it.

Echidna

Female monster who is a beautiful woman from the waist upward and a serpent below. She has a number of equally monstrous children by the dreaded Typhon, including the Chimera, the Hydra, and Cerberus, the three-headed guardian of the underworld. She is finally caught asleep by Argus of the one hundred eyes, and killed.

Echo

Nymph who attends on Hera, and infuriates the goddess by chattering when she is trying to spy on Zeus's amours. In punishment for her loquacity, Hera deprives her of normal speech, so that she can only repeat the words of others. She falls in love with Narcissus and, when he fails to respond, pines away until she is only an echoing voice.

Egeria

Italian water-goddess, worshipped in conjunction with Diana at Aricia. She is the advisor and lover of the early Roman king Numa, and is so distraught at his death that Diana turns her into a fountain.

Electra

Daughter of Agamemnon and Clytemnestra, who is either enslaved or married off to a peasant after Clytemnestra and her lover Aegisthus have murdered Agamemnon. She is not mentioned in Homer, but in later Greek literature, and particularly the trage-

Above This Roman sculpture group shows Electra towering over her brother Orestes.

dies by Sophocles and Euripides, she becomes the prime mover of her brother Orestes' vengeance on their mother. She recognizes Orestes, when he returns with his cousin Pylades from many years of exile, and helps to plot Clytemnestra's death. Orestes is pursued by the Furies for his act of matricide, and Electra follows him in his tormented wanderings until he is purified by Apollo. She then marries Pylades. In Euripides' *Electra* she is shown as a character obsessed with hatred and a desire for revenge, and then with guilt and remorse. She figures as such in two operas, Mozart's

Idomeneo and Richard Strauss's *Elektra*, where the realization of her long-desired vengeance is too much for her, and she falls dead. The American playwright Eugene O'Neill retells the story of Orestes and Electra in the setting of nineteenth-century New England in *Mourning Becomes Electra*.

Endymion

Variously a shepherd or a king of Elis, with whom the moon-goddess Selene falls in love as he sleeps on a mountainside and she descends from the skies each night to enjoy his company. She cannot bear the thought of his dying, and puts him into an everlasting sleep so that she can always look at his beauty. In another version, the dreams

Selene gives Endymion are so enthralling that he begs Zeus for perpetual sleep. Keats uses the story for the framework of his allegorical poem *Endymion*, reflecting the poet's quest for ideal beauty.

Eos

Greek goddess of dawn, known as Aurora to the Romans. Homer describes her as "rosy-fingered dawn," who drives her chariot across the morning sky. The daughter of Titans, she is the sister of Helios, the sun, and Selene, the moon. She offends Aphrodite by her amorous liaison with Aphrodite's lover Ares, and her other love affairs tend to end tragically. She carries off Cephalus and, when he pines for his wife Procris, jealously causes him to kill her. She takes the giant hunter Orion to Delos, an island sacred to Artemis, and Artemis puts him to death. She goes so far as to marry the mortal Tithonus and asks Zeus for immortality for him, but neglects to ask for eternal youth as well and has to watch him decline into perpetual senility.

Epimetheus

Brother of the Titan Prometheus, whose name means "forethought," whereas Epimetheus means "afterthought." The gods create Pandora, the first mortal woman, and offer her to Epimetheus as a bride in order to punish Prometheus for the help he has given to man. Pandora brings with her a box, which she has been told must remain closed, but she cannot contain her curiosity and opens it. From it emerge all the troubles which subsequently afflict the human race. Pyrrha, daughter of Pandora and Epimetheus, marries Deucalion and they are the only humans saved from the flood which Zeus sends to the world.

Erato

Muse of lyric and love poetry, and inventor of the lyre and the lute. She is usually shown as crowned with roses and myrtle and supported by Cupid holding a burning torch.

Erebus

Primeval god of darkness and son of Chaos, who fathers Aether, the atmosphere; Hemera, day; and Charon, the ferryman of the dead, by his sister Nyx, night.

Erectheus

Legendary king of Athens, often confused with Ericthonius and like him born directly from the earth rather than of human parentage. Athena rears him and he is worshipped with her on the Acropolis at Athens; the temple of the Erectheum there dates from the fifth century BC but is believed to stand on the site of an older royal palace. During his reign in Athens, war breaks out with the neighboring kingdom of Eleusis, and the oracle at Delphi promises victory if Erectheus sacrifices one of his daughters. This he does and Eleusis becomes Athenian territory, but retains the right to celebrate the mysteries of Demeter. Procris, tragic wife of the hero Cephalus, is another of Erectheus's daughters.

Erginus

King of the Minyans, who invades and defeats Thebes and subjects the Thebans to an annual tribute of 100 cattle. Heracles meets Erginus's messengers on their way to collect the tribute, cuts off their ears and noses, hangs them round their necks and sends them back to Erginus. When Erginus again attacks Thebes, Heracles takes the Thebans' part and Erginus is defeated and in turn forced to pay tribute. Im-

Below The Greek moon-goddess Selene gives eternal sleep to Endymion.

Above Erato, part of the decorative scheme for the Paris Opera.

poverished and grown old, he consults the Delphic oracle, which advises him to fit a new tip to his plowshare; he duly marries a much younger woman and she bears him two sons.

Ericthonius

One of the first kings of Athens and the son of Hephaestus who, repulsed by Athena, fathers him on Ge, the earth. Ironically, Ericthonius is given to Athena to raise, and she entrusts him, hidden in a basket, to the daughters of Cecrops, forbidding them to look inside. Of course they disobey, and find the baby guarded by two snakes (or alternatively with a snake's tail instead of legs). They go mad and throw themselves off the Acropolis, and Athena resumes charge of Ericthonius. He succeeds Cecrops as king of Athens, promotes the cult of Athena there and institutes the principal festival, the Panathenaea. In one story he invents the chariot because he has a snake's tail rather than feet, and on his death is turned into the constellation Auriga, the Charioteer.

Erinyes

See Furies.

Eriphyle

Sister of Adrastus, leader of the Seven against Thebes. When she marries the seer Amphiarus, he agrees that she shall be the arbiter in any dispute between the two men. Adrastus wants Amphiarus to join the expedition against Thebes but Amphiarus foresees his own death. The exiled Theban prince Polynices persuades Eriphyle to decide in favor of her brother rather than her husband by giving her the necklace of his ancestress Harmonia, wife of Cadmus. Amphiarus swears his son Alcmaeon to avenge his death; and Alcmaeon kills his mother on returning from Thebes, and is in turn pursued by the Furies.

Below Erisicthon felling a tree sacred to Demeter.

Eris

Greek goddess of discord, the daughter of Nyx, night. She comes uninvited to the marriage of Peleus and Thetis and flings a golden apple inscribed "For the Fairest" into the gathering. Aphrodite, Athena, and Hera all claim the apple, and Zeus appoints the Trojan prince Paris as arbiter. He awards the prize to Aphrodite, who promises him the most beautiful woman in the world, Helen of Sparta, as his reward. From this stems the Trojan War.

Erisicthon

A prince of Thessaly who cuts down the sacred grove of Demeter in order to build a banqueting hall. The goddess punishes him with perpetual hunger and he squanders all his possessions to gratify his endless appetite. His daughter Metra prays to her lover, Poseidon, for help. Poseidon gives her the power to change herself into different animal shapes, enabling her father to sell her over and over again to gullible passers-by. Finally Erisicthon starts to devour his own limbs and dies.

Eros

Greek god of love, called Cupid or Amor by the Romans. His powers and role evolve considerably. In the earliest myths, he is born directly of the primeval Chaos and brings about the union of Uranus, sky, and Ge, earth; as such he is little more than the generative force of nature. Later he is identified as the son of Aphrodite, goddess of love, either by Ares or Hermes, and represented as a handsome and athletic young man, the particular protector of homosexual love. In the later Greek and Roman periods, Eros appears more often as a winged baby or child, with a quiverful of arrows which he mischievously uses to trouble the hearts of humans. Some of these are gold-tipped and cause passionate love, others are tipped with lead and provoke equal repulsion. Even the gods are not immune from his tricks; he causes Apollo, Zeus, and even his own mother to fall in love against their will. Beneath the innocence of childhood, the cruel, whimsical, and powerful god still lurks.

Eryx

Son of Aphrodite and Poseidon and king of part of Sicily, where he gives his name to Mount Eryx and establishes a famous sanctuary for the worship of his mother. A champion wrestler, he challenges all comers to a match, and is finally defeated and killed by Heracles on his way home with the cattle of Geryon.

Eteocles

Theban prince, product of the incestuous relationship between Oedipus and his mother Jocasta. After the incest is revealed and Oedipus has blinded himself in remorse, Eteocles and his brother Polynices insult their father by offering him an inferior cut of meat instead of the royal portion, Oedipus curses them both, praying that each will die by the other's hand. Once the two brothers are old enough to rule Thebes, they agree to share the kingship, each ruling for a year. Eteocles rules first, but at the end of the year refuses to give way to Polynices. Polynices meanwhile has married the daughter of Adrastus, king of Argos, who collects an army against Eteocles, including the seven champions who give their name to Aeschylus's play

Above Bronze *Sleeping Eros*, dating from about the third century BC.

The Seven Against Thebes. The expedition is a disaster, as predicted by the seer Amphiarus, who foretells his own death. All the Seven are killed, and Polynices and Eteocles meet at the gate of the city and kill each other, fulfilling Oedipus's curse. Jocasta's brother Creon, who has already ruled as regent during the brothers' minority, again takes over the reins of government, and orders that Eteocles shall be buried with full honors, but that Polynices' body shall be left to rot where it lies. See Antigone.

Eumaeus

Faithful swineherd to Odysseus, who entertains his returned master in his hut without recognizing him, until Odysseus reveals himself. Eumaeus then helps him to defeat the many suitors to Odysseus's wife Penelope. In Virgil's *Odyssey*, Eumaeus tells of his own royal birth and abduction by Phoenician slave traders, who sell him to Odysseus's father Laertes.

Eumenides

Careful Greek euphemism for the Furies; it means "the kindly ones."

Europa

Princess of Phoenicia, with whom the irrepressible Zeus falls in love when he sees her playing with her attendants by the sea. He takes on the shape of a tame white bull and joins their games, playing so sweetly that Europa eventually climbs on his back, whereupon he instantly walks into the sea and swims straight to Crete, there revealing himself as Zeus. Europa has three sons, Minos, Rhadamanthys, and Sarpedon, and Zeus gives her the bronze man Talos to guard the coasts of Crete and keep her and her children safe. Asterius, the king of Crete, marries Europa and adopts her children as his own. Meanwhile Europa's father Agenor has sent his sons, including Cadmus, to search for their sister, with instructions not to return without her; he never sees any of them again. Europa is worshipped as a goddess on Crete, and her story may be a Greek explana-

tion for the bull-dancing ritual they found there (see Minotaur).

Eurus

The east wind, son of Eos, goddess of the dawn.

Euryclea

Nurse to Odysseus, who recognizes him on his return from the Trojan War before his wife Penelope does, from the scar on his leg.

Eurydice

Nymph or dryad who marries the great musician Orpheus. She dies as the result of a snake bite – according to Virgil she was trying to escape from the orchard-god Aristaeus – and Orpheus ceases to make music in his misery. Finally he makes his way to the underworld to beg her release, and enchants even Charon and Cerberus, guardians of the gate, with his melodies. Even Hades and Persephone, rulers of the kingdom of the dead, are touched, and grant him Eurydice on condition that

Above A sentimental nineteenth-century view of the death of Eurydice, bitten by a snake, by B. Burroughs.

he leads her out of the underworld without looking at her. According to the oldest version of the story Orpheus succeeds, in testament to the power of Dionysos, of whom he is a devotee. As told by the Roman writers Virgil and Ovid, however, Orpheus turns impatiently to look at his wife and loses her for ever.

Eurylochus

A companion of Odysseus, the only one who resists drinking the magic potion of Circe and is not therefore turned into a pig. When they arrive at the island of the sun-god Helios, however, Eurylochus and his shipmates kill the sacred cattle for food, even though Odysseus has been warned not to do so. They are punished by a great storm, from which only Odysseus escapes.

Eurystheus

King of the Argolid, ruler of Tiryns and Mycenae, who is set by Hera to rule over Heracles. As Heracles, Zeus's son, is about to be born to Alcmene, Zeus boasts that the baby born that day will rule all those around him. The jealous Hera succeeds in delaying the birth of Heracles, much to Alcmene's discomfort, and accelerating that of Eurystheus, who is only of seven months' gestation, so that it is Eurystheus who fulfils the prophecy of Zeus. When they both reach adulthood, Eurystheus orders Heracles to perform the Twelve Labors, a series of tasks so formidable that only a son of Zeus can possibly succeed. Eurystheus proves a coward, however, and takes shelter in a bronze storage jar when Heracles brings Cerberus up from Hades at his command. After that he refuses to let Heracles enter the city, instead sending his herald to deal with him. Even after Heracles has been received as a god on Olympus, Eurystheus continues to persecute his children, and is finally killed in battle by Heracles' son Hyllus. His head is sent to Alcmene who, remembering all the cruelties her son has patiently suffered at Eurystheus's hands, tears out the dead man's eyes.

Euterpe

Muse of music, regarded as the inventor of the flute and all wind instruments.

Evander

An early king in Italy, believed to be of Greek origin. He settles on the Palatine hill, in what is later to become Rome, and teaches the natives the hitherto unknown arts of writing and music. When Heracles comes to Italy, Evander purifies him of the murder of Cacus and, recognizing his divine origins, institutes a cult in his honor. By the time Aeneas arrives in Italy, Evander is an old man, but he welcomes Aeneas and gives him a contingent of troops under his son Pallas to help him subdue the unco-operative local tribes.

Below Euterpe, Muse of music, with Polyhymnia.

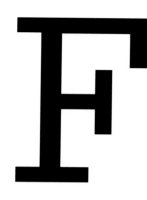

Fates

See Moirae.

Fauna

Roman goddess, also known as the Bona Dea or good goddess, she is the wife of Faunus and has the power to foretell the future. She is said not even to have looked at a single man after her marriage, and is accorded divine honors for her chastity.

Faunus

Italian god of the countryside and shepherds, identified with the Greek Pan. The son of Picus and the grandson of Saturn, he is often represented as having a human body and goat's legs, a creature subsequently named a faun, similar to but gentler than the Greek satyr.

Flora

Roman goddess of flowers and the spring. She is pursued by the wind-god Zephyr while still a nymph, and on marrying him is transformed into Flora, whose very breath becomes petals, and whose footprints turn into flowers.

Fortuna

Roman goddess of fortune, portrayed with a cornucopia, indicating the riches she can bestow, and a rudder, symbolizing her power to steer lives. She is also often shown blind, as in blind chance, and with a wheel in her hand to illustrate her inconstancy. Her nearest Greek counterpart is Tyche.

Above Flora, Roman goddess of spring, from a wall-painting at Pompeii.

Furies

The Furies, known as the Erinyes to the Greeks, or by the euphemistic name of the Eumenides (kindly ones), are female spirits of justice and vengeance, and personify the fundamental idea of retribution. They were believed to have been born from the blood shed by Uranus upon the earth, Ge, when his son Cronos castrated him, and were represented in classical art as winged spirits, with hair entwined with snakes, and holding whips or torches in their hands. Their essential role is to punish those who transgress "natural" law, particularly the laws of kinship, and their principal venom is reserved for matricide. They persecute Alcmaeon, who kills his mother Eriphyle on the instruction of his father, whom she has betrayed. Orestes, who kills his mother Clytemnestra, is pursued inexorably by the Furies, regardless of his plea of mitigation, and even Apollo is hard put to it to pacify them, since they are representatives of an older power than the Olympian gods. Finally they accept the verdict of the ancient Athenian court of the Areopagus, and in gratitude for the cessation of their persecution, Orestes sacrifices to them and renames them the Eumenides.

They are also, however, the instruments of the gods' vengeance, and as such mercurial in their selection of victims. It is they who instigate Althea's destruction of her son Meleager, and they who cause the misfortunes which plague the family of Agamemnon after the sacrifice of Iphigenia to ensure calm weather for the Greek embarkation for Troy. In a precarious and defensive society, their role was to punish all crimes likely to disturb the hard-won social order, whether excessive pride, or *hubris*, the over-accurate foretelling of the future, or straightforward murder. They drive their victims mad before them, until someone can be found with the power and the will to purify them.

Below The Furies pursue Orestes.

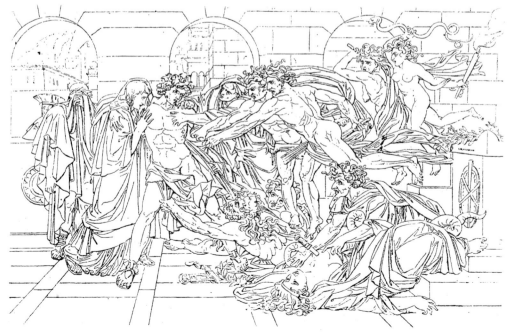

G

Galanthis

Servant of Alcmene. When her mistress is in labor with the hero Heracles, son of Zeus, Hera, always vindictive toward Zeus's lovers, sends Ilithyia, the goddess of childbirth, to sit outside Alcmene's door in the guise of an old woman with her legs crossed, thus preventing the unfortunate Alcmene from giving birth. Galanthis realizes that the old woman seated outside is somehow connected with Hera's jealousy and her mistress's travails, and rushes out crying that the child has been born. Ilithyia leaps up to see for herself, her hold on Alcmene is released, and Heracles is finally born, but in spite Ilithyia turns Galanthis into a weasel.

Galatea

Sea-nymph who lives off Sicily, where the Cyclops Polyphemus pastures his sheep and goats. He falls madly in love with her but she treats him with disdain, much preferring the attentions of the shepherd Acis. Polyphemus in rage crushes his rival under a huge rock; the broken-hearted Galatea causes a spring to flow from under the rock, and Acis becomes the god of the stream. Handel's *Acis and Galatea* celebrates the idyllic nature of pastoral life.

Galatea

The name of the statue of a beautiful woman with which the sculptor Pygmalion falls in love. He prays for her to be brought to life and the gods answer him; she marries him and has a son, Paphos.

Above Galatea, a seventeenth-century statue in the garden of Versailles.

Ganymede

Trojan prince carried off by the gods to serve as the cupbearer of Zeus, in exchange, variously, for a pair of immortal horses or a golden vine. In later legend it is Zeus alone, attracted by his beauty, who abducts him in the form of an eagle. Ganymede was held throughout the Middle Ages to typify homosexual love, but Renaissance theorists read a more spiritual meaning into the myth, seeing it as a symbol of the soul's ascent to the absolute.

Ge

The Earth in Greek mythology, also known as Gaia. She is the first to be born from the primeval Chaos, together with Tartarus, the underworld; Nyx, night; and Erebus, darkness. Alone she conceives and bears Uranus, the sky, and Pontus, the sea; she then couples with Uranus and bears the 12 Titans, of whom Cronos is the youngest. Uranus insists that all 12 should remain entombed within their mother's body, and only Cronos dares to defy him. Ge gives him a sickle and he castrates his father, but the blood from the wounding falls upon Ge and fertilizes her; this time she bears the Furies, or Erinyes, the giants, and the nymphs. Her fecundity undiminished, she then

Above Zeus battles with the giants, copied from the Pergamum altar.

Left The Rape of Ganymede by the sixteenth-century Italian painter Correggio.

gives birth to five marine deities, including Nereus, by Pontus. When Cronos proves as much of a tyrant as his father, swallowing all his children by Rhea because it has been predicted that one of them will supersede him, Ge masterminds a second revolution.

She hides Rhea's last child, Zeus, and when he has grown to manhood, advises him that he will only overcome Cronos if he enlists the aid of the Titans. After a long war, Zeus finally prevails, and imprisons Cronos and those Titans who have supported him in Tartarus. Ge is offended by this and mates with Tartarus, producing the monsters Titan and Echidna as her champions, inciting the giants to rebel against Zeus, but again he is the victor, and imprisons the giants in the earth from which they have come.

The cult of Ge the earth mother is one of the earliest in Greece, but in most places she is superseded by later gods. It is she, for example, who originally delivers the oracle at Delphi, until Apollo kills the serpent Python, a creature of the earth. Apollo has to do penance for this. The early kings of Athens, such as Ericthonius and Erectheus, with their serpent tails, are creatures of Ge. Later her cult becomes absorbed into that of deities such as Demeter and Cybele.

Geb

Egyptian earth-god, product with the sky-goddess Nut of the union of Shu and Tefnut, air and moisture, who in turn had risen from Nun, the primeval waters which the Egyptians believed surrounded the world. Geb and Nut are the parent deities of Egyptian mythology, the equivalent of Cronos and Rhea; their children are Isis, Osiris, Seth, and Nephthys.

Geryon

A monster with three bodies from the hips upward, who lives on an island far to the west beyond the Pillars of Heracles (in late legend said to be Spain), where he keeps herds of cattle. One of the Labors of Heracles is to steal the cattle of Geryon; he is pursued by their owner and shoots him with a fatal arrow dipped in the blood of the Hydra.

Giants

Children conceived by Ge, the earth, when the blood of Uranus, the sky, falls

*Glaucus de Pescheur qu'il eftoit, deuient **Dieu Marin**, pour auoir mangé d'vne certaine Herbe, qui auoit redonné la vie a de petits Poiffons. Ouid. Metam. l. 13. Nonnus. l. 35.*
Auec priuilege du R.   *A Paris chez P. Mariette le fils, rue S. Iacques aux Colomnes d'Hercule.*   *C. Blomart fculp.*

Above The sea-god Glaucus, shown in a seventeenth-century engraving.

on her. They are of human form, although vast, but have serpents' tails attached to their legs or feet. When Zeus offends Ge, his mother, by confining Uranus and the Titans in Tartarus, she stirs the giants to rebellion against him. The gods know they cannot win without the help of a mortal hero, and so Zeus sleeps with Alcmene and fathers the mighty Heracles. The giants pile Mount Pelion on top of Mount Ossa in order to try and reach Olympus, home of the gods, and the battle of the gods and giants ensues. The gods finally gain the day, with Heracles stationed by Zeus's chariot, finishing off with his poisoned arrows the giants that Zeus stuns with thunderbolts. The battle of the gods and the giants became a favorite subject for sculptured groups, as on the frieze of the Siphnian treasury at Delphi and the altar at Pergamum.

Glaucus

A sea-god, who starts life as a fisherman. He observes that all the fish he catches and lays on the grass seem to acquire new vigor and leap back into the sea. He tastes the grass himself, and is at once consumed with the desire to leap into the sea, sprouting a tail and fins as he does. The sea deities Oceanus and Tethys make him a god, and he falls in love with the nymph Scylla. When she rejects him he consults the sorceress Circe, who in turn falls in love with him, and transforms Scylla into a monster from the waist down.

Gordius

A Phrygian peasant, who is acclaimed king in fulfilment of a prophecy that the next king will arrive riding in his chariot – or, in this case, his farmer's cart. He dedicates his cart to Zeus, and the yoke is tied to the pole in such a way that it cannot be untied. Word spreads that he who undoes the Gordian knot will conquer all Asia, and when Alexander the Great passes through, he solves the problem and claims the prophecy by cutting the knot with his sword. Gordius's son is Midas, who becomes king of Phrygia after him.

Gorgons

Three monstrous sisters living in the far west, the offspring of sea-gods. Instead of hair they have live snakes curling about their heads and their necks are covered with dragons' scales; they also have tusks like a boar's, bronze hands, and golden wings. Of the three, Medusa has the power to turn to stone anyone at whom she gazes, but she is mortal; her sisters Stheno and Euryale are immortal. Medusa is killed by Perseus, but she is pregnant by Poseidon when she dies, and her decapitated corpse gives birth to the winged horse Pegasus. In some accounts the Gorgons are beautiful women, and Athena gives Perseus the help he needs to kill Medusa because she has boasted herself more exquisite than the goddess. Certainly Perseus gives the head of Medusa to Athena, after he has used it to save Andromeda, and she attaches it to her breastplate. The Gorgons are popular subjects in classical art, appearing both in vase painting and in sculpture.

Graces

Daughters of Zeus, they are named Aglaia, Euphrosyne, and Thalia, and personify beauty, charm, and friendship. They are the attendants of Aphrodite but play little part in myth.

Graeae

Three crones in Greek mythology, sisters of the Gorgons and ancient from the moment of their birth. They live in a cave in Atlas's mountain, and are blind and toothless apart from one eye and one tooth, which they share. They have knowledge of all living things, however, and when Perseus comes seeking the way to Medusa, he steals the eye, only returning it in exchange for the information he needs. In one story, they tell Perseus about the winged sandals and the helmet of invisibility he will need for his quest.

Above *The Three Graces* by Raphael.

Right A Gorgon's head used as architectural decoration by the Etruscans.

Gyges

Mythical king of Lydia in Asia Minor, who is originally a shepherd. The reigning king is so proud of his wife, and so confident of his power, that he summons Gyges to see her naked. The queen is so outraged by this that she orders Gyges to kill either himself or the king; Gyges, not surprisingly, chooses the second, marries the queen, and founds a dynasty.

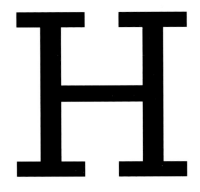

Hades

Greek god of the dead and ruler of the underworld, which also becomes known as Hades. He is the brother of Zeus and Poseidon, and after they have overthrown their father Cronos and defeated the giants, they share the universe, Zeus taking the sky, Poseidon the sea, and Hades the underworld. His queen is Persephone, daughter of Demeter, whom he steals from her mother and keeps by his side for half the year. The story of Persephone is one of the few myths in which Hades

Below Hades enthroned in his kingdom of the dead.

figures actively; although not an evil figure, he is considered to have no interest in the living and so no temples are dedicated to him. His name is considered unlucky, and not usually spoken out loud for fear of arousing his anger. Instead he is called "Pluton," the rich, which translates into Latin as "Dis," short for "*dives.*"

The shades of the dead cross the River Styx, conveyed by the infernal ferryman, Charon, and meet the three judges of the underworld, Minos, Rhadamanthys, and Aeacus. The vast majority of these shades stay for ever on the Plain of Asphodel, prevented from returning to the living world by the three-headed guard dog Cerberus. The lowest level of the underworld, Tartarus, is reserved for the spectacularly wicked, such as Tantalus, Sisyphus and those Titans who rebeled against the gods. Very few living mortals penetrate Hades and escape. Orpheus, at least in one version of the story, achieves the release of his wife Eurydice in a unique act of mercy by Persephone; Odysseus comes to consult the seer Tiresias; and Aeneas is guided there by the Cumaean Sibyl to speak with the shade of his father Anchises. Theseus and Pirithous, grown reckless in their later years, try to steal Persephone and are imprisoned by Hades in chairs of forgetfulness. They are finally released by Heracles when he carries off Cerberus.

Haemon

Son of Creon, king of Thebes, about whom there are two different stories. In one he is devoured by the Sphinx and in revenge Creon promises his kingdom to whomever will deliver Thebes of the monster. The deliverer is Oedipus, who unknowingly marries his own mother and has children by her. In the other, Haemon survives and falls in love with Oedipus's daughter Antigone, and kills himself when Creon condemns her to death.

Halirrhothius

Son of Poseidon and the nymph Euryte, he rapes Alcippe, daughter of Ares, for which Ares kills him. Poseidon summons Ares to trial, which is held near the Acropolis in Athens, on the spot where the rape took place. Ares is acquitted by the gods, and the site becomes the origin of the Areopagus, the court which tries homicide cases in Athens.

Hapi

The god of the River Nile, who brings fertility to Egypt with his annual inundation of the river valley. He is represented as a plump, well-fed god, holding ears of corn and a cornucopia.

Harmonia

Daughter of Aphrodite by her lover Ares, Harmonia seems nonetheless to be regarded as human rather than divine. Zeus arranges her marriage to Cadmus, founder of the city of Thebes and brother of Europa, whom Zeus abducted in bull form. All the gods come to the marriage feast and bring gifts, including a necklace made by the smith-god Hephaestus. In some versions of the story, Hephaestus, angry at his wife Aphrodite's infidelity with Ares, curses the necklace, and it brings misery to Harmonia's children and to subsequent owners (see Alcmaeon). Cadmus and Harmonia themselves, however, remain happily married and devoted to each other.

Harpalyce

Thracian princess, whose mother dies when she is a child and who is brought up by her father and taught how to fight. She becomes a skilled warrior,

Above Undated engraving of a harpy with dragon's wings, lion's paws, and a serpent's tail.

Hecate

Primitive pre-Greek earth-goddess, variously believed to be the daughter of Zeus or of a Titan, and honored by Zeus more highly than any other god, being given power over land, sea, and sky. She is associated with Demeter through her role as a fertility-goddess, and with Artemis for her interest in animals. She plays an important role in human affairs, granting prosperity, eloquence and victory in battle. She has the power to make cattle grow fat or lean, and to enlarge or reduce the fisherman's haul. She is also connected with sorcery and black magic; Medea invokes her in weaving her enchantments, and she is sometimes portrayed as mother of Circe. As a magician, she presides over crossroads, where she is represented as having three heads, and becomes associated with the world of the dead. In Shakespeare's *Macbeth* she makes two brief appearances to direct the sinister activities of the three witches.

Below Hebe, the cupbearer of the gods. Based on a sculpture by Antonio Canova.

and rescues her father from death when the Getae invade Thrace. After he is dethroned they take refuge in the woods and she supports them by hunting until accidentally killed by local shepherds. A cult grows up around her tomb.

Harpies

Originally wind spirits, their initial role is to carry to Hades the souls of the dead, and they are named as Aello (rain-squall), Celaeno (storm-dark), Okypete (swift-flying), and Podarge (swift-foot). In later myth they feature as monstrous birds with women's faces, similar to the Sirens, sent by Zeus to steal the food that the Thracian king Phineus sets before the Argonauts. They also plague Aeneas on his way to Italy, and are responsible for the disappearance of whatever cannot be found.

Hathor

Egyptian fertility-goddess, she is represented either as a cow with a solar disc or as a woman with cow's horns and the solar disc between them. She

is also the goddess of beauty, love, marriage, and childbirth, and is sometimes identified with Isis. On one occasion, however, she shows a less munificent aspect to mankind. The sun-god Re becomes convinced that men are plotting against him, and he sends the Eye of Re in the form of Hathor to destroy the impious. She undertakes her task with a will and Re begins to fear universal destruction, so he floods the fields with beer, dyed with red ocher to resemble blood. The vengeful Hathor is fascinated by her reflection and becomes drunk, forgetting her gruesome purpose. Many Egyptian myths focus on the renewing Nile flood.

Hebe

Personification of youth, usually held to be the daughter of Zeus and Hera, although in one version she is conceived by Hera after eating lettuces. Ever fair and youthful, she serves as cupbearer to the gods until Zeus dismisses her for falling drunkenly down while serving nectar at a feast, and she is succeeded by Ganymede. She continues to prepare her mother's chariot and harness her peacocks. When Heracles is raised to the rank of a god, he marries Hebe, and as a favor to him she restores his nephew Iolaus to youth so that he can aid Heracles' children.

Above Classical sarcophagus showing Hector's body being dragged behind Achilles' chariot.

Hector

Eldest son of King Priam and Queen Hecuba of Troy, and the Trojan hero of the *Iliad*. Although he deplores Paris's seduction of Helen of Sparta and proposes that she should be returned to her husband, he becomes the Trojans' war leader, and it is he who kills the first Greek to step ashore at the start of the Trojan War. While he knows Achilles to be active on the Greek side, however, he keeps the Trojan forces penned inside the city, for despite the protection that Apollo gives him, he knows he is fated to die at Achilles' hands. It is only when Achilles retires from the conflict after his quarrel with Agamemnon that Hector leads his men out of Troy; Zeus instructs the gods, most of whom support either the Greeks or the Trojans, to let Hector have the victory as long as Achilles is absent. He kills many Greeks in the course of the war, and challenges any Greek hero to single combat. Ajax accepts and the fight continues all day, until finally at nightfall the two heroes recognize each other as equal adversaries and exchange presents.

Hector's sortie against the Greeks is so successful that he is on the point of destroying their fleet when Poseidon rallies the Greeks, and Patroclus, who has failed to persuade his friend Achilles to fight, marches out in Achilles' armor. In the ensuing combat, Hector kills Patroclus and strips him of his armor. The loss of his friend finally brings Achilles back into battle. Despite the prayers of his parents, Hector refuses to retire into the city to escape the rage of Achilles, and the two circle the walls three times. Athena assumes the form of one of Hector's brothers and urges him to stand and fight; when she vanishes, Hector understands that the fated moment has come. The gods abandon him and Achilles is able to strike a fatal blow. As Hector lies dying he begs that his body shall be returned to his parents, but Achilles refuses, and drags the dead Hector in cruel triumph around the walls of Troy, until his mother Thetis persuades him to yield to the supplications of the aged Priam, Hector's father. Achilles then announces a truce of 11 days for the funeral games. The *Iliad* ends with the funeral of Hector, but the Trojans know that his death heralds the fall of Troy. When this takes place, the Greeks put to death Hector's son Astyanax to ensure the end of his line.

Hecuba

Tragic queen of Troy, who bears 19 children to King Priam, only to see most of them die during or after the Trojan War. When she is pregnant with her oldest son Paris, she dreams that she gives birth to a burning torch which destroys Troy and the surrounding country. On the advice of soothsayers who foretell the fall of Troy, she and Priam abandon Paris, but he is rescued and returns to the city as a young man, fulfilling the prediction by carrying off Helen of Sparta and precipitating the Trojan War. After her second son Hector is killed and Troy has fallen, Hecuba and her daughter Polyxena are given to Odysseus as slaves. On the way back to Greece, the victors land in Thrace to honor the grave of Achilles and the shade of the dead hero appears to them demanding the death of Polyxena to ensure favorable weather. When, on top of this, the body of her youngest son Polydorus, who is supposedly in the safekeeping of the Thracian king Polymestor, is washed ashore, Hecuba is driven mad with grief and, going to Polymestor's court, she tears out his eyes and kills his children. Pursued by a stone-throwing mob, she is transformed into a bitch and drowns herself.

Helen

Daughter of Leda and Zeus, princess of Sparta, and the cause of the Trojan War, Helen is a curiously ambiguous character in Greek myth, renowned for her peerless beauty and the object of much unrequited passion. Her mother Leda marries Tyndareos, king of Sparta, but is seduced by Zeus in the guise of a swan and gives birth to Castor, Pollux, and Helen by Zeus, and Clytemnestra by Tyndareos (in some accounts Castor too is of human birth). Helen is brought up as Tyndareos's daughter, and even at the age of 12 is so ravishingly beautiful that the now ageing hero Theseus and his inseparable companion Pirithous abduct her, but she is rescued by her brothers. When she reaches marriagable age, Sparta is overwhelmed with suitors, to the point that Tyndareos becomes anxious that those who are rejected will become troublesome. Odysseus, who is one of them (or in some versions Agamemnon, already married to Helen's younger sister Clytemnestra), suggests that all the suitors be bound by an oath to support and protect Helen and her husband, whoever he may be. She chooses Menelaus, and the fact that he is a dispossessed younger son suggests that this is a love match. Tyndareos adopts Menelaus as his successor to the throne of Sparta, and aids Menelaus's brother Agamemnon to regain his kingdom.

On the other side of the Aegean sea, however, Aphrodite has promised Paris the most beautiful woman in the world as his prize for awarding the apple inscribed ''for the fairest'' to her in preference to Athena and Hera. Presently Paris arrives in Sparta in search of his reward, and Aphrodite causes Helen to fall in love with him, abandoning husband and daughter, Hermione, to elope with Paris to Troy. There her welcome is by no means uniformly warm, as her arrival has been foretold to herald the fall of Troy, but she marries Paris. After an interval of negotiation, the vast Greek armada sets sail for Troy. In the course of the ten-year siege, Helen's loyalties seem to have wavered; in the *Iliad* she sometimes reproaches herself for her weakness and wickedness in staying with Paris, and when Odysseus, disguised as a beggar, comes to spy out the Trojan defences, she does not betray him; and yet she stands on the walls of Troy and points out the Greek leaders for the Trojans to aim at.

There is a touching moment in Homer when the old men of Troy agree that it is worth fighting such a war just to keep her in Troy, but her beauty is never described in the *Iliad*. Toward the end of the war, after Paris has been killed by the poisoned arrow of Philoctetes, Helen marries his brother Deiphobus, and when the Wooden Horse is pulled inside the walls, with Greek warriors hidden inside it, she is suspicious enough to try to spring the trap the Greeks have set by calling each Greek leader in a perfect imitation of his wife's voice. And yet she then hides Deiphobus's weapons, allowing Menelaus to kill him after the storming of the walls. Menelaus intends to kill her too, for the pain and the deaths she has caused, but on seeing her he is so captivated by her beauty that the sword falls from his hand and they are reconciled. The Greeks too abandon their intended vengeance when they set eyes on Helen, and she and Menelaus return to domestic bliss in Sparta, where they are found by Telemachus many years later when he comes in search of his father Odysseus.

Helenus

Son of Priam and Hecuba of Troy, twin brother to Cassandra and, like her, gifted with the power of prophecy. He foresees the disaster tht will ensue

Below The abduction of Helen by Paris, on a Greek relief sculpture.

from Paris's voyage to Sparta, but fights bravely in the Trojan War that follows. He is angered by Helen's marriage to Deiphobus after the death of Paris, however, and when captured by the Greeks foretells the conditions that must be fulfilled before Troy can fall. These include the theft of the Palladium, the luck of Troy, from Athena's temple; the presence of Philoctetes with the bow and arrows of Hector; and the building of the Wooden Horse (see Odysseus). After the fall of Troy, Helenus becomes the slave of Achilles' son Neoptolemus, and endears himself to him by warning him to go home overland, thus avoiding the storm sent by the angry Athena to destroy the Greeks. In gratitude Neoptolemus frees him and gives him his brother Hector's widow Andromache as his wife. Helenus is the only one of Priam's sons to survive the ruin of his country; he rules over part of Epirus, and receives the Trojan hero Aeneas on his way to Italy.

Heliads

Children of the sun-god Helios. When their brother Phaethon steals the chariot of the sun, losing control and being destroyed by Zeus's thunderbolt, the Heliads mourn for him on the banks of the River Eridanus until the gods take pity on them, transforming them into poplars and their tears into amber.

Helios

Greek sun-god, probably pre-dating Apollo, since he is a Titan and not one of the Olympian gods. He is portrayed as a young man with rays of light streaming from his head, who drives his chariot of fire each day across the sky from east to west, preceded by Eos or Aurora, the goddess of dawn. The Greeks were much exercised as to how he returned at night from west to east, and in one version of the legend he floats round on the stream of the Ocean in a large cup, which Heracles borrows on his way to the Hesperides. He is worshipped particularly in Rhodes, ostensibly because he was away driving his chariot through the sky when Zeus divided the lands between the gods, and so Zeus created an island for him in recompense. The *Colossus* of Rhodes, one of the wonders of the ancient world, was a statue of Helios.

Helle

Helle and her brother Phrixus are the children of Athamas and his first wife Nephele. Athamas abandons Nephele and marries Ino, who plots against her stepchildren. Just as they are about to be sacrificed on the order of a false oracle, Hermes, at the prayer of Nephele, sends a golden ram to rescue them. As they fly over the sea on the back of this magic creature, Helle loses her hold and falls into the sea, which becomes the Hellespont.

Hellen

Oldest son of Deucalion and Pyrrha, who are saved by the gods from the flood they send to punish the impieties of man. He gives his name to Hellas, Greece, and his children are Dorus, Aeolus, and Xuthus, mythical forebears of the three great branches of the Greek race.

Hephaestus

Greek god of fire and a metal-smith, the son of Zeus and Hera or, in one account, of Hera alone in response to Zeus's creation of Athena. He is invariably portrayed as lame, having taken Hera's side in a quarrel with Zeus over another of Zeus's children, Heracles, and been thrown by Zeus in fury out of Olympus, landing on Lemnos after falling for a whole day. In another story, he is born lame and cast out by Hera in

Above Hephaestus, the smith-god, shown on a Greek kylix or cup.

Right Hera, queen of the Greek gods, in a Roman copy of a Greek statue.

disgust, falling into the sea and being brought up by the Oceanids. He learns the art of smithing from them, and makes a golden throne for his mother which imprisons her when she sits in it. The gods plead with Hephaestus to release her, and are forced to send Dionysos to invite him back to Olympus. He marries Aphrodite, but she continues her longstanding affair with Ares, the god of war. Hephaestus builds great halls and palaces for the gods, and forms Pandora, the first woman, out of clay. His workshops are in the volcanoes, where he creates many miraculous artifacts, including the armor of Achilles, the great chain that binds Prometheus to Mount Caucasus, and the thunderbolts of Zeus. In later stories he is helped in his forge by the Cyclops, and there are a number of post-Renaissance paintings on this theme.

Hera

Originally a pre-Olympian goddess associated with women and marriage, whose name simply means "lady," Hera is absorbed into the Olympic pantheon as the wife of Zeus. She is also Zeus's older sister, swallowed at birth, like her other siblings, by her father Cronos and released by Zeus.

Although Zeus has affairs with a number of other goddesses, he decides that only Hera is great enough to be his consort. In one version of their marriage, Hera is wandering in the woods near Argos, when Zeus causes a rainstorm, disguises himself as a cuckoo, and hides in her dress, where he resumes his true form and swears to marry her. Many places, including Crete, Samos, and Naxos, claim to be the location for their wedding, and the rite of the sacred marriage was widely performed in Greece to commemorate it.

The peacock, symbol of ostentatious pride, is sacred to Hera. As patroness of women and marriage, Hera is a model of chastity and is outraged by Zeus's constant infidelities. She is often motivated by jealousy to take revenge on Zeus's lovers and their children, in particular Leto, mother of Apollo and Artemis; Semele and her son Dionysos; and Alcmene and her son Heracles. Hera's persecution of Heracles is so vindictive that Zeus punishes her by suspending her from a pinnacle of Olympus by the wrists. She also plays a role in the Trojan War, pursuing the Trojans with implacable hatred in vengeance for Paris's having failed to award her the golden apple intended for the fairest.

Heracles

The most famed and popular of all Greek heroes, who becomes a god after his death. The son of Zeus and Alcmene, he is intended by his father to become a great ruler, and ultimately to aid the gods in their battle with the giants, but the machinations of Hera ensure that instead he becomes for a time the slave of Eurystheus. Even when he is a baby Hera tries to destroy him, sending two serpents which twine themselves around the infant Heracles and his twin brother Iphicles, son of Alcmene's lawful husband Amphitryon, but the hero proves his divine paternity by strangling them. His first heroic deeds on reaching manhood are the killing of the lion of Cithaeron, which has been savaging the countryside, and the defeat of Erginus, who has been exacting an annual tribute from Thebes. In gratitude the Theban king, Creon, gives Heracles his daughter Megara as wife. When Creon dies and the usurper Lycus tries to seize the throne, Heracles kills him, but in the rejoicing that follows, Hera

again takes a hand; she strikes him with a fit of madness, and he shoots both Megara and their three children. It is when he consults the Delphic oracle, in penance for this act of homicide, that he is ordered to perform the famous Twelve Labors for Eurystheus.

The first labor is the killing of the Nemaean lion, whose skin cannot be pierced, so Heracles strangles it, flays it, and is often portrayed wearing its skin as a cloak. The many-headed Hydra of Lerna is the second task, and Heracles needs the aid of his nephew Iolaus to cauterize the necks as he cuts off the heads, because otherwise they grow again at once. He dips the tips of his arrows in the Hydra's poisonous blood. Next is the hunting of the Erymanthian boar, which he brings back to Eurystheus on his shoulders, and the capture of the hind of Ceryneia, which he hunts for a year. The fifth labor is the cleansing of the stables of Augeas, which Heracles achieves by diverting the River Alpheus through them, and the sixth is the killing of the Stymphalian birds, which infest the shores of Lake Stymphalus in Arcadia, and which he scares with a rattle given him by Athena, shooting them as they fly away. Next he kills the fire-

Above Heracles fights Apollo for the sacred tripod. Greek vase-painting.

Right   Heracles and Iphitus by Antonio Canova (1757-1822).

breathing bull that is ravaging Crete, and captures the man-eating mares of King Diomedes of Thrace. The ninth labor is to steal the girdle of Hippolyta, queen of the Amazons, which Eurystheus's daughter wants for herself.

The last three tasks all take the hero outside the Greek world. To steal the cattle of Geryon he has to go to the far west, in some versions traveling there in the floating cup of Helios, and killing the monster Cacus on his way back. For the golden apples of the Hesperides he takes the place of Atlas, holding up the world while Atlas fetches the apples for him, and finally he descends into the underworld to carry off the guard dog Cerberus, defeating and wounding Hades, king of the dead, and so confirming his own claim to immortality. While there he rescues Theseus, who tried to steal Persephone, queen of the dead, and promises the shade of Meleager that he will marry Meleager's sister Deianira.

Many other legends are told about

Heracles. He joins the expedition of the Argonauts, but stays behind to search for Hylas, the boy he loves, who is captured by nymphs. When Apollo refuses him purification for the killing of Iphitus, he steals the sacred tripod of Delphi and the two sons of Zeus fight until separated by a thunderbolt thrown by their father. He serves the Lydian queen Omphale disguised as a woman, a bizarre episode which later moralists cited as the enslavement of a strong man by woman's wiles, and descends into the underworld a second time to rescue Alcestis.

Heraclids

The children of Heracles, particularly the descendants of Heracles and Deianira, who colonize the Peloponnesus. They too are pursued by Eurystheus, finally taking shelter in Athens, where Theseus or his sons agree to protect them. Eurystheus declares war on Athens, but his five sons are killed and he himself is killed by Heracles' son Hyllus. Three generations pass, and many unfavorable oracular pronouncements are given, before the Heraclids finally defeat the Peloponnesians and build an altar to Zeus in thanks.

Hermaphroditus

Son of Aphrodite and Hermes, an exquisitely beautiful young man with whom the nymph Salmacis falls in love. Hermaphroditus rejects her, but then makes the mistake of swimming in the lake that is sacred to her. She embraces him and pulls him down into the deep, praying to the gods that their bodies shall be forever joined. The gods combine them into a single being, with female breasts and proportions but male genitals.

Hermes

Greek messenger-god, also the god of travelers, merchants, and thieves, Hermes was originally a phallic god of protection, whose statue was set up at roadsides. The son of Zeus by the nymph Maia, he is extraordinarily precocious; born in the morning, he has invented the lyre by midday and stolen 50 cows from the herd of Apollo by

Left The nymph Salmacis pulls Hermaphroditus down into her lake and they become one body.

evening. When Apollo comes searching for his cattle, he is so taken with the lyre that Hermes persuades him to overlook the theft in return for the gift of the instrument. In recognition of this ingenuity, Zeus gives him the broad-brimmed hat and winged sandals in which he is usually shown. He acquires his characteristic snake-entwined staff or *caduceus* by striking a bargain with Apollo, who wants the syrinx or pan-pipes that Hermes has invented. Apollo offers the golden crook with which he tends the sheep of Admetus, and Hermes accepts as long as he can be taught the art of prophecy as well. He even manages to avoid the anger of Hera that falls on so many of Zeus's love children, by disguising himself as Ares, Hera's own child, so that she suckles him and thus becomes his foster-mother.

As messenger of Zeus, Hermes saves the infant Dionysos from the vengeance of Hera, and accompanies Zeus in his travels across the earth. He organizes the beauty contest between Hera, Aphrodite, and Athena, decided by the Judgment of Paris, and escorts Priam to Achilles to recover Hector's corpse. In the battle of the gods and the giants, he wears the helmet of Hades, which renders the wearer invisible, and so kills the giant Hippolytus. His greatest service to Zeus is when the monster Typhon cuts out Zeus's sinews and hides them in a cave, completely incapacitating him, until Hermes discovers and returns them.

He has many lovers, principal among them being Aphrodite, the goddess of

Below Hermes with the Infant Dionysos, possibly an original marble by Praxiteles.

love herself. At first she rejects him, but Zeus sends one of his eagles to steal her golden sandal, and when Hermes offers it back in return for a night with her, she is amused by his impudence and succumbs, bearing him Hermaphroditus and Priapus. He is the father of Pan and of Daphnis by nymphs, and his children by mortal women include Cephalus, from his affair with Herse; the thief Autolycus; and Heracles' armbearer Abderus.

Hermione

Daughter of Helen and Menelaus of Sparta, who is nine when her mother abandons her and goes to Troy with Paris. She is pledged in marriage to her cousin Orestes, son of Agamemnon, but during the Trojan War Menelaus promises her instead to Neoptolemus, son of Achilles, whose support is essential if Troy is to fall. When Neoptolemus visits Delphi after the war to ask the oracle why he and Hermione

Below Egyptian mummy in the shape of a hawk, representing Horus.

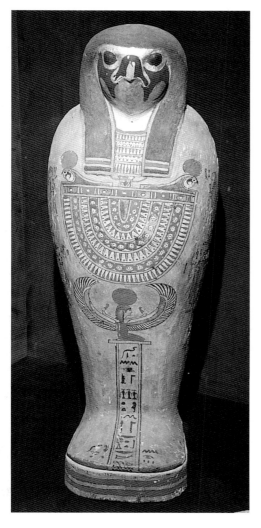

have no children, he is killed, possibly by Orestes, whom Hermione subsequently marries.

Hero

Priestess of Aphrodite at Sestos, who falls in love with Leander, a young man of Abydos, on the other side of the Hellespont (Dardanelles). She is barred from marriage, and instead Leander swims the strait to spend each night with her in secret, guided by a light in her window. One stormy night the light blows out and Leander is drowned; next morning Hero sees his body on the beach and throws herself into the sea.

Herse

Princess of Attica, daughter of Cecrops and the lover of Hermes, with whom she has a son, Cephalus. Hermes first discloses his passion for Herse to her sister Aglaurus, in the hope that she will help him, but instead she tells her father, for which betrayal Hermes turns her into a stone. When Athena gives the infant Ericthonius to Cecrops to look after, Herse disobeys her father's order and spies on the baby; she is driven mad and leaps to her death from the Acropolis.

Hesione

Early Trojan princess, daughter of Laomedan. Apollo and Poseidon build the walls of Troy for Laomedan, and when he refuses to pay the agreed fee, Troy is punished with a plague and a sea monster. Hesione is about to be sacrificed to the monster when Heracles offers to kill it in return for the mares that Laomedan received from Zeus in exchange for his son Ganymede. Again Laomedan reneges on the bargain, however, and Heracles returns with an army and sacks Troy. The first man over the walls is Telamon, and in reward Heracles gives him Hesione in marriage.

Hesperides

Nymphs of the evening and daughters of Atlas, who guard the golden apples that Zeus gives Hera as a wedding gift. Heracles steals some of the apples as his twelfth labor, with the help of Atlas, but Athena makes sure that they are returned.

Hippodamia

Princess of Pisa in Elis, daughter of Oenomaus. Her father is warned that he will die at the hand of his daughter's child, and so he makes all suitors for her hand – of whom there are many as she is extremely beautiful – compete with him in a chariot race. Since his horses are a gift from Ares, he invariably wins and kills the loser. When Pelops arrives to compete, however, Hippodamia falls in love with him and bribes her father's charioteer Myrtilus to replace his lynchpins with wax. In the course of the race, Oenomaus's chariot overturns and he is killed. Pelops then kills Myrtilus, either because the price of his disloyalty is too high or because he tries to rape Hippodamia. As he dies Myrtilus curses Pelops, and this is the origin of the misfortunes which dog the descendants of Pelops and Hippodamia. Among their children are Atreus and Thyestes, whom Hippodamia persuades to kill Chrysippus, Pelops' love child. She is banished and dies, and her sons quarrel and bring another curse on their family. See Atreus.

Hippolyta

Queen of the Amazons, whose girdle Heracles steals as his ninth labor. She subsequently attacks Athens in retribution for Theseus's abduction of Antiope, and in some versions marries Theseus and has a son, Hippolytus. The wedding of Theseus and Hippolyta forms the context for Shakespeare's comedy *A Midsummer Night's Dream.*

Hippolytus

Son of Theseus, king of Athens, and Hippolyta, queen of the Amazons. Like his mother, he is a noted hunter, a devotee of Artemis, and scorns love. Aphrodite punishes him by making his stepmother Phaedra fall passionately in love with him. When he rejects her, she accuses him to Theseus of rape, and Theseus calls on Poseidon to punish Hippolytus. Poseidon sends a sea monster, which frightens Hippolytus's horses as he drives along the seashore and causes his death, and Phaedra then kills herself. One of Euripides' greatest plays is devoted to the story, which in turn inspired Racine's tragedy *Phèdre.* In the Roman version

of the legend, however, Hippolytus is restored to life by Artemis/Diana and carried off to her sacred grove in Aricia.

Horae

Greek goddesses of the seasons, daughters of Zeus and the Titan Themis. Devoted to the natural order, they control the growth of plants, oversee the stability of human society, and guard the gates of Olympus.

Horus

Egyptian falcon-headed sky-god, conceived by Isis by magical means after the death of her brother and consort Osiris. She takes refuge in the Nile delta and raises Horus in total secrecy. When he reaches manhood, Horus challenges Seth, his father's murderer, and in the combat he loses an eye but succeeds in killing or castrating Seth, and is adjudged the winner by the other gods. Seth restores Horus's eye, but he gives it to the restored Osiris and replaces it with the divine serpent, which then acts as a symbol of royalty.

Hyacinthus

A beautiful young man beloved of Apollo. One day the two are practising throwing the discus when a gust of wind (or possibly a rejected suitor, the wind-god Zephyrus) catches the discus that Apollo has thrown and whirls it around so that it hits Hyacinthus on the head and kills him. Unable to revive him, Apollo causes a new flower, the hyacinth, to grow from his blood. The myth probably grew out of the cult of a pre-Hellenic deity taken over by that of Apollo.

Hyades

Nymphs, daughters of Atlas, to whom the infant Dionysos is entrusted after the death of his mother Semele. They become afraid of the jealousy of Hera and pass the child to Semele's sister Ino, who pays the price for her family loyalty. The Hyades are changed by Zeus into a cluster of stars in reward for their service, or alternatively as consolation for the death of their brother Hyas.

Above Hippolytus is dragged to death by his horses, which have been panicked by a sea monster sent by Poseidon. Engraving after a painting by Peter Paul Rubens (1577-1640).

Hydra

Monstrous many-headed offspring of Typhon and Echidna, which Heracles is sent to kill as his second labor. A serpent with the body of a hound, it was reputedly bred up by Hera with the specific purpose of destroying Heracles, the bastard son of her husband Zeus. As Heracles cuts off one head, two more grow, and he has to call on his nephew Iolaus to cauterize each neck to prevent this. When he returns to Eurystheus, who has imposed the labors on him, Eurystheus refuses to count the killing of the Hydra, because Heracles has received help.

Hygeia

Roman goddess of health, the daughter of Asclepius, or Aesculapius to the Romans. She is shown holding a cup in one hand and a serpent in the other, and is usually veiled; Roman matrons cut off and dedicated their hair to her.

Hylas

Son of Theodamas, king of the Dryopes, whom Heracles kills after stealing one of his oxen. Hylas is so beautiful that Heracles carries him off to be his squire. Hylas accompanies him on the voyage of the Argonauts and during a landing is asked to draw water from a spring. The water-nymphs fall in love with him and pull him under the water, where he drowns. Heracles is desolated and, with the help of Polyphemus, searches everywhere for him; meanwhile the Argonauts sail on without their comrades.

Hyllus

Son of Heracles and Deianira. When Heracles lies dying from the poisoned shirt that Deianira has been tricked into giving him, he commands Hyllus to marry Iole, whom he won in an archery contest and who provoked Deianira's jealousy and thus the death of Heracles. Eurystheus continues to persecute the children of Heracles, and they take refuge with Theseus in

Below Hymen and Cupid, undated engraving based on a work by William Hogarth (1697-1764).

Athens. Hyllus finally succeeds in killing him and marries Iole. He is determined to claim Heracles' right to the Argive kingship and consults the Delphic oracle, which tells him to march "after the third fruit." Hyllus takes this to mean three years, but is killed when he invades the Peloponnese, and it is his grandson Temenus who finally conquers the Peloponnese 100 years later; the oracle meant the third generation.

Hymen

Greek god of marriage, whose name comes from the Greek for a wedding song. A late myth recounts that he is a young Athenian, too poor to marry the girl he loves, who succeeds in killing the pirates that carry her off and is then accepted as a suitable son-in-law.

Hyperboreans

Mythical nation living far to the north or west of Greece; *hyper boreas* means beyond the north wind. Apollo flies there with his team of swans immediately after his birth, and stays there until his triumphal entry into Delphi, returning there to spend the winter. Homer says the Hyperboreans live in a land shrouded in mist, but other accounts see them as a happy people untouched by illness and living in a country of perpetual sunshine. The basis for the legend has been variously

interpreted as the amber route to the Baltic, or the rich cornlands of Central Europe.

Hyperion

One of the Titans and an early sun-god, father of Helios, the sun; Eos, the dawn; and Selene, the moon. In the *Odyssey* he keeps his sacred cattle on a fertile island, possibly Sicily, and is identified with Helios. In Keats's unfinished poem *Hyperion* he is the last of the Titans, who is about to be deposed by the Olympian sun-god Apollo.

Hypermnestra

Eldest daughter of Danaus, king of Argos. When she and her 49 sisters marry the 50 sons of Danaus's brother Aegyptus, she is the only one to disobey her father's order that they all murder their husbands. She helps Lynceus to escape and he avenges the death of his brothers, but they are eventually reconciled with Danaus, and Lynceus succeeds him as king of Argos.

Hypnos

Greek god of sleep, son of Nyx, the night, Hypnos lives in a cave on the island of Lemnos, or possibly in the far-off land of the Cimmerians. He lies on a soft couch, surrounded by his children, the Dreams, and Lethe, the river of forgetfulness, flows through the cave. At the command of Hera, he sends one of his sons, Morpheus, to impersonate Ceyx and tell Ceyx's wife Alcyone of his death by drowning. On another occasion Hera, by promising him the nymph Pasithae as wife, persuades him to lull Zeus to sleep during the Trojan War so that Poseidon can intervene on behalf of the Greeks, who have been driven back to the shore by the valor of Hector.

Hypsipyle

Queen of Lemnos. When the women of Lemnos neglect the cult of Aphrodite, the goddess punishes them by making them smell so foul that their husbands refuse to come near them. In revenge the women massacre all the men, except for the king, Troas, Hypsipyle's father, whom she saves by hiding him in a chest which she sets adrift. She rules in his place, and when the Argonauts pass on their journey to Colchis (see Jason), the women entertain them for a year, having presumably appeased Aphrodite and become desirable again. Hypsipyle bears Jason two sons, but after the Argonauts leave, Troas reclaims his kingdom and Hypsipyle flees and is captured by pirates, who sell her as a slave to Lycurgus, king of Sparta. She becomes nurse to his son Archemorus, and is warned by an oracle never to place the child on the ground. When the Seven Champions, on their way to attack Thebes, ask her for water, however, she forgets and places Archemorus on the ground while she shows them a

Below left Roman statue of Hypnos, with a burned-out torch symbolizing sleep.

spring. A serpent kills the boy, and the prophet Amphiarus sees this as portending the failure of the Seven. Hypsipyle's children by Jason save her from Lycurgus, and take her back to Lemnos.

Hyreus

First king of Hyria on Boeotia. He is a peasant when he is visited by Zeus, Poseidon, and Hermes, whom he entertains as generously as he can. When they offer him a gift, he asks for a son, as his wife is lately dead and he has promised her never to remarry. The gods each urinate on to the hide of a dead bull, and tell him to bury it. Nine months later, Hyreus digs it up and finds the child Orion (from *ouria*, urine), who grows into a giant.

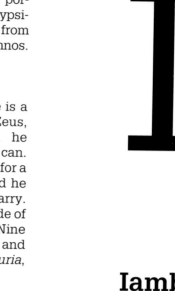

Iambe

Servant maid of Metanira, queen of Eleusis, and daughter of Pan and Echo, she tries to cheer Demeter when she pauses for a while at Eleusis in her search for Persephone. From the jokes and stories which she tells comes the term "Iambics," free and satirical verse.

Iapetus

A Titan, the son of Uranus and Ge, and the father of Atlas, Prometheus, and Epimetheus by Themis. He fights on the side of the giants in the great battle with the gods, and is thrown into Tartarus by Zeus when the giants are defeated.

Below The wounded Aeneas is treated by Iapis. Wall-painting from Pompeii.

Iasius

Son of Zeus and Atlas's daughter Electra, he falls in love with Demeter, goddess of harvests and fertility. In some stories she rejects him and Zeus strikes him dead for his boldness, but in others he makes love to the goddess in a fallow field that she has plowed three times, and she bears Plutus, wealth. In yet another version, it is not Demeter but Cybele with whom Iasius sleeps, and she bears two sons and a daughter, Atalanta, whom Iasius exposes on the mountainside because he wants only male children, but she survives to become a famed huntress.

Icarius

Spartan prince who, with his brother Tyndareos, is driven out of Sparta. He marries a water-nymph and among his children are Troas and Penelope. Icarius is so fond of his daughter that, when she grows up and marries Odysseus, he first tries to persuade the couple to live with him, and then follows the bridal chariot begging her to stay. Odysseus rather generously gives his bride a free choice to go or stay. Penelope blushes deeply and covers her face with her veil, indicating her intention of going with her husband, and Icarius is so charmed that he builds a temple to the goddess of modesty on the spot.

Icarus

Son of the brilliant Greek inventor Daedalus, who offends Minos king of Crete. He and Icarus are both imprisoned, but Daedalus makes wings of feathers and wax with which they fly from their jailer. He warns Icarus not to fly too close to the sun, as the wax will melt, but Icarus finds the experience so exciting that he forgets the warning; the wax melts and he plunges into the sea and drowns.

Idas

Prince of Messenia and twin brother of Lynceus, Idas is one of the bravest and strongest Greek heroes, but also known for his rash behavior. Idas and Lynceus sail with the Argonauts and join the hunt of the Calydonian boar, two of the great epics of Greek mythology. Idas wins the Greek princess Marpessa as his wife in a chariot race, because he borrows the winged chariot of Poseidon and defeats her father. She is also courted by Apollo, however, and when Apollo still pursues her, Idas challenges him and is turned into a kingfisher for his insolence, but Zeus intervenes and asks Marpessa her views. She chooses Idas, because he will grow old when she does. A quarrel then arises between Idas and Lynceus and their cousins the Dioscuri, Castor and Polydeuces. In some stories this is over the division of some sheep they have stolen, but in others it is brought about by Castor and Polydeuces carrying off the daughters of Leucippus whom Idas and Lynceus had been about to marry. Either way, both brothers die in the feud that results, and Marpessa kills herself in grief.

Idmon

Prophet son of Apollo and the nymph Cyrene, he accompanies the Argonauts on their expedition to recover the Golden Fleece (see Jason), even though he foresees his own death; he is killed by a wild boar when the *Argo* docks at Bithynia.

Idomoneus

King of Crete, grandson of Minos and, since he was one of the suitors of Helen, the leader of the Cretan forces which assist the Greeks in the Trojan War. He acquits himself honorably in battle and is on his way home when his

Below Icarus falls to his death when the sun melts the wax of his artificial wings.

fleet is threatened by a terrifying storm, and Idomoneus rashly promises to sacrifice to Poseidon the first living creature that he meets in Crete, in return for a safe landfall. Inevitably this is his son. When Idomoneus postpones the sacrifice, Poseidon sends a plague to afflict the land; when Idomoneus finally fulfils his oath, however, the Cretans are so horrified by his brutality that they depose him, and he travels to Italy and founds a city there.

Ilia

The mother of Romulus and Remus, also known as Rhea Silvia, in which guise her story is rather different. Ilia is the daughter of Aeneas and his Italian wife Lavinia, and is loved by Mars, the Roman god of war, who is the father of her twins. Amulius, king of Alba, imprisons Ilia and exposes the twins on the mountainside, where they are suckled by a she-wolf. In some versions of the story, Ilia marries the god of the River Tiber.

Ilus

Founder of Troy. He migrates from his homeland to Phrygia and competes in the local games, where he wins 50 youths, 50 girls, and a dappled cow. An oracle tells him to found a city where the cow sits down, which it does on a hill near Mount Ida. Ilus asks Zeus for a sign, and the Palladium, a wooden image of Athena, drops from the sky. Ilus dedicates a temple to Athena on the spot, and the Trojans believe that as long as the Palladium is safe in the temple, Troy cannot fall.

Inachus

River-god, the son of Oceanus and Tethys, and mythical first king of Argos. When Hera and Poseidon argue about which one of them should claim the land of Argos, Inachus awards it to Hera, in punishment for which Poseidon dries out his river each summer. His daughter Io is loved by Zeus and turned into a heifer to protect her from Hera; Inachus mourns his daughter and curses the god, so Zeus sends the Fury Tisiphone to drive him mad.

Ino

Daughter of Cadmus and Harmonia, and sister of Semele. She plots to kill the children of her husband Athamas's first wife, but they are rescued by a golden ram (see Helle, Phrixus). When Semele is killed by the sight of Zeus in his divinity, Ino shelters her son Dionysos from the jealousy of Hera, although she herself doubts Dionysos's divinity. When Hera discovers the trick, she sends Ino and Athamas mad. First Ino and her sisters Agave and Autonoe kill Agave's son Pentheus in a bacchic frenzy (probably also a punishment for failing to recognize the divinity of Dionysos); then Ino and Athamas kill their own children in their madness.

Io

Priestess of Hera, the daughter of Inachus, king of Argos. Zeus falls in love with her and spreads a cloud over the woods so that he can make love to her in secret. Hera becomes suspicious, however, and Zeus transforms Io into a white heifer to protect her. Hera is not deceived, and sets Argus of the one hundred eyes to watch her and prevent Zeus approaching her. Hermes, at Zeus's command, strikes off Argus's head, but Hera then sends a gadfly to torment Io so that she is driven through Europe and as far as Egypt. There she is restored to her normal shape and becomes the mother of Epaphus, ancestor of Danaus.

Iolaus

Nephew and charioteer of Heracles, who accompanies him on most of his Labors, and helps in the battle with the Hydra by burning the stumps left when Heracles cuts off its many heads, before new heads can grow. He also joins the hunt of the Calydonian boar. When Heracles goes mad and kills his children by Megara, he passes Megara on to Iolaus, who marries her. After the death of Heracles, Iolaus helps his children, the Heraclids, in their long struggle to claim their kingdom. In one story, he is restored to youth and vigor for one day by Hebe, at the request of the now deified Heracles, in order to kill Heracles' old enemy Eurystheus.

Iole

Lover of Heracles, who wins her in an archery contest staged by her father, but then has to abduct her when her father refuses to give her up. Heracles' wife Deianira tries to win back her husband's love from Iole by sending him a tunic which the centaur Nessus has told her restores true lovers to each other. Nessus has poisoned the tunic, however, and Iole thus becomes the cause of the hero's death. His dying wish is that Iole should marry his son Hyllus.

Ion

Grandson of Erectheus, one of the first kings of Athens, Ion gives his name to the Ionians, who colonized the western part of Asia Minor (modern Turkey). In Euripides' play *Ion*, he is the son of Erectheus's daughter Creusa and Apollo, conceived and born in a cave on the Acropolis and abandoned by his mother, who assumes that Apollo will look after his own. This he does; Ion is taken by Hermes to Delphi and brought up by the priestess, and is finally recognized by Creusa and adopted by her husband Xuthus.

Iphicles

Half-brother of Heracles, whose mother Alcmene gives birth to twins. One, Iphicles, is the son of her husband Amphitryon, the other, Heracles, is the offspring of Zeus. When Hera, jealous of her husband's love child, sends two snakes to kill the boys, Iphicles betrays his human origins by screaming, while Heracles strangles the snakes. Iphicles accompanies his brother on several of his Labors, and his son Iolaus becomes Heracles' charioteer.

Iphigenia

Youngest daughter of Agamemnon, king of Mycenae, and Clytemnestra, she is summoned to Aulis, where the Greek fleet lies becalmed on its way to Troy. An oracle has ordained that the goddess Artemis will only send a favorable wind if Iphigenia is sacrificed to her. At first Agamemnon refuses to send for his daughter, but finally he gives way to pressure from the other generals, telling his wife that Iphigenia is to be the bride of Achilles. In one version of the story, Iphigenia is indeed sacrificed and Clytemnestra, with her lover Aegisthus, exacts a fearful and final vengeance on Agamemnon for the death of their daughter when he finally returns from the Trojan War. In another, Artemis takes pity on the girl and snatches her away at the

Above Iphigenia as a priestess in Tauris, by the engraver Josef von Keller (1811-73).

last minute, substituting a deer. Iphigenia becomes a priestess at a temple in Tauris where all strangers are sacrificed to an effigy of Artemis. After many years, Iphigenia's brother Orestes comes to Tauris, driven by the Furies and seeking expiation for murdering his mother, who in turn had killed his father. Iphigenia recognizes him and flees with him, taking with her the effigy of Artemis, and they return to Greece.

Iphis

A Cretan girl, whose father has no interest in daughters and wants only sons. She is therefore dressed as a boy by her mother to save her life and brought up as her father's son. When Iphis grows up she is betrothed by her father to the beautiful Ianthe, and the two fall in love, but her mother, afraid of the consequences of discovery, keeps postponing the marriage ceremony. Finally the goddess Isis comes to the rescue, changing Iphis into a boy.

Iris

Greek goddess of the rainbow and messenger of the gods; the Greeks saw the rainbow as connecting heaven and earth, and so Iris is the personification of communication. She is linked particularly with Hera, and has the role of cutting the thread which detains the souls of the dying in their bodies. She marries Zephyrus, the god of the west wind, and is believed to supply the clouds with water to make rain.

Isis

Egyptian mother-goddess, universally worshipped in Egypt and whose cult was also widespread in the Greek and Roman worlds. She is the daughter of Nut, the sky-goddess, and the earth-god Geb, and achieves deification in her own right by discovering the ineffable name of the sun-god Re. Collecting some of his spit, she mixes it with earth to create a serpent, which she leaves in Re's path. Poisoned by its bite, Re is persuaded by Isis to speak his secret name, since its power gives life and health to the speaker, and she in turn appropriates some of Re's divinity. She becomes the consort of her brother Osiris, and together they are represented as the ox and the cow, bringing fertility and wealth to the earth. When Osiris is murdered and dismembered by Seth, Isis's tears of despair are said to cause the life-giving floodwaters of the Nile. She painstakingly collects all the pieces of her husband's body, and conceives her avenging son Horus by the dead god. As the goddess of fertility and regeneration, Isis becomes identified with many other deities, including Aphrodite, Athena, Cybele, Diana, and Bellona.

Ismene

Theban princess, daughter of Oedipus through his incestuous union with his mother Jocasta. She and her sister Antigone help their father, after he has blinded himself on discovering who he has married, but when Antigone wishes to bury their brother Polynices, whose body has been left to rot for rebellion against the state, Ismene refuses her support. Antigone is punished by being walled up alive, and Ismene insists on joining her.

J

Janus

One of the most ancient of the Roman gods, represented as having two faces, one looking forward and one back, either because he knows both past and future, or because he is identified with the sun, which opens the day with its rising and closes it with its setting. He is the god of beginnings, gates, and avenues, and only through him can prayers reach the other gods, and so he is always named first in Roman ritual. He is supposed to have entertained Cronos (Saturn in Roman mythology)

Below Sculpture of Janus with his two heads.

Above Ixion bound to his burning wheel. Seventeenth-century engraving.

Itys

Son of Tereus, king of Thrace, and the Greek princess Procne. He is killed, cooked, and served up as a meal to his father by Procne and her sister Philomela in revenge for Tereus's rape of Philomela.

Ixion

King of the Lapiths, and supposedly the first man to murder a blood relative, the Greek equivalent of Cain. He marries Dia and invites her father to a feast to collect the bride-price, but treacher-ously digs a pit and fills it with burning coals, in which his father-in-law dies. The neighboring monarchs are so shocked by this that they refuse the normal rites of purification, and Ixion becomes an outcast. Zeus takes pity on him and carries him to Olympus to be cleansed of his sin, but Ixion, un-daunted, tries to seduce Hera. When she complains to Zeus, he creates a cloud in her form to test his protégé; Ixion makes love to this creation and is caught in the act by Zeus and con-demned to perpetual torment in Tarta-rus, being fastened to a continuously rotating burning wheel. The cloud, Nephele, bears a son, Centaurus, who mates with the wild mares of Mount Pelion to produce the centaurs.

when Cronos was driven from Greece by his son Zeus, and to have derived much of his power from this ancestral god. He saved Rome from the Sabines by dispelling them from the Capitol by a jet of hot water, and henceforth the doors of the temple of Janus were only ever closed in times of peace.

Jason

Celebrated Greek hero, the son of Aeson, rightful king of Iolcos in Thessaly, who has been deposed by his half-brother Pelias. Jason's mother Alcimede does not trust the usurper and sends her son away to be educated by the centaur Chiron, telling Pelias that the boy has died. Many of Jason's fellow pupils later accompany him on his most famous exploit, the recovery of the Golden Fleece. When Jason has grown to manhood, the Delphic oracle warns Pelias to beware of a descendant of Aeolus (the grandfather of

Below Jason pours out a drug for the dragon guarding the Golden Fleece.

Aeson) who wears only one sandal. Jason resolves to make himself known to Pelias, his uncle, and establish his claim to the throne, and sets off from Mount Pelion, where Chiron lives, to Thessaly. On the way he has to cross the flooded River Anaurus. As he prepares to wade through, an old woman asks him to carry her over. This he does, despite her extraordinary weight, and loses a sandal in the flood. He continues on his way, unaware that the old woman is Hera, who resents Pelias's neglect of her rites and smooths Jason's path.

Pelias is alarmed at Jason's ominous arrival in Iolcos but does not dare to kill him outright, and instead sends him on a quest to avenge the death of Phrixus, kinsman to both of them, who has been killed by Aeetes, king of Colchis, after flying to his kingdom on a golden ram. Jason is to carry back to Iolcos the magic Golden Fleece of this ram, and in return, Pelias, believing the task to be impossible, promises to resign the throne to him. In some versions of the story, it is Hera who suggests this

course to Pelias, because she foresees that Medea will return with Jason and kill Pelias.

Jason assembles a band of the noblest heroes in Greece for the quest of the Golden Fleece, including the shipbuilder Argus, who builds the *Argo* to carry them to the far end of the Black Sea where Colchis lies. Other warriors who sail with Jason include Zetes and Calais, the winged sons of Boreas; Castor and Polydeuces, twin sons of Leda; Heracles; Hephaestus; Peleus; Telamon; and, the musician Orpheus. The full crew numbers 56 men, of whom 54 row in pairs, while Tiphys the helmsman steers and Orpheus sits in the bows, stilling the sea and giving the time to the oarsmen with his music.

The Argonauts pass through many adventures before arriving in Colchis. Their first landfall is on Lemnos, whose women have offended Aphrodite and killed all their men; the Argonauts stay long enough to repeople the island. After passing the Hellespont, they land at Salmydessus, where the king,

Phineus, who is a prophet, is plagued by the harpies for betraying Zeus's secret plans for humanity. He forecasts the *Argo*'s course and advises them how to avoid the clashing rocks at the mouth of the Bosphorus, and in return Calais and Zetes drive away the harpies. On reaching the mouth of the Bosphorus, Jason releases a dove, which flies between the rocks (sometimes interpreted as ice floes from the Russian rivers), causing them to smash together. The *Argo* tries to sail through as the rocks withdraw, but is held back by a huge wave, and only the intervention of Athena, from whose sacred wood the ship is built, ensures their survival, with just the tip of the stern oar being crushed.

When the *Argo* finally arrives in Colchis, Jason assures the suspicious Aeetes that the winning of the Golden Fleece is his sole purpose, and Aeetes sets him the task of yoking a team of fire-breathing bulls to a plow, tilling a field, sowing it with dragons' teeth, and then killing the host of armed men which will spring from the ground. With the help of Aeetes' sorceress daughter Medea, who has fallen in love with Jason, he succeeds, but Aeetes does not yield the fleece and instead starts to plot the destruction of the Greeks. Medea learns of this by her witchcraft and, in return for Jason's solemn oath before Hera that he will marry her, she puts to sleep the unsleeping serpent that guards the tree on which the Golden Fleece is hung, and they take flight in the *Argo*.

The voyage home proves quite as eventful as that to Colchis. First Zeus ordains that Jason and Medea must be purified by Circe (who is Medea's aunt) for Medea's murder of her brother Absyrtus. They arrive anonymously on Circe's island and she carries out the purification, only afterward asking who they are. On hearing the crime of which they have now been cleansed, she is so horrified that she sends them away without hospitality.

When they have nearly reached Greece, they are blown off course as far south as Libya, carried inland by a huge wave, and dumped in a desert. The Argonauts carry the *Argo* for nine days until they reach an inland lake, where they pray to the gods of the place and are rescued by Triton, who pushes them down a river to the sea. The final hazard is a dense darkness which surrounds the ship so that steer-

ing is impossible. Jason prays to Apollo, who fires a blazing arrow which lights them to shore.

In Iolcos Jason discovers that Pelias has murdered his father Aeson, but by now Medea is the driving force both in the relationship and in the myth. In revenge for the death of Aeson, she persuades Pelias's daughters that she can rejuvenate their father if they first kill him and throw him into her magic cauldron. The Iolcans are so shocked at the savage death of Pelias that they drive Jason away, despite his claim to the throne, and Hera also now abandons him. He and Medea take refuge at the court of Corinth and Jason finally abandons Medea for the king's daughter, who dies by Medea's vengeful hand.

Above The moment of horror when Jocasta and Oedipus recognize their incestuous relationship.

Jason lives on in obscurity, and is finally killed by a rotting timber from the *Argo*, which falls on his head.

Jocasta

Tragic queen of Thebes, wife of the accursed Laius. After Laius has been killed by a stranger, who also rids Thebes of the sphinx that plagues the city, Jocasta marries the conqueror in accordance with the promise made by the regent, her brother Creon. Her new husband is none other than her son by Laius, Oedipus, who had been destined from birth to kill his father and so had been exposed on a mountainside, and assumed to be dead. Jocasta has two sons, Eteocles and Polynices, and two daughters, Antigone and Ismene, by Oedipus before a plague that descends upon Thebes leads to the truth being revealed. In despair at her own unwitting but mortal sin, she hangs herself.

Juno

Originally an Italian goddess of women and childbirth, the wife of Jupiter, she becomes associated with the Greek Hera. One myth that seems specifically to concern Juno and not Hera is the birth of Mars. Juno is offended when Jupiter bears Minerva from his head without female assistance, and complains to Flora, who rubs Juno's stomach with a magic herb so that she becomes pregnant with Mars. Juno is associated particularly with married love, and her festival, the Matronalia, takes place in the month dedicated to Mars. The Romans believed that each woman had her own protective spirit which they called *iuno*.

Above Roman bronze head of Juno Lucina, in her aspect as goddess of childbirth.

Left *Jupiter and Io* by Antonio Correggio (1489-1534).

Jupiter

The principal Roman god, originally a sky-god connected with rain, storms, and thunder, who becomes associated with the chief Greek god Zeus and has hardly any separate mythology. His chief temple stood on the Capitoline Hill, dedicated to "Jupiter Optimus Maximus."

Juturna

Italian water-nymph, sister of the Italian prince Turnus, whom she aids against Aeneas when he arrives in Italy after the fall of Troy. Jupiter pursues her, and she hides in the River Tiber but is betrayed by Lara. Jupiter compensates Juturna for the loss of her virginity by granting her power over streams and rivers. She disguises herself as the charioteer Metiscus in order to protect Turnus, but is warned by a Fury sent by Jupiter to give up the struggle to save him, and sinks lamenting into her spring.

K L

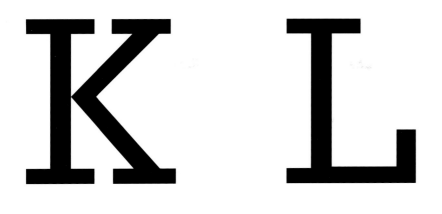

Khepra

Egyptian god of the dawn, a facet of the sun-god Re, represented as a scarab beetle pushing the sun across the sky like a ball of dung. Like the young scarab, which emerges spontaneously from its ball of dirt, Khepra arises self-generated from the primeval waters.

Below Khepra the scarab beetle pushes the sun up toward Nut, the sky-goddess.

Lacedaemon

Son of Zeus and the mountain-nymph Taygete, one of the Pleiades, who is raped by Zeus while unconscious and hides under the mountain Taygetus in shame. Lacedaemon gives his name to the people of Latonia in the southern Peloponnesus, the Lacedaemonians. He marries Sparta and names his capital city after her, and it becomes the chief rival to Athens in historical times.

Lacinia

Surname of the chief Roman goddess Juno from her temple of Lacinium in Italy.

Laertes

King of Ithaca and ostensibly the father of the Greek hero Odysseus, although in some versions Anticlea is already pregnant by Sisyphus when she marries Laertes. He acknowledges Odysseus as his heir and yields the throne to him when he reaches maturity, living in miserable retirement during Odysseus's absence in the Trojan War, unable to defend Odysseus's wife Penelope from her many suitors. When Odysseus returns, Athena gives Laertes a magic bath which restores him to vigor and enables him to assist his son in defeating and killing the suitors.

Laestrygones

A race of man-eating giants who live in Sicily, where, according to Homer, the nights are so short that shepherds bringing their flocks home at sunset meet those going out in the morning. Odysseus drops anchor in an apparently safe harbor in the course of his wanderings after the end of the Trojan War, and sends envoys to the Laestrygonian king, who at once eats one of them. The giants then bombard Odysseus's fleet with rocks, sinking all but Odysseus's own ship, which manages to escape.

Laius

King of Thebes and father of Oedipus. As a young man, Laius is forced to flee to the court of Pelops when his throne is usurped by Amphion and Zetus in revenge for the torments which their mother Antiope suffered at the hands of Laius's uncle Lycus. On Laius's return to Thebes he carries off Pelops's young son Chrysippus, with whom he has become infatuated, and as a result falls under a curse that dogs the whole Theban dynasty. Once re-established in his own kingdom, he marries Jocasta, but the marriage is childless. On consulting the Delphic oracle, he is bluntly warned that his son will cause his death and he resolves not to sleep with Jocasta, but forgets his decision when drunk. When Oedipus is born, he

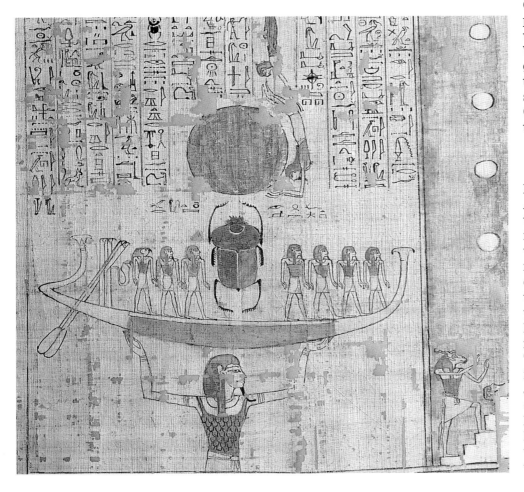

is at once abandoned on a hillside and his feet are staked to the ground to speed his death, but shepherds hear his screams and save him.

The curse laid on Laius takes the form of a sphinx, which settles in Thebes and devours all travelers who do not correctly answer the riddle it poses. Laius decides to travel to Delphi for advice on how to rid his kingdom of this menace, and on the way meets an unknown young man who refuses to give ground to him. This, of course, is his son Oedipus, returning from Delphi after learning that he will kill his father and marry his mother. The two argue and Laius is duly killed.

Lampetia

Daughter of the sun-god Helios and the nymph Naera, she tends her father's sheep in Sicily until Odysseus and his starving companions steal and kill some of the animals. She complains to her father, who makes the flesh of the stolen sheep bellow as it cooks, and the thieves take flight. They are pursued by a storm, from which only Odysseus himself escapes with his life by hanging on to a broken mast.

Laocoon

Trojan priest of Apollo, who warns the Trojans not to accept the Wooden Horse, which appears to have been left as a peace offering by the departing Greeks but is in fact a trap (see Odysseus). Athena, who supports the Greeks, sends two huge serpents, which seize and strangle Laocoon's two young sons and then also kills him when he tries to save them. The Trojans take this as a sign that the Horse should be accepted.

Laodamia

Devoted wife of Protesilaus, the first Greek warrior to set foot on Trojan soil, who is soon killed by Hector. Laodamia is desolate with grief and the gods, moved to pity, send Hermes to restore the shade of her husband to her for three hours, after which she insists on accompanying him to the underworld.

Laodice

Daughter of the Trojan monarchs Priam and Hecuba, she falls in love with Acamas, the son of Theseus,

when he comes as ambassador to Troy, and bears him a son. When Troy falls, the earth opens and swallows her.

Laomedon

King of Troy and father of Priam, notorious for his treachery. Apollo and Poseidon, who have been banished from Olympus for rebelling against Zeus, agree to build a wall round Troy for an agreed fee; when they have finished, however, Laomedon not only refuses to pay, but threatens them with slavery. They punish his kingdom with plague and a sea serpent, to which a virgin has to be sacrificed. When the lot falls on Laomedon's daughter Hesione, he gladly accepts Heracles' offer to kill the serpent, in return for the magic horses that Zeus gave him in exchange for Ganymede. Once the serpent is dead, however, he again fails to fulfil his side of the bar-

gain. Heracles therefore besieges Troy and kills Laomedon, setting his youngest son Priam on the throne instead.

Lapiths

Mountain people who live in Thessaly and are supposedly descended from Lapithes, son of Apollo and the river-nymph Stilbe. When their king Pirithous marries Hippodamia, they invite their neighbors the centaurs to the marriage feast, but the centaurs get drunk and try to carry off the Lapith women. The ensuing battle between the Lapiths and the centaurs was a popular subject in Greek sculpture.

Right above   Latinus welcomes Aeneas.

Right below   Roman statue of a lars or household god.

Below   Greek statue of *Laocoon*.

Lara

Italian river-nymph, the daughter of Tiber. When Jupiter falls in love with the nymph Juturna, he asks her kindred to help. Not only does Lara refuse, but she tells Juno of her erring husband's intentions; in punishment, Jupiter cuts out Lara's tongue and orders Mercury to conduct her to Hades. On the way Mercury falls for her, and she bears him the Lares, the Roman household gods.

Lares

Minor Roman gods who preside over households and crossroads; each household supposedly had its *lars familiaris* or divine protector.

Latinus

King of Latium when Aeneas arrives in Italy, and variously described as the son of Circe and Odysseus or of Faunus and a nymph. He welcomes Aeneas and gives him his daughter Lavinia as wife, but later turns against him and forms an alliance with the local king Turnus of the Rutuli. Aeneas defeats them both and becomes king of the Latins.

Laverna

Roman goddess of thieves and cheats, who protects all those who plot or deceive. Her worship was very popular, and the Romans raised an altar to her near one of the gates of the city, which as a result became known as the gate of Laverna.

Lavinia

Daughter of the Italian king Latinus, who is promised to Turnus, king of the Rutuli. An oracle orders her father to marry her to a foreign prince, however, and so Latinus betroths her to the Trojan Aeneas.

Leander

Young man of Abydos, who falls in love with Hero, a priestess of Sestos on the other side of the Hellespont. Each night he swims the straits to spend the night with her, guided by her lamp, but one night the lamp blows out, he cannot find the shore in the darkness, and drowns.

Leda

Queen of Sparta, the wife of Tyndareos, who is observed and desired by Zeus when she is a few days pregnant, bathing naked in a stream. Zeus persuades Aphrodite to change herself into an eagle, and to give chase to Zeus in the form of a swan. The subtle swan flies at once to Leda, who shelters it from the eagle, and Zeus makes good use of the opportunity. Nine months later, Leda gives birth to two eggs, from one of which come the immortal Castor and Helen, the children of Zeus, from the other Polydeuces and Clytemnestra, the children of Tyndareos. The subject of Leda and the swan was popular in Roman, Renaissance and post-Renaissance art.

Below Leda with all four of her children, by a follower of Leonardo da Vinci.

Lemures

The Romans believed that the spirits of the dead wandered over the world after death and disturbed the peace of the living, rather than being shipped to Hades as in Greek mythology. The benign spirits were called the Lares, whereas the Lemures were the maleficient ones, who haunted the good and cursed the wicked. The festival of Lemuralia in May was intended to exorcize these evil spirits for the following year, and while it was observed the temples were shut and marriages were prohibited.

Lethe

Greek goddess of oblivion, the daughter of Eris, who gives her name to one of the six rivers of the underworld, from which the dead must drink so that they can forget their previous existence and be born again.

Leto

Titan woman, the mother of the archer-gods Artemis and Apollo by Zeus. When she is due to give birth, the jealous Hera, knowing that Leto's children will be greater than her own, forbids every country to shelter her, ordains that the birth may not take place anywhere where the sun shines, and sends the monstrous serpent Python to pursue Leto. Zeus intervenes, however, ordering Poseidon to carry Leto to Ortygia, the floating island created when Leto's sister Asteria fell into the sea in the form of a quail. There he makes a wave curve over Leto so that she is hidden from the sun while she gives birth, and afterward the island is fastened down and becomes Delos. Unlike most of the Greek gods, Leto and her children retain a close family loyalty. Apollo kills the Python which pursued his mother, and he and Artemis cruelly punish Niobe when she boasts her superiority as a mother over Leto.

Leucippus

Young Greek who falls in love with the nymph Daphne and disguises himself as one of her female attendants. Apollo also has designs on Daphne, however, and engineers the revelation of Leucippus's sex while the nymphs are bathing. In punishment, they kill him.

Leucippus

Descendant of Bellerophon, who offends Aphrodite and is caused to fall in love with his own sister. They become lovers, but the man she is to marry discovers the truth, and accuses her to her father Xanthius of having a lover, without naming the man. Xanthius hides himself in his daughter's room and kills her, thinking that he has killed her lover; Leucippus in turn kills Xanthius, not realizing that it is his father. He flees to Crete, but is refused shelter because of the heinousness of his crime, and finally dies in misery at Ephesus.

Leucothea

Name given to Ino, the daughter of Cadmus, after she has been driven

Above Leto with the Infant Twins Diana and Apollo by the seventeenth-century French painter Simon Vouet.

mad by Hera, in punishment for her protection of the infant god Dionysos, and has thrown herself into the sea. She becomes a sea-goddess, and the son she has killed in her insanity becomes Palemon, a minor sea deity. Leucothea means "white goddess," perhaps referring to the sea foam, and she guides sailors through storms. In the *Odyssey*, she rises from the waves in the form of a sea mew when Odysseus's raft breaks up, and gives him her veil to tie round his waist, enabling him to swim to safety.

Levana

Roman goddess who presides over the first time that a newborn baby is picked up after the midwife has laid it down. This was usually done by the father, and so rigorously observed was the ceremony that a child's legitimacy could otherwise be disputed.

Libertas

Roman goddess of freedom, shown holding a rod in one hand and a cap in the other. These are both symbols of liberty; the rod was used by magistrates when freeing slaves, and the cap was worn by slaves who were soon to

be given their liberty. She is also associated with the cat, a creature that prizes its independence.

Libitina

Roman goddess who presides over funerals; her shrine was in a sacred wood, the meeting place of the undertakers.

Lichas

Herald to Heracles, who brings to the hero the poisoned shirt sent by his wife Deianira (who believes it will restore Heracles' love to her). Heracles puts on the clean shirt in order to make a sacrifice to Zeus, but is instead seized by the burning agony of the poison and, grabbing Lichas by the ankle, whirls him round three times and casts him out to sea, where Lichas is transformed into a rock.

Linus

Greek musician, about whom several conflicting stories are told, possibly reflecting the diverse origins of the myth of the harvest song, a lament for the end of the year. In one version he is the child of Apollo and an Argive princess, but is abandoned and eaten by dogs, whereupon Apollo sends a plague to ravage the country, and is only propitiated by the institution of an annual dirge to be sung in memory of his dead son. Another story makes Linus the son of the Muse Urania, who is killed by Apollo for claiming to sing as sweetly and is mourned in song by his people. Linus is credited with the discovery of the rules of harmony.

Lucina

Roman goddess, daughter of Jupiter and Juno, who supposedly bears her without pain, and so Lucina becomes the presiding deity of labor and childbirth.

Luna

Roman goddess of the moon, identified with Selene.

Lycaon

An early king of Arcadia and father of the nymph Callisto. When Zeus and Hermes travel through the world to

Above Undated engraving showing Lycaon transformed into a wolf for impiously testing the gods' omniscience.

test the virtue of mankind (see Baucis), Lycaon serves them human flesh to test their divinity. He is turned into a wolf for his rash impiety, and henceforth each time that a sacrifice is made at the Arcadian temple of Zeus, a man is turned into a wolf. If after eight years the wolf has not eaten human flesh, however, it is turned back into a human, in one version of the werewolf tradition.

Lycomedes

King of the Aegean island of Scyros, who is secretly entrusted with the care of the young hero Achilles by Achilles' mother Thetis, in an attempt to avoid his predestined death in the Trojan War. Odysseus sees through Achilles' female disguise, and Lycomedes' daughter Deidamia bears Achilles a son after his departure. Later, when Theseus is driven from his kingdom of Athens, he too takes shelter with Lycomedes, but the king distrusts his powerful and devious guest and throws him into the sea.

Lycurgus

King of Thrace, who refuses to welcome the wine-god Dionysos on his triumphant return from the East. He drives away the god with an ox-goad, alarmed by the abandoned behavior of Dionysos's followers and accusing the god of encouraging immorality. He also imprisons Dionysos's followers, the Maenads. Dionysos is so frightened by Lycurgus's rage that he takes shelter in the sea, where the sea-god Thetis, mother of Achilles, welcomes him, and the Nereids give him shelter. Lycurgus's prisons cannot hold the Maenads, however, and the walls turn into vines and release the women. Dionysos then returns and either sends Lycurgus mad, or makes him so drunk that he tries to rape his mother and kills his son Dryas, thinking he is a vine. An oracle tells the Thracians that they cannot taste wine until their king is dead, and so they bind him and leave him on Mount Pangaeus, where he is devoured by wild horses. The Lycurgus Cup in the British Museum, a superb example of Roman glassware, shows a different version of his fate, ripped apart by a vengeful vine.

Lycus

King of Thebes, who forcibly marries his niece Antiope in punishment for her affair with Zeus, and forces her to abandon Amphion and Zetus, her two sons by Zeus. She is cruelly treated by Lycus's first wife Dirce, but is finally avenged by her sons, who put Lycus to death.

Lynceus

The only one of the 50 sons of Aegyptus to be spared on his wedding night. His 49 brothers are all killed by their brides on the instruction of the girls' father Danaus, but Lynceus survives through the love of Hypermnestra, and succeeds Danaus as king after they are reconciled.

Lynceus

Greek hero renowned for his keen sight; he can see through the earth itself and distinguish objects at a distance of nine miles. He takes part in the hunt of the Calydonian boar (see Meleager) and the quest for the Golden Fleece (see Jason). He and his brother Idas are killed by Castor and Polydeuces as they are about to marry the daughters of Leucippus.

Lyncus

Greek king turned into a lynx by Demeter for trying to steal her gift of corn from Triptolemus.

M

Maat

Egyptian goddess of truth, daughter of the sun-god Re, she personifies the harmonious order established by Re at the time of the creation of the world. The pharoah derives his authority to rule by upholding the laws of Maat, and Egyptian temple decorations show the monarch presenting the effigy of Maat to the deity of the sanctuary. She is invariably shown wearing a feather, which she uses to tip the balance when the souls of the dead are weighed in the underworld for the judgment of Osiris.

Macaria

Daughter of Heracles and Deianira who, pursued by the vengeful Eurystheus, imposer of the Twelve Labors,

Above Dancing Maenad, on a Roman wall-painting found at Pompeii.

Left The goddess Maat wearing the feather of truth.

takes refuge in Athens with her kin after her father's death. An oracle declares that the descendants of Heracles will only gain victory over Eurystheus and reclaim their Peloponesan kingdom if one of them voluntarily submits to be sacrificed. Macaria offers herself, and in consequence the Athenians and the Heraclids defeat Eurystheus.

Machaon

A celebrated physician, the son of the healing-god Asclepius, who is one of the suitors to Helen and is therefore bound by oath to fight in the Trojan War (see Agamemnon). There he cures the wounds of Telephus, Menelaus, and Philoctetes, and is himself wounded by Paris and cured by Nestor. He is killed by the Amazon queen Penthesilea, his bones are taken back to Greece by Nestor, and a healing shrine established at the site of their burial.

Maenads

Female followers of Dionysos, Greek god of wine, who celebrate his rites with music and dance in a state of ecstatic frenzy. They roam the mountains dressed in animal skins, crowned with vine leaves or ivy, and carrying torches, snakes, and bunches of grapes. They possess more than human strength and are capable of tearing wild beasts apart and devouring them, and can inflict the same fate on a human who tries to resist them; see Pentheus. The first Maenads were the nymphs who guarded Dionysos in Asia.

Maia

Eldest of the Pleiades, daughters of Atlas, she lives in a mountain cave in Arcadia, where Zeus falls in love with her and visits her late at night when his wife Hera is asleep. Maia bears Hermes by Zeus, but seems to have been immune from the jealousy which Hera normally visited on her husband's lovers, and is able to give shelter to the less fortunate Callisto's child, Arcas.

Manes

Roman spirits of the dead, who are believed to become a collective underworld deity which presides over burial places and must be propitiated with offerings.

Below Roman head of Mars, dating from the first century AD.

Manto

Greek seer and daughter of the Theban prophet Tiresias, who is captured when the sons of the Seven against Thebes conquer the city (see Adrastus). They dedicate her to Apollo at Delphi, as the finest prize, together with many other Thebans, and there she perfects her gift of prophecy and gives birth to the prophet Mopsus. Apollo then sends her and the other Thebans to Asia Minor, directing her to found the colony of Colophon.

Marica

Italian water-nymph, she is the mother of the woodland-god Faunus, and is sometimes identified with Circe.

Marpessa

Greek princess whose father is so devoted to her that he challenges all her suitors to a chariot race, which he invariably wins. The defeated suitors are killed and their skulls used to decorate the temple of Poseidon. Poseidon seems unmoved by this ritual fervor,

and lends his winged chariot to Idas to help him win Marpessa. Her father gives chase but cannot catch them, and throws himself into the River Lycormas. Marpessa and Idas live in Messenia, where Apollo sees and falls in love with her. When he tries to carry her off, however, Idas intervenes and god and human wrestle furiously with each other until stopped by Zeus. He acts as arbiter and calls on Marpessa to choose between the sun-god and her husband; she chooses Idas, because they will grow old together.

Mars

Roman god of war, much of whose mythology is derived from that of the Greek war-god Ares, including his love affair with Venus. Mars is the son of Juno, just as Ares is the son of Hera, but Mars is conceived by Juno alone, with the aid of a herb given her by Flora, in payment for Jupiter's single-handed creation of Minerva, whereas Ares is the sole offspring of Zeus and Hera. Mars seems originally to have been a god of agriculture, identified with the pastoral god Silvanus, and he takes on more warlike qualities as the Romans themselves develop from a farming to a conquering nation.

He plays a more important role in Roman mythology than Ares in Greek, being second only to Jupiter in the Roman pantheon, and his worship was of paramount importance in the religion of the Roman state, because by fathering Romulus he founded the Roman race. He gives a sacred shield to the Romans, on the safekeeping of which the fate of Rome is believed to depend, and so the canny Romans make 11 more identical shields and hang them all in the temple of Mars to confuse any potential thief. On only one occasion does he, like Ares, become the butt of the other gods. He asks the aged goddess Anna Perenna to intercede for him with Minerva, and she eventually tells him that Minerva has agreed to be his bride. When he claims his bride and lifts her veil, however, he finds that it is Anna Perenna herself.

The love of Mars and Venus was a subject favored by classical as well as Renaissance painters, and a fresco

Right Mars, aided by a tiny Cupid, lays aside his armor and prepares for the bath. Roman sculpture from a bath building.

from Pompeii shows their courtship. The theme took on a more philosophical significance for the Renaissance, however, with the idea that Harmony is born from the union of Love and Strife, hence such paintings as Botticelli's *Mars and Venus*, in which Mars' helmet and weapons have become playthings for cupids.

Marsyas

A satyr, who finds the flute that Athena has invented but thrown away, because the other gods laughed at the faces she pulled while playing it. Marsyas becomes so proficient on the instrument that he challenges Apollo with his lyre to a contest. The Muses arbitrate, and the rules state that the winner may use the loser as he chooses. Both players perform equally well, until Apollo challenges Marsyas to play upside down, which is possible with the lyre but not with the flute, and so Apollo is adjudged the victor. He ties Marsyas to a pine tree and flays him alive; his blood, and the tears of the nymphs at his hideous death, combine to form the River Meander.

Below Roman marble of Marsyas bound for flaying.

Medea

Princess of Colchis, who learns sorcery from her aunt Circe and becomes a skilful witch and devotee of Hecate. Without her, Jason would not have won the Golden Fleece from her father Aeetes. Hera causes her to fall in love with Jason by sending Eros to her in the form of Circe, and she promises to help him in exchange for his promise of marriage. She advises him how to survive the challenge which Aeetes sets him (see Jason), and drugs the serpent which guards the tree on which the Golden Fleece hangs. Knowing that

Above Medea kills her two sons by Jason, after a painting by Eugène Delacroix (1798-1863).

her father intends to murder the Argonauts, she warns and flees with them. In order to delay pursuit, she dismembers the body of her brother Absyrtus and casts the pieces into the sea, and for this crime she and Jason have to be purified by Circe.

When the Argonauts finally reach Iolcos, Medea rejuvenates Jason's aged father Aeson by drawing all the blood from his veins and replacing it with a magic brew she has made. The daughters of the usurping king Pelias then beg her to do the same for their father, but Medea takes revenge on him for his seizure of Aeson's throne and his plots against Jason by persuading the girls to murder their father and then refusing to bring him back to life. Still Jason does not inherit his father's throne, however, and instead he and Medea are banished to Corinth by Pelias's son Acastus.

Here disaster ensues, for the king of Corinth wants Jason to marry his daughter Glauce and become his heir, and Jason proposes to divorce Medea. This she can neither allow nor forgive, having abandoned her homeland and killed her brother for Jason. She

Below Undated bust of Medusa with her writhing snakes instead of hair.

creates a poisoned wedding dress which destroys Glauce, and even murders her own children by Jason, before escaping to Athens in a chariot drawn by winged serpents. There the aged King Aegeus promises her protection, in return for Medea's assurances that he will father a child (although he is in fact and unknowingly the father of Theseus).

To fulfil her word, she marries him herself and bears Medus. When Theseus arrives to claim his inheritance, Medea recognizes him first and tries to poison him, but Aegeus realizes in time who the stranger is, and Medea flees to Asia, and her end is unreported in myth.

In Euripides' *Medea* she is a complex, passionate, and proto-feminist character, by no means wholly evil, who has been abandoned in a hostile land by the man for whom she has left her homeland, and whose tragedy is to understand, and yet to be unable to control, the forces that impel her to destroy all that she loves.

Medusa

One of the three Gorgons, female monsters who live in the Far West. Although they are sisters, Medusa is the only one who is mortal, and she alone has the power to turn anything that looks at her to stone. In later legend, Medusa is a beautiful girl whose lovely hair rivals Athena's and with whom Poseidon falls in love. In punishment, Athena turns her into a monster and her hair into a mass of snakes. She is killed by the hero Perseus, with Athena's help, and from her severed neck springs the winged horse Pegasus, the offspring of Poseidon. Perseus carries off Medusa's head and uses it to defeat his enemies and rescue Andromeda, finally offering it to his patroness Athena, who attaches it to the center of her shield, where it turns her enemies to stone.

Megara

Theban princess who is the first wife of Heracles, marrying him after he has delivered Thebes from the besieging Minyans. They have several children, but while Heracles is engaged on the last but one of his Twelve Labors, the removal of the three-headed dog Cerberus from Hades, Megara and her children are threatened by a usurper. Heracles returns just in time to rescue them and is about to offer a thanksgiving sacrifice to Zeus when Hera, ever unrelenting to Zeus's love children, sends him mad. Drawing his great bow, he shoots both Megara and their children, believing them to be the family of his tormentor Eurystheus.

Melampus

Greek prophet, whose name means "the man with the black feet;" when he was born, his mother placed him in the shade, but accidentally left his feet in the sun. As a child, he finds the nest of a dead serpent and rears its young, which reward him by licking his ears so that he can understand the speech of birds and animals. When his brother

Above Meleager joins the hunt for the Calydonian boar. Roman mosaic from Tunisia.

Bias falls in love with Pero, daughter of the king of Pylos, who can only be won by the gift of the cattle of Phylacus, Melampus undertakes to seize the cattle, but is caught in the act and imprisoned for a year. At the end of that time, he understands from the woodworm in his cell that the main beam will give way that night, and insists on being moved. Phylacus is so impressed that he challenges Melampus to cure his son's impotence, which he does in exchange for the cattle. When the daughters of Proetus, king of Argos, are driven mad for failing to observe the rites of Dionysos, Melampus is able to cure them, gaining a third of Proetus's kingdom for himself and a third for Bias.

Melanippe

Daughter of the wind-god Aeolus, she bears two sons to Poseidon, for which her father blinds and imprisons her and abandons the babies, who are raised by shepherds. They in turn give the babies to the queen of Icaria, who is about to be denounced by her husband Metapontus for her barrenness. She then also bears two sons of her own, but Metapontus prefers the older two, and the queen plots to kill them. In the ensuing battle, Poseidon brings about the death of the queen and her

boys and finally reveals himself to his own sons, commanding them to rescue their mother. He restores her sight, and Metapontus marries her and adopts the boys.

Melanippus

Theban warrior, one of the men born from the dragon's teeth sown by Cadmus. He helps to defend Thebes in the war of the Seven against Thebes and wounds Tydeus, but is killed by Amphiarus. Amphiarus beheads him and gives his head to the dying Tydeus, who splits his skull and eats his brains, thus foregoing his own chance of immortality.

Meleager

Greek hero and prince of Calydon, son of Oeneus and Althaea, whom the Fates predict will live no longer than the firebrand that is burning when he is born. His mother seizes the brand from the fire and guards it carefully, and Meleager grows to celebrated manhood, taking part in the voyage of the Argonauts (see Jason), and returning to defend Calydon against an invasion instigated by Artemis in punishment for Oeneus's neglect of her rites. Artemis then sends a huge wild boar to ravish the country, and Meleager invites all the heroes of Greece to join in the hunt of the Calydonian boar, one of the great quests of Greek mythology.

Among the warriors who assemble at Meleager's call are Castor and Polydeuces, Idas and Lynceus, Pirithous of the Lapiths, Theseus, Jason, Admetus, the brothers Peleus and Telamon, Adrastus, Amphiarus, and the warrior maiden Atalanta. Together they pursue the boar and it is Meleager who finally kills it. He gives the skin and the tusks to Atalanta, who was the first to wound it, but this partiality for a woman irritates the rest of the hunters, particularly Meleager's uncles. They try to steal the skin from Atalanta, and Meleager, who has fallen in love with her in the course of the chase, defends his gift and kills his uncles.

As Meleager's mother Althaea goes to the temple to give thanks for her son's victory, she meets the corpses of her brothers being born into the city and is told that they were killed by her son. Inflamed with grief, she seizes the firebrand which represents her son's life and thrusts it onto the fire, and Meleager instantly dies.

Melicertes

Greek prince, the son of Ino and Athamas, who is drowned by his mother in the insanity which Hera inflicts on her for her protection of Zeus's love child Dionysos. Poseidon takes pity on both mother and son and transforms them into sea deities; Melicertes becomes Palemon.

Melissa

Princess of Crete who, with her sister Amalthaea, cares for the infant Zeus when he is hidden from the suspicious rage of his father by his mother Rhea. Melissa feeds Zeus on goats' milk and discovers how to collect honey.

Melpomene

Muse of tragedy; see Muses.

Memnon

King of Ethiopia and son of the dawn-goddess Eos, whose skin is black because, like his mother, he is in childhood the constant companion of the sun, Helios. He brings an army to Troy to aid his uncle Priam, wearing armor made for him by Hephaestus at his mother's request. He kills Antilochus, son of the aged Greek king Nestor, and many other Greek warriors, and is then

Above Memnon and Achilles in single combat. Classical Greek vase-painting.

Left Melpomene, Muse of tragedy.

challenged by Achilles, also the son of a goddess, the sea deity Thetis. As the two heroes battle, the two anxious mothers each supplicate Zeus for her son's victory. Zeus weighs the destinies of the two and finds that Memnon's is the heavier, and so Achilles gains the day and Memnon dies. Eos persuades Zeus to grant her son immortality, and he causes the smoke from Memnon's funeral pyre to turn into two flocks of birds, which kill each other and fall into the flames as divine offerings to the dead hero's shade.

Menalippe

Amazon warrior, sister of the queen Antiope, who is captured by Heracles when he makes war on the Amazons and ransomed by her sister, who gives Heracles her own armor and belt instead.

Menelaus

Greek prince, the younger brother of Agamemnon. Menelaus becomes king of Sparta through his marriage to the Spartan king's daughter Helen. He and Agamemnon spend their youth in exile while their uncle Thyestes rules their father's kingdom of Mycenae, and Agamemnon is restored with Spartan help. Menelaus and Helen rule Sparta for many years and have one child, Hermione. When the Trojan prince

Paris arrives in his kingdom, having been promised Helen, the most beautiful woman in the world, by Aphrodite, Menelaus welcomes him, despite an ominous but ambiguous oracle. Summoned to Crete for the funeral of his grandfather, he leaves Paris in Sparta with Helen, only to find on his return that Paris has carried her back to Troy. He and Odysseus visit Troy to demand her return, but are spurned and insulted. On his return to Sparta, Menelaus summons all the princes who had been suitors to Helen and are bound by oath to protect her, and a huge army under the leadership of Agamemnon takes ship against Troy.

Initially the issue is to be decided by single combat between Paris and Menelaus. Menelaus wounds Paris severely, and Paris's protectress Aphrodite envelops him in a cloud and carries him to the safety of Helen's bedroom in Troy. Agamemnon claims that Menelaus is therefore the victor, but as the Trojans hesitate, Pandarus fires an arrow at Menelaus and grazes him, and general battle is joined. Menelaus does not figure as more than a secondary character in accounts of the ten-year Trojan War that follows, but on the fall of Troy it is he who finds Helen in the ruins of the city, now married to Deiphobus after the death of Paris.

He intends to kill her on the spot for her infidelity, but is once more ravished by her beauty and is reconciled with her. He neglects to propitiate the gods of defeated Troy, however, and their journey back to Greece takes eight years. They finally arrive in Sparta 18 years after they left, and when Telemachus passes through Sparta on his wanderings in search of his father Odysseus, he finds them peacefully installed there once again. At the end of his life, Menelaus, as Zeus's son-in-law, is carried off alive to live with the heroes in the Elysian Fields.

Menestheus

Grandson of the primitive Athenian king Erectheus, who lays claim to the Athenian throne when the rightful ruler Theseus is imprisoned by Hades in the underworld. He persuades the Athenians to accept him, because Theseus's theft of Helen of Sparta from her father Tyndareos has caused her brothers Castor and Polydeuces to in-

vade Attica. When Theseus is finally released by Heracles, Menestheus closes Athens against him and persuades King Lycomedes of Scyros to kill him. As one of the suitors of Helen after she has been returned by her brothers to Sparta, Menestheus is bound to fight in the Trojan War, and finds on his return that Theseus's son Demophon has dethroned him.

Menoeceus

Theban prince, the son of Creon and descended from one of the "sown men" whom Cadmus had created from the teeth of a dragon he killed in order to found Thebes. During the siege of

Below Head of Menelaus, undated drawing from a classical Greek statue.

Thebes by seven armies, the prophet Tiresias predicts that the city can only be saved by the voluntary sacrifice of a virgin warrior descended from the dragon's teeth army. The death of Menoeceus propitiates Ares, and the Thebans repel the seven armies.

Mentor

Friend and adviser of Odysseus, who is too old to fight at Troy, and takes charge of Odysseus's household and his son Telemachus in his absence. His name has come to mean a trusted counsellor. Athena takes the shape of Mentor when she accompanies Telemachus on his search for his father.

Mercury

The Roman equivalent of Hermes, god of merchants and traders, and the messenger of Jupiter. His worship was probably brought to Rome by Greek traders. The Romans dedicate the first fig from a fig tree to Mercury, and by extension any first fruit or new work.

Mercury Tresmegistus

Egyptian priest and philosopher in the time of Osiris, who teaches the Egyptians to cultivate the olive and to understand hieroglyphics.

Metis

Daughter of the Titans, or pre-Olympian gods, Oceanus and Tethys, and the first wife of Zeus. Her name means "prudence," "counsel," and it is she who gives Zeus's father Cronos the emetic which causes him to regurgitate Zeus's brothers and sisters, whom he has swallowed. When Metis becomes pregnant, the earth-goddess Ge prophesies that if she has a daughter, the girl will be Zeus's equal in wisdom, and that Metis will then bear a son who will be greater than his father and overthrow him. To avoid this, Zeus in turn swallows Metis. Some time later he is afflicted with an agonizing headache and persuades Hephaestus to split his head open with an ax; out flies Athena, the daughter of Metis, fully grown and armed.

Right Bronze *Mercury* by Italian sculptor Giovanni da Bologna.

Metra

Daughter of the Thessalian prince Erisichthon and loved by Poseidon, she persuades her lover to give her the power to change shape, so that her father can repeatedly sell her in order to feed the inordinate appetite with which he has been afflicted by Demeter. Once sold, Metra assumes a different shape and returns to Erisichthon.

Midas

King of Phrygia in Asia Minor, the son of Gordius, and renowned for his wealth. One day his people capture Dionysos's tutor Silenus and bring him to Midas, chained with garlands of flowers. Midas recognizes him, entertains him lavishly, and returns him to Dionysos in Lydia. In return he is offered his choice of a reward, and rashly requests that all he touches may be turned to gold. This proves inconvenient when his food turns to gold in his mouth, and he begs the god to remove the gift. He is told to wash himself in the River Pactolus, whose sands have been golden ever since.

On another occasion he supports Pan in a music contest between Pan and Apollo, and is punished by being given ass's ears. He manages to hide this deformity by wearing a Phrygian cap. His barber, the only man in on the secret, cannot stay silent, so he digs a pit and whispers the truth into it. From the pit grows a bed of reeds, which broadcast the news of Midas's monstrous ears to all comers. This story, which may well have suggested Nick Bottom's ass's head in *A Midsummer Night's Dream*, may also imply that Midas employed many spies and informers to report any possible signs of sedition.

Miletus

Young Cretan, the son of Apollo and the nymph Acacallis, who is loved by Minos, Rhadamanthys, and Sarpedon, the three sons of Zeus and Europa. He prefers Sarpedon, and they are driven from Crete by Minos, who establishes himself as king. Miletus settles in Caria in Asia Minor, marries the daughter of the river-god Meander, has two children, Caunus and Byblis, and founds the city of Miletus, which becomes an important Greek colony.

Minerva

An Italian household goddess, who becomes identified with the Greek Athena and so develops into a goddess of war as well as of wisdom. She is introduced into the Capitoline Triad with Jupiter and Juno, her worship ousting that of Mars. In post-classical times, while still portrayed wearing a helmet, she is associated more with prudence and wisdom than with battle, as in Mantegna's painting *The Triumph of Wisdom over Vice*, where she is shown routing Venus and her unregenerate supporters.

Minos

King of Crete, one of the three sons whom Europa bears to Zeus after he has carried her away across the sea in the guise of a white bull. Europa sub-

Below Midas turns his daughter to gold, lithograph by Walter Crane (1845-1915).

Above Cretan snake goddess, from the ancient Minoan civilization named after the mythical king Minos.

Left Minerva as the patron of learning and handicraft.

sequently marries Asterion, king of Crete, who adopts her three sons. On his death, each of them claims the kingdom, but Minos prevails by asking Poseidon to provide a suitable sacrificial victim if the kingdom should be his. Poseidon sends a magnificent bull from the sea, and the kingdom is duly accorded to Minos, but the creature is so beautiful that he cannot bring himself to sacrifice it. Poseidon in revenge sends the bull mad, and it lays waste the island until Heracles arrives to carry it off to Greece as one of his Twelve Labors.

In a further twist to Poseidon's punishment of Minos, he causes the queen, Pasiphae, to fall in love with the bull. She persuades the Athenian craftsman Daedalus to create a hollow wooden cow, in which she can hide to satisfy her passion, and as a result gives birth to the Minotaur, half man and half bull. Minos too has many lovers, and is cursed by Pasiphae who, as the daughter of the sun-god Helios, has magic powers, and ensures that he infects with a virulent poison any

Above Theseus kills the Minotaur, on a fifth-century BC Greek vase.

woman he makes love to. He is cured by Procris, to whom he gives a magic spear that never misses its mark.

Minos makes himself lord of the seas surrounding Crete and subjugates much of Greece; the prehistoric Minoan civilization which dominated eastern Mediterranean culture in the second millennium BC is named after him. He is supposed to have retired every nine years to the cave where Zeus was concealed in infancy, in order to pay homage to his father, and Zeus gives him laws by which to rule his kingdom. He is an implacable enemy, however, and wages bitter war on Athens after his son Androgeos has been killed there, exacting an annual tribute of seven boys and seven girls as human sacrifices for the Minotaur.

Theseus, the king's son, finally volunteers to be one of the victims and, with the help of Minos's daughter Ariadne, kills the Minotaur. Daedalus is implicated in their escape and is imprisoned by Minos, but manages to gain his freedom by building wings for himself and his son. Minos continues to pursue him, and finally meets his

death in Sicily while taking a bath, scalded by hot water from the pipes Daedalus has installed. Because he received laws direct from Zeus, he becomes a judge in the underworld realm of Hades, together with his brother Rhadamanthys.

Minotaur

Cretan monster, half man and half bull, the result of an illicit passion conceived by the queen, Pasiphae, for a magnificent bull sent to Crete by Poseidon. Her husband Minos commissions the craftsman Daedalus to create a vast complex of rooms and passages, the Labyrinth, in which the Minotaur is imprisoned, and exacts from Athens an annual tribute of seven boys and seven girls on which it is fed. Theseus finally succeeds in killing it. The Labyrinth has been connected with the great palace excavated at Knossos by Sir Arthur Evans, and with the rites of the *labrys*, the Cretan double-headed ax, which features in many Minoan frescoes along with scenes of bull-dancing and leaping. The Minotaur came to be a symbol of brutality and perversion for later ages, guarding the Seventh Circle of Hell in Dante's *Inferno*.

Minyans

The three daughters of King Minyas, called Leuconoe, Leucippe, and Alcithoe. They mock the rites of the wine-god Dionysos, and in return he inflicts them with an unquenchable desire for human flesh. They draw lots to decide which should give up her son to be eaten by the rest. The lot falls on Leucippe, who cheerfully sacrifices her son, and in retribution they are all three turned into bats.

Mithras

An Iranian god whose cult, being confined to men, appealed particularly to soldiers. It was carried to Rome by the army and spread throughout the empire. A young man who undergoes a trial of strength with the sun-god, Mithras then becomes identified with the sun, and with the fertilizing power of light, in the dualistic battle between the forces of light and darkness. He is always depicted with a bull, which he captures and sacrifices in a ritual of rebirth, and is seen as a savior who offers a route to immortal life. As such, Mithraism was the only serious competitor to Christianity in the Roman Empire. The ritual was kept a closely guarded secret, but included seven ceremonies of progressive initiation.

Mnemosyne

A Titan woman, the daughter of the primitive sky-god Uranus and the earth-goddess Ge. Her name means "memory." Zeus makes love to her on nine consecutive nights, and she gives birth to the nine Muses, the goddesses of the fine arts, music, and literature.

Moirae

The three Fates in Greek myth, known as the Parcae to the Romans, who determine the lifespan of all humans. They are variously described as the children of Nyx (night) and of Zeus and Themis, which raises the question of whether or not they are subject to Zeus's power; many classical writers saw them as superior even to the gods. They are named Clotho (the spinner), Lachesis (the drawer of lots), and Atropos (inevitable), and in later mythology are envisaged as three old women, spinning out and cutting off men's destinies like thread.

Momus

Greek god of blame and satire, originally a powerful and bitter figure, who by Roman times has become a figure of jokes and fun. The son of Nyx, night, he personifies carping criticism. He blames Zeus for placing the bull's horns on its head, rather than on its shoulders where the animal is strongest. He criticizes Hephaestus for creating man without a window in his breast, so that his feelings and motives may be more easily read. He censures the house built by Athena, because she has not made it movable. Even Aphrodite is deemed unsatisfactory because, although Momus can find no fault with her person, he maintains that the noise of her footfall is too loud to befit a goddess of beauty. When Ge,

Left and below The cult of Mithras became very popular during the Roman Empire. The ritual sacrifice of a bull was a key element in the rites.

the earth, complains that mankind is multiplying too rapidly and weighing her down, it is Momus who suggests first the Theban and then the Trojan War to solve the population problem. Finally the gods get tired of him and drive him from Olympus.

Mopsus

Celebrated Greek seer, the grandson of Tiresias and son of Manto, possibly by the sun-god Apollo. Apollo sends Manto to Asia Minor, where she founds the oracle of Clarus near Colophon. By the time the Trojan War has ended, Mopsus is in charge of the oracle, and when the Greek prophet Calchas comes to Colophon, a famous contest takes place between the two. First Calchas asks Mopsus the number of figs on a well-laden tree, and Mopsus gives the right answer. Then Mopsus asks Calchas how many young piglets will be born of a pregnant sow; Calchas says eight, but Mopsus correctly predicts the number to be nine, and Calchas dies of mortification.

Morpheus

God of dreams and the son of Hypnos, sleep. In earlier myth, as told by Homer and Virgil, dreams and visions are supposed to pass through the Gates of Sleep, ivory for false dreams and horn

Below The nine Muses, patrons of music, the fine arts, and literature, with Apollo who is regarded as their leader.

for true ones. It is only in Ovid that the source of dreams is personified as Morpheus, sender of visions to mankind.

Muses

Divine patrons of music, the fine arts, and literature, the Muses are the nine daughters of Zeus and the Titan Mnemosyne, and are also associated with Apollo who, as god of music, is regarded as their leader. They dance with him at festivals on Mount Olympus, and also attend the two great marriages of deity and human, Harmonia to Cadmus, and Thetis to Peleus. They give Hesiod, the earliest Greek poet after Homer, his knowledge and gift of verse, but can be relentless with those who oppose them; when the musician Thamyris challenges them to a contest and loses, they blind him and remove his musical powers. "Possession by the Muses" was long regarded as a form of divine madness, essential for poetic inspiration.

Myrmidons

A Greek people who accompany Achilles to the Trojan War, and whose name has come to suggest faithful but faceless cohorts. In some stories they are originally ants. See Aeacus.

Myrrha

Cypriot princess, who falls madly in love with her own father Cinyras, who has rashly boasted of his daughter's

great beauty and offended Aphrodite. Myrrha persuades her nurse to help her insinuate herself into her father's bed during a festival when married couples have to sleep separately. When, after several nights, he realizes the truth, he tries to kill her, but she escapes to southern Arabia, where the gods turn her into a myrrh tree. She is pregnant with the fertility-god Adonis, however, and when he is ready to be born, the goddess of childbirth splits the trunk of the tree and releases him.

Myrtilus

Charioteer of King Oenomaus of Pisa, bribed by Pelops to tamper with his master's chariot so that Pelops can win the race and so gain the hand of Oenomaus's daughter Hippodamia. Oenomaus recognizes that he has been betrayed and curses Myrtilus as he dies, predicting that he will die at the hands of Pelops. This proves all too accurate; Pelops has promised Myrtilus not only half his kingdom but also a night with Hippodamia in exchange for his treachery, and perhaps in retrospect the price seems too high. He takes Myrtilus for a ride in his chariot, drawn by the magic horses of Ares, and as they cross water he pushes Myrtilus in and he drowns. Drowning, however, he curses not only Pelops himself, but also all his descendants, and many of the most famous Greek myths spring from this curse. See Agamemnon, Atreus, Clytemnestra, Orestes, Thyestes.

N

Naiads

Nymphs who preside over rivers, springs, wells, and fountains, often shown in art as beautiful women holding urns, from which flow the waters sacred to them.

Nais

River-nymph with whom the Sicilian shepherd Daphnis falls violently in love, having boasted his immunity to love's power. At first he does not tell

Right Seventeenth-century French engraving of Narcissus, falling in love with his reflection.

Below A Naiad or water-nymph.

her of his passion, but as he begins to waste away with yearning, she agrees to be his on condition that he foreswears all other loves. A mortal woman, Xenia, tricks him into making love to her, however, and Nais strikes him blind in punishment.

Narcissus

A beautiful youth, the son of a nymph and a river-god, of whom the seer Tiresias predicts enigmatically that he will live a long life as long as he never knows himself. He is sought by many lovers, both male and female, but rejects them all, including Echo, who has been punished for her chattering by Hera with loss of speech. Spurned by Narcissus, she wastes away to nothing but a voice. He is punished for his cold-ness by being condemned to fall in love with his own reflected face in a mountain pool, thinking it to be the nymph of the place, and he too pines away and dies. Medieval writers used the legend to point up the perils of vanity, but post-Renaissance painters were more struck by the pathos of the story.

Nauplius

One of the Argonauts, who then becomes king of Nauplia in southern Greece and a slave-trader. When Auge, daughter of the king of Arcadia, becomes pregnant by Heracles, her father sends her to Nauplius with instructions to drown or sell her. Catreus, son of King Minos of Crete, gives both his daughters to Nauplius, because an oracle has predicted that one of them will cause his death. Nauplius sells Aerope to Atreus, king of Mycenae, and marries Clymene himself. One of their sons, Palamedes, is betrayed to his death by Odysseus at the siege of Troy, and Nauplius takes vengeance on the Greeks by lighting false beacons as they journey home, causing many of them to drown.

Nausicaa

Princess of the Phaeacians, who is playing ball with her attendants when the shipwrecked Odysseus staggers naked and alone from the sea. Her maids run away in fright, but Nausicaa gives him food and clothing and takes him home to her father, Alcinous. Alcinous wants him to marry Nausicaa, but Odysseus is eager to return to his wife Penelope, and so Nausicaa sadly watches him leave. The nineteenth-century British novelist and satirist Samuel Butler argued that the *Odyssey*, usually attributed to Homer, was written by a woman, whom he suggested was Nausicaa.

Neleus

Son of the sea-god Poseidon by the Greek princess Tyro. He and his twin brother Pelias are abandoned by their mother and brought up by horse-breakers. Pelias manages to establish himself in his mother's kingdom, but he drives out his brother Neleus, who in turn conquers and becomes king of Pylos in southern Greece. Neleus marries Chloris, the only surviving child of Niobe, and their children include Nestor, who inherits the kingdom, and Pero, who marries Bias. Neleus and

most of his family are killed by Heracles in revenge for Neleus's refusal to purify him of the murder of Iphitus, brother of Heracles' lover Iole.

Nemesis

Greek goddess of retribution, the daughter of Nyx (night) and in some stories one of the Moirae or Fates. Her main sanctuary was at Rhamnus in Attica, where the statue of her was supposedly carved by the superlative Greek sculptor Phidias, from marble brought by the Persians to Marathon to make a victory monument, on the assumption that they would win that critical battle.

Neoptolemus

Son of the Greek hero Achilles by Deidamia, princess of Scyros. Achilles is destined to die in the siege of Troy, and so his mother Thetis tries to prevent him going to the Trojan War by hiding him in women's clothes at the court of Lycomedes. While there he fathers Neoptolemus, initially known as Pyrrhus. After Achilles' death, Neoptolemus's presence at the siege is predicted as one of the requirements of Greek victory, and Odysseus and Phoenix are sent to fetch him from Scyros.

He is given his father's armor, rapidly wins great renown, and is one of the warriors who hides in the Trojan Horse. At the taking of Troy, it is he who kills the aged Trojan king Priam, on the very altar of Zeus, and also sacrifices Priam's daughter Polyxena at the tomb of Achilles, to satisfy his father's ghost. He takes Hector's wife Andromache as his prize and gets home safely, avoiding the storm sent by the

Above Wooden figure of the Egyptian funerary goddess Nephthys.

Left Nemesis, Greek goddess of retribution.

angry Athena to wreck the Greek ships through the intervention of his grandmother, the sea-nymph Thetis.

In some stories, he is bribed to take part in the siege of Troy by the offer of marriage with Helen's daughter Hermione, who has previously been promised to her cousin Orestes. After the war, when Neoptolemus goes to Delphi to discover why this marriage is childless, he is killed by Orestes, as he killed Priam, on the altar of the god.

Nephele

Greek nymph, and first wife of Athamas, king of Thebes, by whom she has a son and a daughter, Phrixus and Helle. Athamas repudiates her and marries Ino, daughter of Cadmus, who plots the destruction of Nephele and her children. Learning of Ino's plans, Nephele prays to the gods for rescue; her children escape to Colchis on the back of a golden ram, while she is transformed into a cloud.

Nephthys

Egyptian goddess, the sister of Isis and the wife of Seth, although she attracts none of the odium attached to her husband. She is a funerary deity, protectress with Isis of coffins and mortuary jars; the two sisters are often represented as hawks, standing at each end of a bier on which lies the mummified body of the deceased. In the Hall of Judgment in the underworld, she stands with Isis behind Osiris.

Neptune

Italian god of water, who becomes identified with Poseidon, the Greek god of the sea, and grows in importance as Rome becomes a significant maritime power. His sanctuary in Rome was between the Palatine and Aventine hills, where a stream once flowed, and his feast was celebrated in August. Like Poseidon, he is usually portrayed holding a trident and carried in a seashell-shaped chariot drawn by sea horses or dolphins, and is frequently shown on Roman mosaics and reliefs.

Nereids

Sea-nymphs, daughters of the primitive Greek sea deity Nereus, said to be 50 or 100 in number. Most famous among them are Amphitrite, wife of Poseidon; Thetis, mother of Achilles by the mortal Peleus; and Galatea. They were believed to live in their father's palace at the bottom of the sea, each with her own golden throne, and to spend their time spinning, weaving, and riding on dolphins. They were a popular subject, with their flowing draperies, in classical art; the Nereid Monument from Xanthus, now in Turkey, takes its name from the sea-nymphs between its columns.

Nereus

An early Greek god of the sea, sometimes regarded as the original Old Man of the Sea, and usually shown as bearded and riding a Triton. He has the gift of prophecy and warns Paris of the consequences of abducting Helen, though to no avail. He also has the power to change shape, and tries in this way to escape the questions of Heracles, who has to find the Garden of the Hesperides as one of his Twelve Labors. Nereus is a benign deity, however, and finally gives the hero the information he needs.

Nessus

Centaur, or horse with a man's head and trunk. He tries to assault Heracles' wife Deianira and is killed by the hero in revenge, but succeeds in bringing about Heracles' death long after his own, by telling Deianira that his blood-soaked shirt has the power to restore the love of a faithless husband. In fact it is poisoned by the Hydra's blood in which Heracles' arrow was dipped, and when Deianira, many years later,

Below Fountain of Neptune in Bologna, Italy, *c.*1566, by Giovanni da Bologna.

sends the shirt to Heracles to try to rekindle his love, she unknowingly causes his death. The phrase "a shirt of Nessus" became proverbial for a fatal gift.

Nestor

King of the Greek kingdom of Pylos in the western Peloponnese, son of Neleus and the only survivor of Heracles' attack on Pylos. His mother is a daughter of Niobe, and Nestor is granted great longevity by Apollo to compensate for the death of his mother's family at the hands of Apollo and Artemis (see Niobe). In Homer's account of the Trojan War, Nestor is an elder statesman among the Greek warleaders, wise and experienced, though given to long rambling tales about the distant past. He acts as intermediary in the dispute between Achilles and Agamemnon, although he fails to reconcile them. By the end of the war, he has become disenchanted with the Greeks and sails home alone, thus narrowly missing the great storm sent by Athena to punish them.

Nike

Greek goddess, the personification of victory, shown in Greek art as flying at high speed on her great wings to bring triumph to the chosen of the gods. She is supposedly a daughter of the Titan Pallas, but supports the Olympian gods in the battle between the gods and the Titans. It is she who escorts Heracles to Olympus after he is deified.

Niobe

Queen of Thebes, wife of Amphion, by whom she is variously reported to have had six, seven or ten sons and the same number of daughters. On the feast of Leto, mother of the divine twins Apollo and Artemis, she makes the mistake of comparing Leto's maternal fecundity unfavorably with her own. Predictably offended, Leto calls on her children to punish this impious mortal. Apollo and Artemis draw their bows and kill all Niobe's children (except, in some stories, Nestor's mother Chloris) with their avenging arrows. Totally des-

Right above Niobe laments her children, killed by Apollo and Artemis.

Right below Nut, in the tree, refreshes the pharaoh Nespaquachouty.

Niobe.   *Diriguitq̃ malis.*

Ouid. 6. Metam.

troyed by grief, Niobe weeps for nine solid days and nights, until the gods in pity turn her into a stone which still spouts tears. She has remained a symbol of grief; Shakespeare, in *Hamlet*, refers to Queen Gertrude as "like Niobe, all tears," and Byron describes the Greece of his day as "the Niobe of Nations."

Nisus

King of Megara, whose kingdom is attacked by Minos of Crete in revenge for the death of his son Androgeos at the hands of the neighboring Athenians. Nisus has a lock of red hair, upon which his own and his kingdom's safety has been foretold to depend, but his daughter Scylla falls in love with Minos and cuts off the lock while Nisus sleeps, causing the fall of Megara and her father's death. She expects gratitude from Minos, but he is horrified by her betrayal and has her drowned.

Numitor

Prince of the Italian kingdom of Alba, whose younger brother Amulius usurps the throne on the death of their father, and dedicates Numitor's daughter Rhea Silvia to the service of Vesta so that she shall not bear children. Mars becomes her lover, however, and she bears two sons, Romulus and Remus, who cast out the tyrant and restore their grandfather Numitor to his rightful throne.

Nun

The primeval waters in Egyptian mythology, personified as a man standing waist-deep in water, his upraised arms supporting the ship of the sun. There are eight elemental Egyptian water deities, of whom the couples Nun and Naunet and Amun and Amaunet are the more important. The world is believed to be surrounded by water, out of which it was created, and the water-gods are the Egyptian equivalent of the Greek Uranus and Ge.

Nut

Egyptian sky-goddess and mother of the principal Egyptian gods Isis, Osiris, Nephthys, and Seth by her brother Geb, the earth-god. From the primeval water-god Nun is born Shu and Tefnut, air and moisture, and from their union

come Geb and Nut. Nut is show in Egyptian art as a naked giant, supported by Shu, the air, and arched over the body of Geb so that her back supports the heavens. Day and night is explained in terms of a solar rebirth, the sun entering Nut's mouth in the evening, passing through her body and being reborn in the morning.

Nycteus

King of Thebes, who forces his daughter Antiope to abandon the twin sons she has born to Zeus. Antiope takes refuge from her father's anger in Sicyon, where she presently marries the king, Epopeus, but Nycteus is unrelenting in his hostility toward his daughter, marches on Sicyon, and binds his brother Lycus to continue the feud after his own death in battle. See Antiope.

Nymphs

Female spirits of nature in Greek myth, often the daughters of Zeus, and probably originally localized nature-goddesses. They are associated with particular natural phenomena. Dryads are tree-nymphs; Hamadryads inhabit particular trees and die with them; Nereids and Oceanids are sea-nymphs, the daughters of Nereus and Oceanus respectively; Naiads are water-nymphs; while the Meliae, the nymphs of the ash tree, are said to have sprung from the blood of the castrated Uranus. However, nymphs can be harmful to mortals: they drown Hylas, blind Daphnis, and destroy Hermaphroditus.

They are also, however, credited with love affairs with both gods and men; Daphne, Echo, and Eurydice are all nymphs. They appear frequently in classical art and literature and in post-Renaissance painting, and are traditionally linked with shepherds. In late Greek and Roman architecture, a nymphaeum was a city fountain dedicated to the local water-nymph and unconnected with a temple. Examples from Pompeii and Herculaneum are richly decorated with statues and mosaics.

Nyx

Greek goddess of night, one of the earliest deities, who emerges from the primeval Chaos together with Ge, the earth; Erebus, darkness; and Tartarus, the underworld. She in turn is the mother of several powerful personified forces, including Hypnos (sleep), Nemesis (retribution), and Eris (strife), and also in some stories of the three Moirae or Fates.

Below Nymphs decorate this Roman silver dish found at Mildenhall, England.

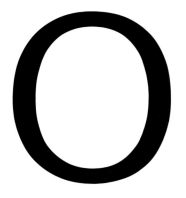

Oceanids

Sea-nymphs, the 3000 daughters of Oceanus and Tethys, who are the guardians of all the waters on the earth. They include Amphitrite, who marries Poseidon; Metis, who becomes Zeus's first wife and conceives but does not bear Athena; Clymene, mother of Phaethon; and Calypso, who rules the island of Ortygia and falls in love with Odysseus.

Oceanus

Primitive Greek sea-god, more element than personality. A Titan, he is born of Ge and Uranus, marries his sister Tethys and fathers all the minor sea- and river-gods. The Greeks believed that he ruled the Ocean, which they envisaged as a great stream encircling the earth. Oceanus and Tethys do not take part in the war of the Titans against the Olympian gods and so are left in peaceful control of their realm.

Odysseus

King of Ithaca, known as Ulysses to the Romans, one of the leading characters in the Trojan War and the central figure in the *Odyssey*, which recounts his ten-year journey from Troy. Although Laertes, king of Ithaca, acknowledges Odysseus as his son, in some accounts Odysseus's mother Anticlea was already pregnant by the trickster Sisyphus when she married Laertes, which is held to account for Odysseus's resourcefulness and cunning. An early example of this is his winning of Penelope to be his wife.

Penelope is the daughter of the Spartan prince Icarius, who loves her dearly and refuses to let her marry. Odysseus therefore joins the suitors wooing Helen, Icarius's niece and daughter of the Spartan king Tyndareos, and it is he who suggests that all the suitors should swear an oath to support whomever Helen chooses, thus avoiding any vengeful repercussions.

In gratitude Tyndareos persuades his brother Icarius to let Penelope marry Odysseus. They have one son, Telemachus, and the marriage is intensely happy; so much so that when Palamedes comes to summon Odysseus to honor his oath and join the Greek expedition to Troy, Odysseus feigns madness to avoid leaving his family. He yokes a horse and ox together and starts to plow the beach of his island kingdom, but Palamedes calls his bluff by placing the infant Telemachus in the path of the plow. Odysseus proves his sanity by halting his team, but never forgives Palamedes for outwitting him and eventually causes his death.

Below Oceanus and Tethys with Hera, whom they sheltered while the gods and Titans fought.

Once he has joined the Greeks, Odysseus proves his worth at once by tricking Achilles, who is hidden at the court of Lycomedes disguised as a woman, into betraying himself. In the *Iliad* he is one of the bravest and wisest of the Greek warriors. When Achilles retires to his tent and refuses to fight, giving Hector the opportunity to gain the upper hand, Odysseus and his friend and companion Diomedes manage to spy out the Trojan dispositions by night, capturing Dolon, who gives them invaluable information about the opposing army. He and Diomedes also penetrate the walls of Troy itself in order to steal the Palladium, a sacred image of Athena without which the city is doomed to fall. Helen recognizes him but does not betray him.

Finally it is Odysseus who has the idea of building a vast wooden horse, ostensibly as a religious offering, which is the immediate cause of the fall of Troy. The Greeks leave the horse outside the city and take to their ships. After much debate, the Trojans decide that the war is over and pull the horse inside the walls, but of course it is a trick; the ships have only sailed into the next bay, and the horse is full of Greek warriors, led by Menelaus and Odysseus, who burst out at night and take the city by storm.

He is also capable of calculating cruelty, however; when Philoctetes is accidentally wounded by one of Heracles' poisoned arrows on the way to Troy, it is Odysseus who suggests abandoning him on the island of Lemnos. And it is Odysseus, many years later, who throws the infant son of Hector, Astyanax, from the walls of Troy so that there shall be no heir to the line of Priam.

The ten years that he spends wandering after the fall of Troy are the result of another act of callousness, the blinding of the Cyclops Polyphemus, for Polyphemus is the son of the sea-god Poseidon, whose anger is so great that Odysseus would never have reached home at all but for the intervention of Athena. Thus his travels become not only a search for his homeland, but also a quest for his own true nature and for an understanding of his relationship with the gods. Homer shows an increasingly mature and serene character, who survives extraordinary adversity to come to a full appreciation of hearth and home.

Odysseus's first landfall after escaping from Polyphemus is on the island ruled by Aeolus, lord of the winds, who gives Odysseus a bag containing all the unfavorable winds, to ensure that only the west wind will blow and see him safely home. While he sleeps, however, his sailors open the bag in the hope of finding gold and cause a storm that blows them totally off-course. They finally anchor in the harbor of the Laestrygonians, savage man-eating giants who crush all but one of the ships with rocks and devour most of the crew.

Only Odysseus and a handful of his men escape, and arrive next on the island of the sorceress Circe. She turns their scouting party into pigs, but Odysseus is given a magic herb by Hermes which helps him to resist her spells; instead she promises to help him and he stays with her for a year, in some stories fathering her child. Homer makes much of the fact that the two women with whom Odysseus has affairs, Circe and Calypso, are both immortal and therefore irresistible; at heart Odysseus remains faithful to Penelope.

On Circe's instructions, Odysseus makes the terrible journey to the edge of the Ocean, the stream that encircles the world, where the souls of the dead come to meet him. Among them is the seer Tiresias, who instructs him how

Above Odysseus bound to the mast, listening safely to the Sirens' song, while his men's ears are plugged with wax. Roman mosaic.

to get home, and warns him on no account to interfere with the cattle of Helios. Odysseus also talks with the shade of his mother, who warns him that Penelope is besieged by suitors, and with Agamemnon, killed by his vengeful wife Clytemnestra, who counsels extreme caution on his return to his native hearth.

Odysseus and his few remaining men then take ship, successfully passing the island of the Sirens, whose singing lures men to their doom, and negotiating the dangerous straits of Scylla and Charybdis. An adverse wind forces them to land on the island of Helios (probably Sicily), and despite Odysseus's prohibitions, his starving men kill and eat some of the magic cattle while he sleeps. When they re-embark, they are wrecked by a ferocious storm sent by Zeus at the demand of the outraged Helios. Only Odysseus survives, by lashing himself to a makeshift raft, and drifts for nine days until he lands on the island of the nymph Calypso.

She falls in love with him and persuades him to stay with her for seven years, but finally his longing for his wife moves the gods, who send

Hermes to bid her release him and help him rebuild his raft. Still Poseidon has not finished with him, however; yet another storm throws him naked and half-dead onto the coast of Scheria, where he is found by Nausicaa, the king's daughter. She persuades her father Alcinous to help him, and after a hospitable welcome Alcinous sends Odysseus home to Ithaca on one of his ships. In a final, if belated, blast of petulance from Poseidon, the ship is turned to stone on its way back to Scheria.

Athena appears to Odysseus on the shores of Ithaca, warns him of the many suitors to Penelope who have taken over his court, and disguises him as a beggar. He reveals himself only to his faithful swineherd, Eumaeus, and his son, Telemachus, but tells Penelope that he has news of her husband's imminent return. She has finally despaired of seeing him again and agreed to hold a contest between the suitors and marry the one who can bend and fire Odysseus's great bow. He urges her to proceed with the plan, promising her that Odysseus will rescue her

Below Oedipus and the Sphinx, on a third-century BC Greek sarcophagus.

from an unwelcome second marriage.

None of the suitors can bend the bow, but Telemachus insists on letting the "beggar" try, who fires it with ease and then turns on the suitors, aided by Athena in the guise of Telemachus's tutor Mentor. Penelope will not at first believe that it is he, but is finally convinced.

The *Odyssey* ends with the defeat of the suitors, the reconciliation of Odysseus and Penelope, and peace in Ithaca, but later stories tell how Odysseus placates Poseidon, ensuring himself a peaceful old age and a natural death, by following the instructions that the seer Tiresias has given him. This is to cross to the mainland carrying an oar, and to walk inland until he meets a people who live so far from the sea that they take the oar for a winnowing fan. There he plants the oar in the ground and sacrifices a ram, a bull, and a boar to Poseidon, who is finally appeased.

In the Middle Ages, Odysseus (more commonly known then by his Roman name of Ulysses) was seen as the archetypal con-man; the rare term "ulyssean" still features in a few dictionaries as meaning crafty, deceitful. Later treatments of him, as in Shakespeare's *Troilus and Cressida*, Monte-

verdi's opera *Il Ritorno d'Ulisse in Patria* and the scenes from the *Odyssey* by the sixteenth-century Italian painter Piero di Cosimo, revert to Homer's more heroic view. More recent writers have focused on Odysseus as the perpetual traveler, the wanderer in search of knowledge and his own identity, as in Tennyson's poem *Ulysses*. James Joyce's epic novel of the same title follows closely the thread of the *Odyssey*, with almost every character and event drawn from Homer, but crams the 19 years of Odysseus's wanderings into one day in the life of its hero, Leopold Bloom.

Oedipus

King of Thebes, son of Laius and Jocasta, a tragic hero in the classical mold, who suffers both for his father's and for his own unwitting misdeeds. Laius has brought a curse on his house by abducting his host's son while he was a refugee at the court of Pelops. When he returns to Thebes and marries Jocasta, an oracle tells him that he will die at the hands of their son, and he therefore has the infant Oedipus exposed on a mountainside, with a spear through his feet to hasten his death. The baby is rescued by a shepherd and taken to the king of Corinth, Polybus, who adopts him and names him Oedipus, "swollen feet."

Brought up as the childless Polybus's heir, Oedipus is one day taunted with being a bastard and asks the oracle at Delphi for reassurance. Instead he is told that he will kill his father (whom he still believes to be Polybus) and marry his mother. Determined to avoid this by never returning to Corinth, he sets out toward Thebes. At a crossroads he meets a stranger driving a chariot who orders him to make way, and when he refuses drives over his foot. Infuriated, Oedipus kills the driver, unaware that this is his true father, Laius, on his way to Delphi to seek advice about the sphinx which is devouring his people.

Oedipus continues his journey to Thebes, where he finds the citizens terrorized by the monstrous sphinx, which sits on a rock outside the city and eats any passer-by who cannot answer the riddle it sets. Oedipus too is challenged to say what it is that goes on four legs in the morning, two at noon, and three in the evening. He correctly replies man, who crawls in

Above Oedipus and the Sphinx by the nineteenth-century French painter Ingres.

infancy, strides in adulthood, and hobbles on a stick in old age.

The sphinx screams with rage, falls from its rock and is dashed to pieces, and Oedipus is hailed as the liberator of Thebes. He learns that the king has died on the way to Delphi and that the regent, Creon, has offered the widowed queen Jocasta as wife to whoever kills the sphinx. Oedipus therefore unknowingly marries his mother and they have four children, Antigone, Ismene, Eteocles, and Polynices.

Oedipus rules in peace for some years, but then a plague descends on Thebes, and the Delphic oracle warns

that this will only be removed when the killers of Laius are driven from the country. This is the point at which Sophocles' play *King Oedipus* begins; determined to discover the truth, Oedipus orders that all efforts be made to identify the killer of Laius, but is furious when the seer Tiresias tells him that he is the murderer.

Meanwhile Polybus dies and the Corinthians believing Oedipus to be his heir, summon him to rule them. He refuses, explaining that he is doomed to marry his mother, whom he believes to be Polybus's widow, but the shepherd who delivered him to Polybus as a baby denies that he is Polybus's son, and the complex and appalling truth is revealed. Jocasta hangs herself and Oedipus blinds himself

with her brooch. Creon again assumes the regency for his young nephews, and carries out the will of the oracle by banishing Oedipus.

He is led into exile by Antigone, finally reaching Colonus in Attica after many years of wandering, where he is given sanctuary by Theseus. Meanwhile his sons have grown to manhood and agreed to rule Thebes year and year about. Eteocles, after his year in office, refuses to surrender the throne to Polynices, who therefore calls on his father-in-law, Adrastus, king of Argos, to support him with an army, the famous Seven against Thebes.

An oracle predicts that the side that has Oedipus's support will gain the day. Polynices therefore comes to Colonus to seek his father's blessing, but instead receives his curse for allowing him to be driven into exile, and Creon and Eteocles try to kidnap Oedipus, but are driven off by Theseus's troops. He dies at Colonus, bestowing his blessing on the land that has given him shelter.

The story of Oedipus became a source of fascination for twentieth-century writers with its reinterpretation by Freud, who gave the name "Oedipus complex" to what he saw as the repressed hostility of a son toward his father as the rival for his mother's affection. This is explored by Jean Cocteau in his play *The Infernal Machine* and his libretto for Stravinsky's opera *Oedipus Rex*; by film-maker Pasolini in *Oedipus Rex*; and by André Gide in the play *Oedipe*, in which the incest is of secondary importance, and Oedipus is a symbol of man's desire for liberation from accepted beliefs and traditions.

Oeneus

In Greek myth, the king of Calydon and father of the hero Meleager and the much sought-after Deianira, whose hand is finally won by Heracles. In some stories, it is the wine-god Dionysos and not Oeneus who is Deianira's father; when Dionysos comes to Calydon, Oeneus hospitably allows him to sleep with his wife Althaea, and in return is given the first vine. Oeneus incurs the anger of Artemis by forgetting to name her during the harvest celebrations, and she sends a wild boar to devastate his kingdom, which is finally killed by Meleager after most of the Greek heroes have joined in the hunt of the Calydonian boar.

Oenomaus

King of Pisa and the son of Ares, he has a beautiful daughter, Hippodamia. An oracle warns that he will be killed by his son-in-law. As he is a skilled chariot-driver, he challenges all claimants to Hippodamia's hand to a chariot race, the loser of which must die. Pelops bribes Oenomaus's charioteer to tamper with his master's chariot, which crashes, killing Oenomaus, but Pelops in turn incurs a curse for his faithlessness. See Myrtilus, Pelops.

Oenone

Greek nymph who lives on Mount Ida, near Troy, and marries Paris while he still believes himself to be a shepherd. She has the gift of prophecy, and tries to dissuade him from seeking out Helen, queen of Sparta, whom Aphrodite has promised him as wife. She also predicts that he will return to her for her medicinal skill. Many years later, after he has abducted Helen, provoked the Trojan War, and been wounded by the poisoned arrow of Philoctetes, Paris returns to Oenone in the hope of a cure but she, bitter at his betrayal, refuses to help him. By the time she has repented of her harshness, Paris is dead, and Oenone kills herself in grief. The nineteenth-century poet Alfred, Lord Tennyson tells her sentimental story in *Oenone*.

Below Hercules enslaved by Omphale. Undated illustration.

Above Orestes, pursued by the Furies, is comforted by his sister Iphigenia.

Oenopion

Son of Ariadne and Dionysos and king of Chios, his daughter Merope is sought in marriage by the giant Orion; he does not dare refuse so formidable a lover, but is reluctant to acquiesce, so he gets Orion drunk and blinds him.

Omphale

Queen of Lydia in Asia Minor (Turkey), she buys Heracles as a slave after the Delphic oracle has condemned him for the murder of Iphitus. He clears her kingdom of various pests, including the outlaw Syleus and a monstrous serpent, and she bears him a son, Lamus.

Orestes

Son of Agamemnon and Clytemnestra, who avenges his father's death at the hands of his mother by killing her and her lover Aegisthus. Orestes is still a child when Agamemnon returns from the Trojan War and is murdered by Clytemnestra. As the heir to the kingdom, he is taken for safety to the court of Strophius, king of Phocis, by his sister Electra. He stays there until he reaches manhood and Strophius's son Pylades becomes his close friend, accompanying him through all the horror that follows.

Orestes asks the Delphic oracle, the mouthpiece of Apollo, what he should do about his father's murderers, Clytemnestra and Aegisthus, who are still ruling Mycenae. He is told to kill them, so he and Pylades go secretly to Mycenae, enlisting the aid of Electra, and Orestes appears before Clytemnestra disguised as a traveler who brings the news of his own death. Clytemnestra is delighted and summons Aegisthus to hear the good news, whereupon Orestes kills him. He almost spares his mother, until reminded by Pylades of the oracle's instructions.

The earliest account of the story, by Homer, describes this as a praiseworthy act of vengeance, for which no harm comes to Orestes. In classical Greek drama, however, where Orestes appears more frequently than any other character, he is bitterly punished for his matricide. According to Aeschylus and Euripides, the Furies afflict him with madness and pursue him through Greece and beyond. He finally goes to Delphi to ask Apollo's aid, since it was he who ordered the deed for which Orestes is being punished, and is sent for trial before the Athenian homicide court of the Areopagus.

There the Furies urge continuing punishment, while Apollo acts as Orestes' advocate. When the Athenian jury gives a hung verdict, Athena uses her casting vote in Orestes' favor, calms the Furies, settles them in a shrine and renames them the Eumenides (the kindly ones), symbolizing the triumph of the Olympian gods over the primitive deities of blood-guilt and vengeance.

According to Euripides, however, Orestes is still not fully absolved, and must travel to Tauris, where he finds and is rescued by his long-lost sister Iphigenia and finally returns to rule Mycenae and Argos and to marry Helen's daughter Hermione. In Sophocles and Euripides, the Furies appear only as the imagined torments of Orestes' guilty and remorseful conscience, and the real interest focuses on the contrast between his suggestible and Electra's more dominant character.

Orion

Giant hunter, born to Hyreus by the intervention of the gods after the death of his wife. Orion is so tall that he can walk on the sea-bed with his head and shoulders out of the water. He marries the nymph Side, but she rashly boasts herself more beautiful than Hera and causes her own death. Orion then falls in love with Merope, daughter of the king of Chios, and is promised her as wife in exchange for ridding the island of wild beasts. This he does, but while he lies sleeping the king blinds him, in order to avoid carrying out his side of the bargain (or alternatively as a punishment for raping Merope).

Orion follows the sound of hammering to a nearby forge, where he picks up the smith's son Celadion as guide and wades into the sea eastward, following the sun's rays, which restore his sight. He joins the company of Artemis in Crete and hunts with the goddess herself. There Eos, goddess of the dawn, falls in love with him and carries him off to the island of Delos, but Artemis is offended at his defection and kills him with her arrows.

In another version, it is Artemis who falls in love with Orion, and even contemplates marriage, but is tricked by Apollo into killing her beloved and in her grief places him in the sky as a constellation.

Orpheus

Supreme musician of Greek mythology, son of the Muse Calliope, possibly by Apollo. Orpheus's love for his wife Eurydice forms one of the most

Below Orion crossing the sea, shown on the back of an Etruscan bronze mirror.

romantic and popular Greek myths. Born in Thrace and a follower of the wine-god Dionysos, he is given the first lute by the gods, and plays so exquisitely that he can charm wild beasts and make rocks and trees move. He accompanies the Argonauts on their quest for the Golden Fleece, lulling the waves in their path and singing so sweetly that his music drowns even that of the Sirens, who entrap men to their doom.

On his return to Thrace he marries the nymph Eurydice, and is devastated by her accidental death. Finally he makes his way into the underworld, charming even Charon and Cerberus (a scene most beautifully conveyed in Gluck's opera *Orfeo*), and persuades Hades and Persephone to let Eurydice go, on condition that he leads her out of Hades without looking back at her.

In the earliest versions of the stories he succeeds, a testament to the power of Dionysos over death, but according to Virgil and Ovid he becomes convinced that she is not following him and turns to reassure himself, only to see her fading wraithlike back into Hades. He tries to follow, but this time the way is barred. He wanders the hills of Thrace like a lost soul, avoiding above all the company of women. This offends the Maenads, followers of Dionysos, with whom Orpheus often celebrated the god's orgiastic rites, and they tear him to pieces. The Muses gather the fragments of his body and give him honorable burial.

The Greek mystic cult of Orphism, the first Greek religion to lay down its doctrines in texts, claimed Orpheus as its founder, and the author of these texts, from as early as the seventh century BC. Orphic literature is one source for the cosmogony of the Greek world, but its particular contribution to religious thought was the idea that the soul of man contains elements both of divinity and of evil, and that those who follow the right path, which includes abstaining from killing animals or eating flesh, can be reborn to a higher life.

Osiris

Egyptian savior-god of death and resurrection, the chief deity of death, and the only god to rival the solar cult of Re. He is the oldest child of Geb and Nut, and marries his sister Isis. He is initially a grain-god, worshipped in the form of a sack filled with seed which sprouts green. His brother Seth becomes jealous of his regenerative power and persuades him during a drunken party to step into an exactly-fitting sarcophagus. This Seth then nails up and throws into the Nile, and so the drowning of Osiris, symbolizing the flooding of the land, makes a new harvest possible.

The sarcophagus floats from the eastern delta to the Mediterranean sea, is washed ashore in the Lebanon, and becomes encased in the trunk of a growing tree. Eventually this is cut down and used as a pillar in the local king's palace, and it is here that Isis, after many years of searching, finds

Below Osiris, in an Egyptian wall-painting from a tomb at Thebes.

P

Above   The Death of Orpheus, painted by the French artist Emile Levy (1825-90).

Paeon

Ancient Greek god of healing, who cures Hades after he has been wounded at the gates of the underworld by the arrows of Heracles. In later myth his name becomes attached as an epithet to Apollo and Asclepius, both associated with medicine.

Palamedes

Greek chief, son of Nauplius, one of the principal Greek warriors at the Trojan War. He is sent to Troy to persuade Helen to return to Menelaus. When that fails, he is sent by Agamemnon to summon all the Greek leaders to join the fleet sailing on Troy. Odysseus feigns madness in order to avoid leaving his wife and newborn son, Telemachus, but Palamedes sees through the deception, incurring Odysseus's bitter enmity. He serves bravely in the Trojan War, but eventually Odysseus effects his revenge. He forges a letter from Priam to Palamedes promising him gold in exchange for betraying the Greeks, and hides the same amount of gold in Palamedes' tent. No amount of protestation by Palamedes will convince the Greeks that he is not disloyal, and they stone him to death.

Palemon

A minor sea-god, originally called Melicertes, the son of Ino and Athamas. Hera drives his parents mad in revenge for their assistance to Zeus's lover Semele and her child Dionysos. Ino leaps into the sea with Melicertes in her arms, and they are transformed into deities.

the body of her husband/brother. She brings the body home, breathes life into it, and succeeds in impregnating herself with Osiris's semen, bearing the falcon-headed god Horus to avenge Osiris's death. Meanwhile Seth has found Osiris's body, dismembered it, and scattered the pieces along the valley of the Nile, again an agricultural simile for the scattering of the grain.

Isis manages to recover and bury all the parts of Osiris's body except his penis, which she replaces with a replica that becomes a focus of the cult of Osiris. After this second death, Osiris embraces the underworld and becomes its ruler, sitting enthroned in the Hall of Judgment as the souls of the newly dead come to be weighed in the balance. In Egyptian art Osiris is represented as a dead king, with crown and shroud, and holding a crook and flail to indicate his agricultural origins. By the late Egyptian period, Osiris had superseded Re as chief god.

Above Pan and Aphrodite playing knucklebones, on the back of a Greek bronze mirror.

Palinarus

The steersman of Aeneas on the voyage from Troy to Italy. He guides the ship safely through the storm sent by Hera to wreck them after they have left Carthage, and to punish him Hera sends Somnus, god of sleep, to lull him to sleep at the helm, so that he falls overboard. He is cast ashore and killed by local tribesmen. When Aeneas is guided by the Sibyl to the Elysian Fields to learn what fate is predicted for him, the shade of Palinarus begs to be taken across the Styx, but is sternly refused by the Sibyl because he has not had proper burial.

Pallas

Title given to the goddess Athena, of unknown origin. In one story Pallas is the daughter of Triton and the ward of Athena. One day the two women argue and Pallas strikes at the goddess with her spear. Athena kills her instantly, but then regrets her death. She takes her name in commemoration and makes an image of her, the Palladium, which Zeus later throws down to the Trojans as a sign of his blessing, and which is stolen by Odysseus in order to capture Troy.

Pan

Greek god of shepherds, pastures, and the rural life, whose father is variously said to be Hermes, Zeus, or Apollo, and who is usually shown as having goat's horns, ears, and legs. He is held responsible for the fertility of the flocks, and is distinctly amorous himself. He pursues the nymph Syrinx, who is turned into a reed-bed to escape him, moving him to cut the reeds and invent the panpipes. He loves the moon-goddess Selene, and tempts her into the wood with him by turning himself into a snow-white goat which she takes to be a moonbeam. He can also be dangerous when angry, stampeding flocks and inducing irrational "panic" fear in men. He becomes the patron of pastoral poetry from classical times onward, as the god of untamed nature in an idealized Arcadia.

Pandarus

Trojan archer, who learns his skill from the archer-god Apollo. In Homer it is he who breaks the truce between the Greeks and Trojans, on the instructions of Athena, by firing an arrow at Menelaus. Only in later myth is he the uncle of Chryseis (Cressida) and her go-between in her affair with Troilus, hence the continued use of the word "pandar" to mean a procurer.

Below Pandora's Box by Walter Crane.

Pandora

The first woman in Greek mythology, the equivalent of the biblical Eve, she is created by Hephaestus on the orders of Zeus to punish mankind, after the Titan Prometheus has been too liberal in the bestowing of gifts. Her name means ''all gifts;'' she is given life and clothes by Athena, beauty by Aphrodite, and guile by Hermes. She is married to Prometheus's foolish brother Epimetheus, who is given a box as a wedding gift which he is forbidden to open. Despite Prometheus's warnings, she lifts the lid and out fly all the troubles and diseases which henceforth afflict the world, accompanied only by Hope to bring some solace.

Parcae

Three Roman goddesses of destiny, identified with the Greek Moirae as spinning out the lifespan of all mortals. They were originally the attendant spirits of childbirth.

Paris

Younger son of Priam and Hecuba, rulers of Troy, Paris causes the Trojan War by his abduction of Helen. When she is pregnant, his mother dreams that she gives birth to a firebrand which destroys the city, and so the infant is given to a shepherd to abandon on Mount Ida. He is suckled by a she-bear, however, and the shepherd, finding him alive after five days, brings him up as his own son. He grows into a brave and handsome youth, attracting the love of the nymph Oenone, whom he marries.

When Hera, Aphrodite, and Athena contest for the golden apple marked ''for the fairest'' which Eris throws down at the wedding of Peleus and Thetis, Zeus chooses Paris to be the adjudicator, and it is from the Judgment of Paris that the Trojan War ensues. Each goddess appears to Paris and promises him immense rewards if he chooses her. Hera will make him ruler of the world; Athena will give him victory in battle; but Aphrodite offers him the most beautiful woman in the world as his wife, and she gains the day.

Unfortunately the most beautiful woman in the world, Helen of Sparta, is already married to Menelaus but, guided by Aphrodite, Paris sets out to win her, despite the doom-laden warnings of the prophetess Cassandra and the tears of Oenone. He arrives in Sparta as his father's ambassador, and is entertained hospitably by Menelaus. Aphrodite causes Helen to fall in love with him, and they flee together to Troy.

Thereafter his role becomes less than noble, perhaps because he has forfeited the qualities that Hera and Athena offered him. The only single combat he undertakes is with Menelaus, and Aphrodite has to rescue him from death by wrapping him in a thick mist. With the aid of Apollo, he causes

Below Paris and Helen by the French painter Jacques Louis David (1748-1825).

Above Pasiphae with Daedalus and the bull, from a Roman wall-painting.

throughout the war, and when Achilles retires from battle as a protest against Agamemnon's theft of his mistress, Patroclus follows.

He cannot bear to see the Greeks worsted, however, and, failing to persuade Achilles to rejoin the battle, begs at least for the loan of his armor. This is granted on condition that he does no more than relieve the besieged Greek ships, but Patroclus gets carried away by his success, advances to the walls of Troy, and is killed by Hector.

Pax

Roman goddess of peace, to whom Augustus dedicated an altar to commemorate the end of the Civil Wars. She is represented holding an olive branch and with the horn of plenty.

Pegasus

A winged horse tamed by the hero Bellerophon so that together they may overcome the monstrous fire-breathing Chimera. Pegasus is born from the drops of Medusa's blood that fall on the ground when she is killed by Perseus, and soars up to the top of Mount Helicon, where he creates the fountain of the Muses, the spring Hippocrene (seen by poets as the source of their inspiration) with one stamp of his hoof. After the death of Bellerophon, Pegasus flies to Olympus and is placed by Zeus among the constellations.

Peleus

Notable Greek hero and one of the few humans to marry an immortal, the Nereid Thetis, Peleus is banished at an early age from his island home of Aegina because he accidentally kills his half-brother. He is purified by Actor, the king of Phthia, and marries his daughter Antigone as his first wife. He takes part in the expedition of the Argonauts, joins the hunt of the Calydonian boar, and is involved in the battle of the centaurs and the Lapiths.

When he visits Acastus, a fellow Argonaut, Acastus's wife Astydamia falls in love with him, and in response to his refusal sends word to Antigone that he has been unfaithful, whereupon she hangs herself. Astydamia also accuses Peleus to Acastus, causing a bitter war between the two friends which ends with the defeat of Acastus and the death of Astydamia.

the death of Achilles, but soon after receives his death wound from the bow of Heracles in the hands of Philoctetes. He has himself carried up Mount Ida in the hope that Oenone will use her medical skill to heal him, but she bitterly refuses him and he dies.

Pasiphae

Queen of Crete, the wife of Minos, and daughter of the sun-god Helios. She bears him Ariadne, Phaedra, and Androgeos, but is then caused by Poseidon to fall in love with a magnificent bull, in punishment for Minos's failure to sacrifice the animal to him. With the help of the master craftsman Daedalus, she mates with the bull and gives birth to the Minotaur. She is wearied by Minos's constant infidelities and afflicts him with a painful disease, which he passes on to all his lovers and which is finally cured by Procris.

Patroclus

Friend and companion of Achilles and often described, though not by Homer, as his lover. He is the son of the king of Opus, and as a youth accidentally kills another boy in a quarrel over a game of dice. He is sent to Achilles' father Peleus for purification and the two boys become inseparable. When, years later, Achilles joins the Greek army besieging Troy, Patroclus goes too, although the quarrel is none of his. They fight shoulder to shoulder

Peleus returns to Phthia, where he is now king, and is rewarded by Zeus for his virtue in repulsing Astydamia with marriage to Thetis. This munificence is not quite what it seems, as Zeus had considered marriage with Thetis himself until warned that her son will be greater than his father. In order to win her, Peleus has to catch her in her sea-cave and hold on to her while she changes shape. She finally agrees to marry him, and it is at their magnificent wedding that Eris, the goddess of strife, who has not been invited, disrupts proceedings by throwing down the Apple of Discord.

Thetis gives birth to the hero Achilles, who will indeed be greater than his father, but returns to the sea when Peleus interferes with her attempts to make Achilles immortal. He stays in Phthia until driven out by the sons of Acastus after the death of Achilles and the fall of Troy, and is finally summoned by Thetis to join her in immortality under the sea.

Pelias

One of twin sons born by Tyro to Poseidon, Pelias and his brother Neleus are raised by a horse-breeder. They are reunited with their mother as young adults, and punish her cruel step-mother Sidero, who had forced her to abandon her babies, even though Sidero has taken refuge on Hera's altar. Pelias thus incurs Hera's implacable hatred. Tyro later marries the king of Iolcos and bears him three sons. One of these, Aeson, succeeds to his father's kingdom, but is dispossessed by Pelias and entrusts his son Jason to the centaur Chiron for safekeeping.

Years later Jason returns and demands his father's kingdom from Pelias, but the ingenious monarch sends him on the quest for the Golden Fleece, in the expectation that he will not survive. With the help of the sorceress Medea, however, Jason comes back to Iolcos, and it is Medea who effects Hera's revenge on Pelias. She persuades his daughters that they can restore his youth by killing him, cutting up his body, and cooking it with magic herbs, but then withholds the recipe.

Pelops

An early Greek hero, who founds the Pelopid family after whom the Peloponnesus is named, but brings a curse on his descendants which is only finally exorcized by the purification of Orestes. He is the son of Tantalus, king of Lydia in Asia Minor, who is honored by a visit from the Olympian gods, and decides to test their omniscience by serving up the body of his own son at the welcome feast.

The gods bring Pelops back to life and continue to take an interest in him, giving him a team of winged horses in which he flies across to Greece after his father has been dispossessed by Ilus, founder of Troy. There he competes for the hand of the princess Hippodamia in a chariot race against her father Oenomaus, which he wins by bribing Oenomaus's charioteer.

Instead of paying his debt, however, he drowns the charioteer, Myrtilus, who curses him and his house. Pelops

Below Bellerophon and Pegasus by Walter Crane (1845-1915).

BELLEROPHON ON PEGASVS

succeeds Oenomaus, ruling wisely as king of Elis and Arcadia and extending his power over the whole of southern Greece. Of his children, Atreus, Thyestes, and Astydamia are the three on whom the curse falls most heavily, while Hippodamia is motivated by jealousy of his bastard, Chrysippus, to leave Pelops.

Penates

Minor Roman gods who preside over the household and the domestic affairs of families, from *penus*, store cupboard. The Penates of the Roman state are given special importance and believed to be the household gods of Aeneas, which he bore from the burning ruins of Troy and established in the city he founded in Latium.

Penelope

Queen of Ithaca and faithful wife of Odysseus. Her father Icarius, a Spartan prince, is deeply reluctant to let her leave for Ithaca with Odysseus, and

Right The faithful Penelope, engraving from an undated Greek statue.

Below Proserpina, the Roman Persephone, by Dante Gabriel Rossetti.

she proves a staunch wife, ruling Ithaca and fending off a host of suitors for the 20 years of Odysseus's absence. At first she tells them that she must finish a shroud for her father-in-law, Laertes, before taking another husband, but unravels each night what she has woven during the day.

Betrayed by one of her maids, she is finally prompted by Athena, after 20 years, to agree to marry whichever of the suitors can string Odysseus's great bow and fire an arrow through a row of double-headed axes. Unknown to her, Odysseus is present at the contest disguised as a beggar, and when all the suitors fail, he seizes the bow and turns on the suitors. Penelope cannot believe that her long ordeal is over, despite the reassurances of Odysseus's old nurse, who recognizes a scar on his leg, and it is only Odysseus's description of their marriage bed, formed from a living tree, that finally convinces her he is genuine.

Penthesilea

Queen of the Amazons and daughter of Ares, Greek god of war. An ally of the Trojan king Priam, she brings an army to aid him against the Greeks. She meets Achilles in fierce single combat, finally receiving a death-wound, and Achilles falls in love with her on seeing her face.

Pentheus

King of Thebes, grandson of Cadmus and Harmonia, who offends Dionysos by refusing to recognize the wine-god's divinity when he returns from his conquest of Asia. Dionysos is already determined to revenge himself on Pentheus's mother Agave for her failure to support her sister Semele, Dionysos's mother, and he now includes Pentheus in his retribution. Thrown into jail by Pentheus when he comes peaceably to the city, Dionysos escapes by causing the doorframe of his prison to turn into a vine and release him.

He inspires the Theban women, including Agave and her sisters, with a Dionysiac ecstasy, and they join the Maenads in their revels in the mountains. The puritanical Pentheus, deeply suspicious of this heady new cult, is persuaded by a disguised Dionysos to dress as a woman and spy on the Maenads' orgies, but they in their frenzy think he is a lion and tear him to pieces.

Persephone

Daughter of the Greek mother-goddess Demeter, known to the Romans as Proserpina, Persephone was originally a pre-Greek fertility-goddess called Kore, "maiden," whose return to life after burial in the ground represents the germination of the seed-corn. In Greek myth she is carried off by Hades, the god of the underworld, to be his wife, but returns to the world for a part of the year through the intervention of her mother.

She seems to accept her role as queen of the dead, for she is with Hades and intercedes when Orpheus comes searching for Eurydice. She is again the object of an attempted abduction when Theseus and Pirithous each decide to marry a goddess and come to Hades to carry her off, but are instead imprisoned by Hades.

Perseus

Famous Greek hero from Argos, son of Zeus and the princess Danae, with whom as an infant he is cast adrift by Danae's implacable father. They are rescued by a fisherman, Dictys, who lives on the island of Seriphos and brings up the boy, but Dictys's brother Polydectes, the local king, falls in love with Danae and wants to get Perseus out of the way. He therefore sends him on a seemingly impossible mission to fetch the head of the Gorgon Medusa.

Athena, whom Medusa has offended by making love to Poseidon in a temple dedicated to the goddess, promises to help Perseus. She gives him her shield, which is as clear as glass, while Hermes gives him a helmet of darkness to make him invisible, a pair of winged sandals, and a bag. Athena sends him to the Graeae, three aged crones who share one eye and one tooth, for instructions on how to find Medusa. Wearing the helmet of darkness, Perseus is able to steal the eye and force them to direct him to the Gorgons' lair.

He flies over the stream of Ocean in his winged sandals and, finding the two immortal Gorgons asleep, uses his shield as a mirror to avoid the eye of the mortal Gorgon, Medusa, whose glance turns humans to stone, and so is able to kill her.

On his return journey with the Gorgon's head safely in Hermes' bag, Perseus sees Andromeda chained to a rock at the mercy of a sea monster, the gods' punishment for the boastfulness of her mother Cassiopia. He falls in love with her on the spot, kills the monster, and claims her as his bride. When they return to Seriphos, however, they find that Danae and Dictys have been forced by the persecution of Polydectes to take sanctuary in the temple. Perseus displays the Gorgon's head to

Below Perseus carrying the Gorgon's head and shown mounted on Pegasus in this undated lithograph.

Above Phaedra's advances are rejected by her stepson Hippolytus.

Polydectes, turning him to stone, and makes Dictys king in his place.

Athena now takes back Hermes' gifts and her shield, attaching the Gorgon's head to it. Perseus, no longer divinely protected, goes back to Argos in search of his grandfather Acrisius, Danae's father, who flees from him because an oracle has foretold that his grandson will kill him. At a funeral games in Thessaly, Perseus throws a discus which accidentally strikes and kills Acrisius, and so the oracle is fulfilled.

Phaedra

Princess of Crete, the younger daughter of Minos and Pasiphae, whose sister Ariadne helps Theseus to kill the Minotaur but is then abandoned by him. Despite this betrayal, Phaedra marries Theseus once he is established as king of Athens, but falls in love with her stepson, Hippolytus, Theseus's son by his earlier marriage to the Amazon queen Hippolyta. Hippolytus is shocked by Phaedra's declaration and rejects her, and in revenge Phaedra denounces him to Theseus. Hippolytus dies as a result of his father's curse, and Phaedra hangs herself.

The seventeenth-century French dramatist Jean Racine uses the story in his play *Phèdre* to explore the issue of predestination, while the twentieth-century novelist Mary Renault retells the tragedy in more human terms in *The Bull from the Sea*.

Phaethon

Son of the Greek sun-god Helios, who is taunted about his paternity and journeys to Helios's palace in the Far East, at sunrise, to prove it. There he is kindly greeted by Helios and offered one wish. Phaethon asks to drive the chariot of the sun for a day and Helios, though horrified, has to comply. Phaethon proves wholly unable to control the four huge horses who pull the chariot; first they blaze a great gash across the heavens, forming the Milky Way, then they plunge downward and scorch the earth, turning the skins of equatorial races black. Afraid that Phaethon will destroy Olympus, Zeus kills him with a thunderbolt.

Philoctetes

Owner of the great bow of Heracles and one of the Greek leaders in the Trojan War. Heracles, accidentally poisoned by his wife Deianira, is lying in agony on a funeral pyre which none of his followers will light while he is alive. As he is immortal, only fire will burn away his mortal parts and ease his pain, and Philoctetes agrees to perform the service in exchange for Heracles' bow and its poisoned arrows.

Philoctetes is subsequently one of

the suitors to Helen of Sparta and so is bound by oath to take part in the Trojan War. On the way he is bitten in the foot by a water-snake (or in some stories accidentally wounded by one of his own arrows) when the fleet lands to make a sacrifice. The pain of the festering wound is so great, and the smell so unendurable, that Odysseus counsels the Greeks to maroon Philoctetes on the island of Lemnos, where he survives on what he can kill with his bow.

Nine years later the prophet Helenus reveals that the presence of Philoctetes is a prerequisite for the fall of Troy. Odysseus, knowing how much Philoctetes must hate the Greeks for their abandonment of him, persuades Achilles' son Neoptolemus to offer him safe passage home to Greece, but instead to bring him to Troy. Once entrusted with Heracles' bow, Neoptolemus reveals the plot and, ashamed of his part in it, proposes to fulfil his offer, but Heracles appears to Philoctetes and orders him to fight at Troy, where he will be cured. There Philoctetes kills Paris with one of his poisoned arrows, and his wound is finally healed by the physician Machaon.

Philomela

Athenian princess, whose sister Procne marries the Thracian king Tereus. When she visits Procne, she is raped and imprisoned by Tereus, who cuts out her tongue to prevent her accusing him and tells Procne she is dead. Philomela weaves a message to her sister into a piece of tapestry, who rescues her, and they revenge themselves on Tereus by serving him the body of his son at a banquet. Only after he has eaten does Philomela reveal the truth by offering him the boy's head; when he tries to kill her, the gods turn her into a swallow, which has no song but only chatters.

Philyra

A sea-nymph, who meets Cronos while he is disguised as a horse and looking for his infant son Zeus, whom Rhea has hidden from him. Philyra becomes pregnant by Cronos and bears a son who is half man and half horse, the centaur Chiron, tutor to most of the famous Greek heroes. She is so shocked by Chiron's appearance that she prays to Zeus to transform her, and he turns her into a lime tree.

Phineus

King of Thrace and a seer, who incurs the hostility of the gods, either by choosing long life in preference to sight and thus offending the sun-god Helios, bringer of light, or by revealing the gods' plans to mortals. He is plagued by the harpies, who snatch away the food from his plate and foul his table. When the Argonauts visit him on their way to Colchis, he predicts the outcome of their expedition in exchange for being rid of the harpies; Calais and Zetes, the sons of the north wind Boreas, pursue the harpies to the edge of the world, where they take shelter in a cave and promise to leave Phineus in peace.

Phoebe

Early Greek moon-goddess, the daughter of Uranus and Ge and mother of Leto, who in turn has the divine twins Apollo and Artemis. Phoebe, whose name means "shining," is later identified with Artemis.

Phoenix

Tutor and companion to Achilles, who is denied children of his own through a curse laid on him by his father after Phoenix slept with his father's mistress. He is chosen by Peleus to train Achilles in the use of weapons, and despite his age accompanies Achilles to Troy, as his lieutenant.

Pholus

A centaur, who entertains Heracles in his cave during the hero's quest for the Erymanthian boar. Pholus does not offer the hero any wine with his roast meat, even though there is an unopened wine-jar in the cave. When Heracles remonstrates with his host for his meanness, Pholus explains that Dionysos gave the wine to the centaurs communally, but Heracles insists on opening it. The other centaurs, attracted by the rich smell, draw near and a fight breaks out. Heracles drives them off with his poisoned arrows, and Pholus is accidentally killed when he drops one of the arrows on his foot while marveling that such a small thing can cause death.

Phoroneus

Son of a river-god and a sea-nymph, king of Argos, and sometimes claimed to be the first mortal. When Hera and Poseidon dispute the ownership of the Peloponnesus, southern mainland Greece, Zeus chooses Phoroneus as arbitrator. He decides in favor of Hera, who makes him a great leader. He teaches his people how to group themselves together in defensible cities and how to use fire; presumably a folk memory of the move from a pastoral to an urban society.

Below Phaethon felled by Zeus's thunderbolt.

Phrixus

Phrixus and his sister Helle are the children of Athamas, king of Orchomenus, and his first wife, the nymph Nephele. Athamas's second wife, Ino, wants to be rid of them and arranges for a false report from the oracle at Delphi which tells Athamas to sacrifice his children. He is on the point of doing so when Nephele (or Zeus) sends a magic golden ram which carries the children away on its back.

Helle falls off as they are crossing the sea dividing Europe from Asia, but Phrixus is born to the kingdom of Colchis, at the east end of the Black Sea. He is welcomed by the king, Aeetes, who gives him his daughter Chalciope in marriage. Phrixus sacrifices the ram to Zeus and hangs its golden fleece on a tree in the grove of Ares, where it is protected by a fire-breathing serpent.

Some time later Aeetes is warned that a Greek stranger will cause his

Below The Dance of the Pleiades, painted the American by Elihu Vedder (1836-1923).

death, and so he has Phrixus killed, but the stranger in fact proves to be Jason, who leads the Argonauts on the quest for the Golden Fleece and rescues Phrixus's children.

Phyllis

Princess of Thrace, who falls in love with Theseus's son Demophon when he visits her father's court on his way home from Troy. He asks her to marry him, but must first return to Athens to settle his affairs. Phyllis gives him a casket which he is to open only when he has abandoned all intention of returning to her. When the day for his return and then nine more days pass with no sign of Demophon, Phyllis invokes a curse on him and hangs herself. On the same day Demophon opens the casket and is so frightened by the contents that he loses control of his horse, is thrown, and dies. In another version, a leafless almond tree grows from Phyllis's tomb; when Demophon finally returns, he embraces the tree and only then does it bear leaves and fruit.

Picus

An ancient Italian king, father of Faunus and grandfather of Latinus. In one story he is turned into a woodpecker by the sorceress Circe because he refuses her advances, preferring the nymph Canens. Another version has it that he is a pastoral god with the power to change his shape, who chooses the form of the woodpecker, a bird sacred to Mars.

Pirithous

King of the Lapiths in Thessaly, the son of Zeus by the Thessalian queen Dia, Pirithous becomes the close friend of the hero Theseus. When he succeeds to the throne, he is challenged by the centaurs, the offspring of Dia's husband Ixion, who claim a share of the kingdom. After a fierce struggle the combatants reach an agreement and the centaurs settle on Mount Pelion.

Pirithous has heard of the valor of Theseus, king of Athens, and decides to test it by launching a cattle raid on Marathon. Theseus pursues and

catches up with him, but instead of fighting they swear eternal friendship. When Pirithous marries, both the centaurs and Theseus with his Athenians are invited to the wedding. The centaurs, unused to wine, get drunk and try to abduct the bride and her women, leading to the battle of the Lapiths and centaurs, which is a favorite subject with classical Greek sculptors.

In the course of time both Pirithous's and Theseus's wives die, and the two widowers resolve to carry off and marry daughters of Zeus. Theseus chooses Helen of Sparta, already renowned for her beauty; they kidnap her and leave her in the care of Theseus's mother Aethra, as she is too young for marriage. Pirithous sets his heart on Persephone, queen of the underworld, and the two heroes brazenly enter Hades, forcing Charon to ferry them across the Styx and somehow avoiding the three-headed guardian Cerberus.

They appear before Hades himself and demand that he give Persephone up to them, but instead he seats them in chairs of forgetfulness. There they stay until Heracles enters Hades on one of his Labors. In some stories Heracles persuades Hades to release both men, but in others Pirithous is detained in the underworld, where his father Ixion is also condemned to stay.

hero gets Plutus's sight restored at the temple of Asclepius, and thereafter riches go only to the deserving.

Above Pluto or Hades, shown feasting with Persephone in this Greek vase-painting.

Pleiades

The seven daughters of the Titan Atlas and the sea-nymph Pleione, who are turned into stars by Zeus to console them when their father is condemned to hold up the sky. Six of them have previously had children by one or other of the gods, only Merope forming a relationship with a mortal, and Merope's star is supposed to shine less brightly in shame.

Pluto

Roman god of the underworld, identified with the Greek Hades.

Plutus

Greek god of wealth, the son of Demeter and originally associated with agricultural prosperity. In later myth he is believed to have been blinded by Zeus, so that he will visit the good and the evil indiscriminately. In Aristophanes' comedy *Plutus*, the honest

Pollux

Roman name for Polydeuces, one of the Dioscuri. See Castor.

Polydectes

King of the island of Seriphos, who falls in love with Danae when she and her infant son Perseus are cast off by her father and land on his shores. Danae resists him, and as Perseus grows up he supports his mother in her continuing refusals. It is Polydectes who sends Perseus on the quest for the Gorgon's head, in the hope that he will never return, but Perseus succeeds and turns Polydectes to stone with it for his persecution of Danae.

Polyhymnia

Muse of singing and rhetoric, the inventor of harmony. She is represented veiled in white, holding a scepter, and with her right hand raised to address the crowd.

Polymestor

King of Thrace, who marries Priam's daughter Ilione. When the Greeks besiege Troy, Priam sends much of his wealth in the care of his younger son Polydorus to Polymestor for safekeeping. On receiving news of the fall of Troy, Polymestor murders the boy so that he can keep the gold. Priam's widow Hecuba learns the truth when she is brought to Polymestor's court as the slave of Achilles, goes mad with grief, and tears out Polymestor's eyes.

Polynices

Elder son of the tragic Theban king Oedipus by Oedipus's own mother Jocasta. When the incest is revealed and Oedipus blinds himself, Polynices and his brother Eteocles mock their father and are cursed by him. Oedipus is banished and the brothers agree to share the rule of Thebes, each reigning for a year. Eteocles refuses to give way to his brother, who takes refuge with

Above Polyxena laments on the tomb of Achilles.

Adrastus at the court of Argos, bearing with him the magic necklace of Harmonia, first queen of Thebes.

Adrastus gives Polynices his daughter in marriage and agrees to help him regain his kingdom, but the soothsayer Amphiarus foresees disaster and refuses to accompany the expedition. Polynices bribes Amphiarus's wife with the gift of Harmonia's necklace to persuade her husband, but the expedition proves as disastrous as Amphiarus foretold.

Adrastus's army is defeated; Polynices and Eteocles kill each other outside the gates of Thebes; and their sister Antigone is put to death for giving Polynices proper burial.

Polyphemus

A Cyclops, or one-eyed giant, the son of Poseidon, who lives on an island which is probably Sicily. Later legend makes him the rejected lover of the nymph Galatea. Odysseus lands here at an early stage of his journey home from Troy and asks for hospitality, telling Polyphemus that his name is Outis, "nobody." Polyphemus, however, imprisons Odysseus and his companions in the cave in which he keeps his sheep, and starts to devour them one by one.

Odysseus gives him wine and makes him drunk, then blinds him when he is helpless. When Polyphemus yells to the other Cyclops for help, saying that "Outis" is attacking him, they think he is joking. Next morning the ingenious Greeks tie themselves under Polyphemus's sheep to get past the giant sitting at the mouth of the cave, and escape. Polyphemus's father is Poseidon, and Odysseus's subsequent wanderings are his revenge for the blinding of his son.

Polyxena

Trojan princess, daughter of Priam and Hecuba. When the Trojan women are being apportioned to the conquerors after the fall of their city, the shade of Achilles rises from the tomb and demands that Polyxena be sacrificed so that she can be his companion in the underworld. A late story has it that Achilles falls in love with Polyxena when she comes with Priam to plead for the body of Hector, and goes to Troy to meet her, where he is killed by Paris.

Pomona

Roman goddess of fruit trees and gardens, with whom the god of the seasons, Vertumnus, falls in love. He appears to her as a shepherd, a fruit-picker, and a vine-tender, but she remains firmly celibate. He then takes the form of an old woman, and pleads so eloquently that she agrees to yield.

Poseidon

Principal Greek god of the sea and also of earthquakes, whom the Romans identified with the water deity Neptune. He is one of the most powerful gods and seems to have supplanted a number of older and more peaceable sea-gods, such as Nereus and Proteus. The son of Cronos and Rhea, he is swallowed at birth by his father, but is rescued with the rest of his siblings by his ingenious younger brother Zeus.

Below   Pomona and Vertumnus, by the Dutch artist Arent de Gelder (1645-1727).

He is a dangerous, vindictive, and unpredictable god, relentless in his pursuit of those who offend him, including the Trojans (see Laomedon), Odysseus, and Minos. He is also a horse-god, and presents horses to a number of his favorites, including Pelops, who wins Hippodamia as his bride in a chariot race; Idas; and Peleus, to whom he gives the immortal steeds Xanthus and Balius inherited by Achilles.

Priam

Last king of Troy, who sees his city ruined twice. When he is a young man, Heracles saves his sister Hesione from a sea monster in a bargain with their father Laomedon, and ruins the city when Laomedon fails to honor his pledge. Priam is spared the destruction at the plea of his sister, who ransoms him with her veil, and he inherits the throne, rebuilding Troy and Trojan power.

He has over 50 children by his wife Hecuba and his many mistresses, but one of these, Paris, is exposed on the mountainside when Hecuba dreams a premonitory dream. Paris survives, however, and is later acknowledged by his father, who urges him to return Helen to Sparta but ratifies the marriage when Paris refuses.

In the *Iliad*, Homer's account of the siege of Troy, Priam is old and worn by war, but is shown as unfailingly gentle to Helen. He presides over the councils of war, but his view does not always prevail. He suffers the loss of his favorite son Hector, and has to beg his killer Achilles for the body. He finally dies, when Troy is sacked, at the hand of Achilles' son Neoptolemus on the altar of Zeus.

Priapus

A fertility-god from the region of the Hellespont, whose cult only arrives in the Greek world in the third century BC. He is said to be the son of Aphrodite by Dionysos or Hermes, but is disowned by his mother on account of his small gnarled body and grotesquely enlarged phallus. He is generally treated with affectionate disrespect, and used as a scarecrow to scare thieves away from gardens. His sacred animal is the donkey, believed to be the embodiment of lust.

Above Head of the *Poseidon of Artemission*.

Below The aged Priam supplicates Achilles for Hector's body.

Procne

Athenian princess, who marries the Thracian king Tereus. After five years she wants to see her sister Philomela and Tereus goes to Athens to fetch her, but imprisons her in a distant stronghold and tells Procne she is dead. Philomela weaves a tapestry containing a message, and Procne rescues her in the guise of a Maenad during the feast of Dionysos. Together the sisters plot a hideous revenge on Tereus. Procne murders Itys, her only child by Tereus, cooks his flesh, and serves it to Tereus. When he realizes what he has eaten, he tries to kill both women, but the gods transform them into birds, Philomela into a swallow, and Procne into a nightingale, which sings "ityn, ityn" in mourning for the dead Itys.

Procris

See Cephalus.

Procrustes

Robber who preys on wayfarers using the road between Athens and Eleusis. He offers them hospitality, then ties them to a bed, either stretching them on a rack or cutting off their limbs until they fit the bed exactly. Theseus, on his way to Athens to claim his inheritance, gives Procrustes the same treatment by cutting off his head.

Proetus

King of Tiryns and twin brother of Acrisius, with whom he quarrels even in their mother's womb. When they reach maturity, Acrisius accuses his brother of seducing Acrisius's daughter Danae, although Danae herself maintains that Zeus is the father of her son, Perseus. Proetus takes refuge in Lycia, marries the king's daughter, and leads an army against Acrisius, who agrees to divide the kingdom.

Acrisius keeps Argos and Proetus builds the stronghold of Tiryns. His family life is notably unhappy; his wife tries to seduce the hero Bellerophon, and hangs herself when Bellerophon proves unyielding, and his three daughters are driven mad by Dionysos for despising his worship.

Proetus approaches the seer Melam-

Left Eighteenth-century engraving of Prometheus imprisoned by Zeus.

pus for a cure but finds Melampus's price, a third of the kingdom, too high. Dionysos then afflicts many more of the women of Tiryns with madness and Proetus resorts again to Melampus, who this time demands two-thirds of the kingdom, to which Proetus is forced to agree.

Prometheus

A Titan, one of the race of giants, who champions mankind in the face of the gods' hostility and is savagely punished. His name means foreknowledge; in the battle of the gods and giants he advises the Titans to use cunning, and when they ignore his advice he supports the gods. In some stories it is Prometheus who creates man from clay models, into which Athena breathes life, and was thus seen as the master craftsman, teaching humanity many skills.

Zeus becomes jealous of mankind's

Below The shape-shifting sea-god Proteus, lithograph by Walter Crane.

Above Cupid and Psyche by the nineteenth-century English painter Spencer Stanhope.

growing competence and demands more and richer offerings in the hope of starving them. Prometheus arranges a meeting between men and gods to determine which part of the sacrificial meat should be set aside for the gods. He cuts up an ox and divides the meat into two bundles, the larger of which is only fat and entrails. Zeus is deceived and chooses the larger and less choice of the two, and in his anger deprives man of fire.

Again Prometheus intervenes, stealing a spark from Hephaestus's forge and hiding it in a stalk of fennel. For this the gods create Pandora to punish mankind, and Prometheus is chained to a mountain peak next to the stream of Ocean, far away from human habitation. Zeus sends his eagle to gnaw each day at Prometheus's liver, which miraculously grows whole again at night because, as a Titan, Prometheus is immortal.

Finally Zeus is forced to release him, in exchange for the vital information that the son of the sea-nymph Thetis, whom Zeus is considering marrying, will be greater than his father. Heracles is sent to kill the eagle and liberate Prometheus, and in return is advised how best to obtain the apples of the Hesperides, one of his Twelve Labors.

The role of Prometheus as the suffering champion of humanity was first explored by Aeschylus in *Prometheus Bound*, where he supports man against the new Olympian gods who have dispossessed earlier earth and fertility deities. The nineteenth-century English poet Percy Bysshe Shelley further developed this theme in his verse drama *Prometheus Unbound*, where the knowledge Prometheus offers will bring freedom and love. The concept of the independent thinker and champion of freedom has had a wide appeal; the early Christian Fathers saw Prometheus's sufferings as prefiguring the Passion, while in the French writer André Gide's twentieth-century reinterpretation, Prometheus takes a masochistic pleasure in his torments as a symbol of man's self-destructive aspirations.

Proserpina

Daughter of Ceres, and the Roman equivalent of Persephone.

Proteus

Greek sea-god, whose cult probably pre-dates that of the Olympian god Poseidon. He is seen as shepherding flocks of sea creatures, and has the gift of prophecy and the power to change shape. Menelaus persuades him to reveal the safe way home from Troy by disguising himself as a seal, while Aristaeus manages to fetter Proteus while he sleeps on a rock, in order to discover why his bees are dying. Proteus gives his name to the term "protean," meaning variable, versatile.

Psyche

The romantic story of Cupid and Psyche is a late addition to classical mythology, first told by the Roman writer Apuleius, and contains many familiar folk and fairytale elements. Psyche is a king's daughter who is so beautiful that people abandon the worship of Venus in favor of her. This infuriates Venus, who instructs her son Cupid to punish Psyche by making her fall in love with ugliest creature in the world.

When Cupid sees her, however, he falls in love with her himself. He arranges for an oracle to instruct her father to dress her in wedding clothes and stand her on a mountain peak, where she will be carried off by an evil spirit. In much sorrow the king obeys, but Psyche is wafted to a palace in a secret valley, where she is waited on by invisible hands and joined in bed at night by Cupid in human form.

He promises her that they will be happy forever as long as she does not try to see him or discover who he is. Presently she becomes lonely and persuades Cupid to let her sisters visit her, but they are jealous of her good fortune, and tease her about her invisible husband, until one night she lights a candle to look at him. She at once recognizes him as the god of love, and her hand shakes so much that a drop of candle wax falls and wakes him, and he vanishes.

Psyche is desolate and seeks throughout the world for her lost husband, but neither Juno nor Ceres, both patrons of women, will help her because she has offended Venus. Finally she comes to Venus's palace, where she is put to work on impossible tasks. She sorts a roomful of grain with the help of a colony of ants; fetches a skein of wool from the fleece of a man-eating sheep; and fills a jug with the water of the River Styx.

Finally Venus tells her to bring a flask of the water of youth from Proserpina, the queen of the underworld. Psyche despairs, knowing that she must die, and climbs a high tower to throw herself off, but the tower talks to her and tells her how she may achieve her quest, only warning her on no account to open the flask. On the way back her longing for Cupid overcomes her and she opens the flask, instantly falling into a deathlike trance.

Meanwhile Cupid is miserable without her and finally tells Jupiter the truth, begging that he may be allowed to make her his lawful wife. Jupiter agrees, and Cupid wakes Psyche with the tip of one of his arrows. She is reconciled with Venus and all the gods attend the wedding, Jupiter himself giving her the drink of nectar which will make her immortal. The story has often been seen as an allegory of the soul's (*psyche*) journey through life.

Ptah

Egyptian creator- and craftsman-god, worshipped particularly in Memphis and always represented in human form, wrapped like a mummy and with a shaven head and tight cap. His sacred animal is the bull. According to the mythology of Memphis, Ptah is senior to the creator-god Atum, generating himself as a bisexual deity from the primeval chaos, Nun. He then thinks and speaks the cosmos into

Below Pygmalion and Galatea, engraving from a painting by the French artist Girodet-Trioson (1767-1824).

Above Pylades and Orestes, by the American Benjamin West (1738-1820).

Right above Galatea repulses Polyphemus.

existence, an example of the "logos doctrine," according to which the world is created by the divine word.

Pygmalion

A king of Cyprus in late Greek legend, who can find no woman to live up to his ideal and therefore has a sculpture made of her. He falls in love with the statue and Aphrodite breathes life into it, creating Galatea. In nineteenth-century literature Pygmalion becomes a symbol for the romantic lover who can create his ideal beloved through the intensity of his desire. In George Bernard Shaw's play *Pygmalion,* on which the musical *My Fair Lady* was based, the Galatea character, Eliza Doolittle, gains self-knowledge and independence through the education she receives from her Pygmalion.

Pylades

Friend and cousin of Orestes, who is brought up with Orestes after Orestes and his sister Electra have fled Argos on the murder of their father Agamemnon, and aids Orestes' vengeance on his mother Clytemnestra for the murder. In some stories Pylades accompanies Orestes to the Crimea, where they find Orestes' lost sister Iphigenia. After Orestes has been purified of the crime of matricide, Pylades marries Electra.

Pyramus

The tragic tale of Pyramus and Thisbe, used by Shakespeare as the play-within-a-play in *A Midsummer Night's Dream,* is a late story, told only by Ovid. The couple are neighbors and fall in love, but are forbidden to meet by their parents and can communicate only through a hole in the wall between their houses. They arrange to meet outside the city but Thisbe, arriving first, is frightened by a lion and runs, dropping her veil. Pyramus thinks she is dead and stabs himself; Thisbe, when she finds his body, does the same; and the fruit of the mulberry tree growing nearby turns blood-red.

Pyrrha

The daughter of the first woman, Pandora, and the Titan Epimetheus, who is the brother of Prometheus. Zeus is angry with Prometheus for the help he has given men, and is determined to wipe humanity out with a great flood and start again with a more biddable and grateful race. Pyrrha and her husband Deucalion are chosen by the gods to be the sole survivors.

Pythia

The priestess of Pythian Apollo at Delphi, who delivers the god's oracular (and often ambiguous) utterances.

Python

A monstrous snake or dragon which Apollo has to kill before he can found his oracle at Delphi, symbolizing the triumph of the Olympian gods over earlier underworld gods. Because Python is the son of the earth-goddess Ge, and therefore immortal, Apollo has to do penance for the killing. He founds the Pythian games in Python's honor, and takes the name Pythian Apollo.

Below Thisbe finds the dead body of her lover Pyramus.

R

Re

Egyptian sun- and creator-god, also worshipped as Atum, Amun, and Khepri. In some myths he creates himself out of a mound that emerges from the primeval ocean, in others he is born from the original lotus blossom. He in turn creates Shu, air, and Tefnut, moisture, from his own spit, and from their union is formed the material world in the form of the sky-goddess Nut and the earth-god Geb.

He is usually shown in the form of a falcon, carrying the sun on its head, and is also perceived as a god of the underworld and described in some inscriptions as "Re in Osiris, Osiris in Re." In this form he is shown as a human figure with a ram's head, surmounted by the sun disc, riding each night through the underworld in his solar boat. The cult of the "Eye of Re" takes on a power and complexity of its own.

Re is believed to have created mankind from his tears, and pharaohs of the Fifth Dynasty began to style themselves the sons of Re. Layered pyramids were built as vast stairways for the pharaoh to climb into the sky to join his father, while true pyramids represented the rays of the sun-god bathing the earth.

Some later myths see Re as an ageing and somewhat confused monarch, who has control of the junior gods and goddesses. He reveals his true name to Isis, thus giving her divine powers,

Above Egyptian grave-slab showing Re with the solar boat and sun disc.

Below Romulus and Remus fed by the wolf. Etruscan sculpture group.

Above Rhea, early Greek mother-goddess and mother of the Olympian gods.

and entrusts the slaughter of mankind to Hathor in a moment of rage. In later mythology, he is superseded by Osiris, god of death and resurrection.

Remus

See Romulus.

Rhadamanthys

A judge of the dead in Greek mythology, the son of Zeus and Europa. Like his older brother Minos, he is adopted by the Cretan king Asterion, who marries his mother. He is renowned for his justice and wisdom, and is held responsible for the codifying of Cretan law, which served as the model for Greek cities. He becomes a judge in Hades.

Rhea

An early Greek mother-goddess, daughter of Ge, the earth, and Uranus, the sky. She marries her brother Cronos and rules the world with him. Their children are Hestia, Demeter, Hera, Hades, Poseidon, and Zeus, six of the 12 Olympian gods. Cronos has been warned by Ge that one of his children will dethrone him, and so he swallows each one as it is born, until Rhea grows wily and at the birth of Zeus gives Cronos a stone instead. She hides Zeus in Crete, an island which remains sacred to her, until he is old enough to rescue his siblings and wage war on his father.

Rhea Silvia

The mother of the Roman heroes Romulus and Remus, she is the daughter of Numitor, king of Alba Longa, with whom Mars, the god of war, falls in love. Her uncle Amulius dethrones Numitor and makes Rhea a Vestal Virgin to ensure there is no succession. When her pregnancy becomes obvious, he throws both her and her twin sons into the Tiber. The boys are rescued by a shepherd, and Rhea Silvia is borne up by the river-god, who makes her his wife.

Rhesus

A Thracian king, son of the Muse Euterpe, who is given a pair of magnificent horses by Poseidon. He is an ally of the Trojans and comes to their aid in the tenth year of the Trojan War. An oracle predicts that if Rhesus and his horses drink from the River Scamander, on the plains of Troy, they will be invincible and Troy will never fall. Athena warns the Greeks of this, and Odysseus and Diomedes make a nighttime raid on Rhesus's army, killing him and driving off his horses before they can reach the Scamander.

Romulus

The legendary founder of Rome, son of Mars and grandson of Numitor, king of Alba Longa, Romulus is thrown into the Tiber in his cradle with his twin brother Remus, on the orders of Numitor's usurping brother Amulius. The cradle floats on the water and comes to rest under a fig tree, and the babies are suckled by a she-wolf, an animal sacred to Mars, until they are found by a shepherd, Faustulus, and brought up by him and his wife, Acca Laurentia.

When they are grown, they fall out with the shepherds of King Amulius, and Remus is captured. Faustulus tells Romulus the truth about his birth and urges him to rescue his brother, so Romulus leads an attack on the palace, killing Amulius and restoring the rightful king, his grandfather Numitor.

The twins are not content to live at Numitor's court and decide to found a city of their own on the spot where the Tiber cast them up, but they argue over who should be in charge of the building operations, and therefore the official founder of the city, and Romulus kills Remus. Unlike Greek mythology, there is no suggestion that Romulus needs purification for this act of fratricide, and his city is soon completed.

In order to people it, he makes it an asylum for all lawbreakers and fugitives, and finds his citizens wives by inviting his Sabine neighbors to celebratory horse races and carrying off all their unmarried women. When the Sabines march against Rome to recover their womenfolk, Romulus prays to Jupiter for aid, and instead of fighting the two sides become allies. Romulus rules Rome peacefully for 40 years, and then disappears from the Field of Mars in a thundercloud.

S

Sarpedon

Son of Europa and Zeus, who is driven by his brother Minos from the island of Crete after winning the favors of a beautiful boy, Miletus, whom Minos also loves. He establishes himself in southern Asia Minor and founds the kingdom of Lycia.

Saturn

An early Italian god of agriculture, who becomes identified with the Greek Cronos. He supposedly arrives in Italy from Greece after being banished from Olympus, establishes himself on the Capitol, the site of what will become Rome, and is welcomed by the local god Janus. His rule in Latium is re-

Below Saturn, the Roman Cronos, enslaved after his revolt against Jupiter.

Above Greek vase showing the death of Sarpedon.

garded as a golden age; he teaches the natives how to grow crops and cultivate the vine.

Satyrs

Early Greek spirits of woods and hills, represented as half man and half horse or goat, who accompany the Maenads in the revels of Dionysos and are regarded as mischievous and dangerously amorous. In Greek drama they are debased and comic figures, guaranteed to lighten the mood after the performance of a tragedy. In Roman myth they are somewhat more dignified creatures, associated with Pan and Faunus and usually shown with goats' legs and horns.

Scamander

God of the river that flows across the plain of Troy. Zeus creates the stream for Heracles when he prays for water, but Heracles finds its flow inadequate and digs in the ground until he finds a great reservoir. The Trojans call Scamander Xanthus, because his waters stain the sheep that bathe in it tawny-gold, and Aphrodite washes her hair in the river to give it golden highlights before submitting to the Judgment of Paris.

Scamander supports the Trojans in the ensuing war, and emerges in flood to do battle with Achilles when Achilles chokes his riverbed with corpses in vengeance for the death of Patroclus. He is about to drown Achilles when Hera intervenes, sending Hephaestus to dry up the flood and return the river to its bed.

Sciron

A thief and murderer who preys on travelers journeying from Megara to Eleusis. He stops them at a point where the road follows a narrow course above a high cliff overlooking the sea, and makes them wash his feet. As they bend to do so, he kicks them over the cliff into the sea, where a giant turtle devours them. Theseus kills him on his way to Athens.

Scylla

Sea monster who guards one side of the Straits of Messina, with the whirlpool Charybdis on the other side. Scylla has six heads, and round her waist is a ring of barking dogs; as ships pass through the straits, she seizes as many sailors as possible from their decks with her many mouths. Originally she is a nymph, with whom the sea-god Glaucus falls in love. He asks the sorceress Circe for a potion which will make Scylla love him, but Circe wants him for herself and so turns Scylla into the monster.

Selene

A pre-Greek, possibly oriental, goddess of the moon. She is identified by the Greeks with Artemis, and by the Romans with Diana or the old Italian goddess Luna. She has two daughters,

Below left Greek statue of Selene poised in her chariot of the moon.

Herse (dew) and Pandia, by Zeus, and also enjoys an amorous relationship with Pan. When she falls in love with a mortal, Endymion, she lulls him into everlasting sleep so that she can enjoy his beauty eternally. The Greeks saw her as driving the chariot of the moon across the sky, just as Eos drives the chariot of dawn. The sculpture on the east pediment of the Parthenon included at each end the horses respectively of Eos and of Selene, Selene's sinking exhaustedly to rest from their night's labors. The head of one of Selene's horses is among the controversial Elgin Marbles now in the British Museum, London.

Semele

Lover of Zeus and mother of the wine-god Dionysos by him, Semele is persecuted by Hera and finally meets her end at Hera's connivance. She is an early princess of Thebes, the daughter of Cadmus and Harmonia, whom Zeus seduces in mortal form. Unlike many of his human amours, he remains a constant visitor to her, perhaps because she too is partly divine, through her mother Harmonia.

This gives Hera time to disguise herself as Semele's nurse Beroe and persuade the guileless girl to extract from her lover an unnamed boon. When she then demands that he appear to her in his immortal majesty, Zeus tries to dissuade her, knowing that she will be destroyed, but she holds him to his oath, convinced by the false Beroe that she too will attain full divinity.

Instead she is shriveled by the flashes of Zeus's lightning, but he seizes the unborn Dionysos from her body and saves him. When Dionysos grows to manhood, he rescues Semele from Hades and takes her to Olympus to receive immortality from Zeus.

Serapis

Late Egyptian god, seen primarily as a healer of the sick. The Serapeum, or sanctuary of Serapis, at Alexandria was one of the wonders of the ancient world and attracted many pilgrims in search of miraculous cures. The cult of Serapis, originally derived from that of the bull-god Apis at Memphis, was very influential among the Romans until overshadowed by that of Isis.

Below The Egyptian healer-god Serapis.

SERAPIS.

Seth

Ancient Egyptian god who represents chaos, violence, and adversity, and comes to be seen as the natural adversary of his brother Osiris, representing one half of the Egyptians' dualistic world view. Seth is the lord of the desert and the cruel sea, while Osiris is the god of vegetation and the life-giving Nile. Son of the sky-goddess Nut and the earth-god Geb sometimes Seth's sister Nephthys is seen as his consort, but he is also linked with Semitic war goddesses such as Astarte.

He is for a time the ruler of Upper Egypt, his sacred city being Ombos, and is sometimes depicted with a human body, animal head, and long curving snout, sometimes as a fabulous animal with a stiffly erect tail. In the myth of Osiris, Seth murders his brother and usurps the throne of Egypt, but is finally defeated by the son of Osiris and Isis, Horus, who castrates his uncle, although he in turn loses an eye, which is sometimes equated with the "Eye of Re."

Sibyls

Originally there is one Sibyl, a prophetess who lives near Troy and devotes herself to the service of Apollo, expressing her oracles in riddles and writing them on leaves. She gains such renown that her name becomes generic, and a number of places claim Sibyls.

The most famous is the Cumaean Sibyl, who guides Aeneas down into the underworld and shows him how to pluck the Golden Bough as a passport to Hades. She tells Aeneas that Apollo once offered her anything she wanted in exchange for taking him as a lover. She asks to live as many years as there are grains in a handful of dust, but forgets to request eternal youth, and grows so decrepit that she hangs from the ceiling of her cave in a bottle.

Right Bronze and gilt figure of Seth, Egyptian god of chaos and adversity.

Below Roman wall-painting showing Silenus lifting the infant Dionysos so he can pluck a bunch of grapes.

It is this Sibyl who comes to the last king of Rome, Tarquin the Proud, and offers to sell him her nine books of prophecies for a huge sum. He refuses, whereupon she burns three of them and offers him the rest for the same amount; again he refuses, and she burns another three; only then does he agree to buy the remaining three for the price of the original nine. These books were preserved in Rome and consulted by the Senate in times of emergency. The Sibyls came to be linked with Old Testament prophets in Christian art and literature, notably in Michelangelo's scheme for the ceiling of the Sistine Chapel in the Vatican.

Side

The first wife of the giant Orion, she rashly boasts herself fairer than Hera, who in revenge prevails on Zeus to throw Side into Hades.

Silenus

The son of Pan or Hermes and a nymph, Silenus is the companion and tutor of the wine-god Dionysos and in some stories is the king of Nysa, the mythical land in which Dionysos spends his childhood. In early myth Silenus is renowned for his wisdom. King Midas captures him by mixing wine with the waters of a forest spring, and persuades him to impart the secret of human life; that the best thing is not to be born at all, and the next best to die as soon as possible. Later stories show Silenus as a comic, pot-bellied drunkard, riding a donkey and surrounded by carousing satyrs and nymphs.

Silvanus

Italian woodland- and garden-god, son of a shepherd and a nanny goat and so usually shown as having a man's body and goat's legs. He is often identified with Pan.

Sinon

A Greek warrior, not mentioned in Homer, who stays behind on the plains of Troy after the Greeks have built the Wooden Horse and left it there. He allows himself to be captured by the Trojans and assures them that the Horse is an offering to Athena to propitiate her for the loss of the Palladium, stolen by Odysseus and Palamedes,

and that the Greeks have sailed away for good in response to a hostile oracle from Apollo. The Trojans believe him, despite the warnings of Cassandra, and pull the Horse inside the city. In the night Sinon lights a beacon as a signal to the Greek fleet, and releases the warriors who are hidden inside the Horse. See Odysseus.

Sirens

In Greek legend as told by Homer, the Sirens are two or more sisters, half bird and half woman, who live on an island near the straits where Scylla and Charybdis lurk, and sing so sweetly that any sailor who hears them leaps from his ship and swims to the island, where he is compelled to listen for the rest of his life. The ground around the Sirens is white with the bleached bones of dead sailors. Only twice are they circumvented.

When the Argonauts pass, Orpheus's lute surpasses even the Sirens' singing; only one man, Butes, hears them and succumbs, but he is saved by Aphrodite. Odysseus, on his lengthy journey home after the Trojan War, fills his mariners' ears with wax so they are deaf, and has himself bound to the mast to prevent him responding to their music. In non-Homeric Greek legend, the Sirens are

Above Early Greek vase decorated with two Sirens.

the companions of Persephone, who are punished for failing to prevent Hades from carrying her off, and become the escorts of the dead to Hades.

Sisyphus

The founder of the city of Corinth and fabled for his deviousness and low cunning, Sisyphus is supposed to have fathered Odysseus by Autolycus's daughter Anticlea, in return for Autolycus's constant raids on Sisyphys's cattle herds. He is finally condemned by Zeus to Tartarus, the lowest level of the underworld, where he must eternally roll uphill a vast stone which always escapes him just before the top and rolls back to the bottom.

He incurs Zeus's anger when he discloses the nymph Aegina's whereabouts to her father after Zeus has carried her off. Zeus at first sends Thanatos, the god of death, to take Sisyphus to Hades, but Sisyphus manages to trick Thanatos and imprison him, with the result that mortals cease to die. Zeus sends Ares to release Thanatos, who again comes looking for Sisyphus. Again he manages to deceive the gods, however, by giving his wife

Above Sisyphus tormented by demons as he labors to roll his stone uphill.

Merope instructions not to perform funerary rites, leaving his body unburied and his death unmourned.

This lack of the proper observations and offerings infuriates Hades, who allows Sisyphus to return to the world to punish his wife for her neglect, but of course, once safely back in Corinth, he does no such thing and instead lives into riotous old age. His punishment is as much for his outmaneuvering of the gods as for his talebearing against Zeus.

Somnus

Roman god of sleep, the equivalent of the Greek Hypnos.

Sphinx

A winged monster with a human head and the body of a lion, which first appears in Egyptian myth. The Egyptian sphinx is invariably male, and is seen as a benevolent guardian, the embodiment of royal power. Avenues of sphinxes flanked the ceremonial entrances to many Egyptian temples, perhaps the most famous being the Great Sphinx at Giza.

In Greek myth the sphinx is female and malevolent, and usually represents some form of divine punishment. Hera sends a sphinx to plague the Thebans, in revenge for the Theban king Laius's abduction of Chrysippus; she sits by the gate and sets all passers-by a riddle, devouring all those who answer wrongly. Oedipus finally solves the riddle and destroys the sphinx, but the curse at the center of the Theban cycle of legends has still not worked itself out. See Oedipus.

Stentor

Greek herald, with a voice equal to that of 50 men, who fights in the Trojan War. He invents the trumpet, but dies after losing to Hermes in a shouting match. His name survives in the adjective "stentorian."

Styx

Goddess of the river in the underworld across which the souls of the dead are ferried by Charon. The River Styx runs from the Ocean, which the Greeks believed to surround the world, through a wild gorge, and down into the underworld, which it encircles nine times, separating the realm of Hades from the lands of the living.

Styx is the daughter of Oceanus and Tethys and thus an early Greek god; she is one of the first to come to Zeus's aid in the battle against Cronos and the Titans. In gratitude Zeus makes her children including Nike, the goddess of victory, his close attendants, and decrees that an oath sworn by Styx shall never be broken.

Syrinx

An Arcadian nymph and companion of the goddess Artemis, she is pursued by the amorous Pan and begs the earth to help her. She is transformed into a bed of reeds, from which Pan makes a simple instrument of reeds of graduated lengths, panpipes in English, the syrinx in Greek. The subject was a popular one in Renaissance art, as a symbol both of musical inspiration and of the mystic idea of life through death.

Below Roman carving of a Sphinx.

T

Talos

A bronze man given by Zeus to Europa to guard her on the island of Crete. He runs round the island three times a day, and repels all invaders by hurling rocks at them, or by making himself red hot and embracing them. He continues to serve Minos, Europa's son and the king of Crete, but is finally defeated by Medea, who sings him to sleep when the Argonauts wish to land, and then pulls out the nail in his foot which seals his single vein, so that he bleeds to death.

Tantalus

Son of Zeus and the Titan Pluto, Tantalus bitterly offends the gods and his children, Niobe and Pelops, also suffer divine disapprobation. He accumulates great riches and is invited to converse and eat with the gods, thus becoming immortal, but he steals nectar and ambrosia from the gods' table to give to his friends, reveals the secrets that he learns from them and, most heinous of all, serves up the body of his own son as a test of divine omnipotence when the gods accept his hospitality.

Pelops is restored to life, and Tantalus is condemned to suffer in Tartarus, the lowest part of Hades where the Titans are imprisoned. He is immersed up to his chin in water which he cannot drink, and tantalized by branches laden with fruit which are always just out of his reach. The Victorians named a locking decanter case after him, holding wine or spirits which could be seen by all but enjoyed only by the holder of the key.

Telamon

Greek hero, who with his brother Peleus is sent into exile by their father, the king of Aegina, for murdering their half-brother. Telamon settles on the island of Salamis, marries the princess, Glauce, and presently becomes king. He sails with the Argonauts, where he rows alongside Heracles and reproaches Jason for abandoning Heracles after he leaves the *Argo* to search for Hylas. Telamon also joins the hunt for the Calydonian boar, and also aids Heracles in the first sack of Troy, in punishment for the dishonesty of the Trojan king Laomedon.

Telamon is first to enter the city, and at once tactfully builds and dedicates an altar to Heracles the Victor. As reward Heracles gives him Laomedon's daughter Hesione, who bears him two heroic sons, Ajax and Teucer.

Above This engraving shows Tantalus desperately reaching for the fruit which is always just out of reach.

Telegonus

In some stories the sorceress Circe has a son of this name by Odysseus while he is entrapped on her island. Telegonus later goes in search of his father, but unknowingly kills him during a raid on Ithaca and marries Odysseus's faithful wife Penelope.

Telemachus

Only son of Odysseus and Penelope, whom Odysseus leaves as an infant in the care of Mentor when he goes to fight the Trojan War. After the end of the war and when Odysseus fails to return at the same time as the other warriors, Penelope is besieged by suitors

Above Telemachus tells Calypso his adventures, in another variant on his myth.

who take over the court of Ithaca and whom Telemachus is too young to challenge.

He sails to the courts of Nestor in Pylos and Menelaus at Sparta to seek for news of his father, and avoids an ambush laid for him by the suitors on his return with the help of Athena. When he reaches home, Odysseus has already landed, and father and son plot together to defeat the intruders.

Traditions then diverge; he marries either Nestor's daughter Polycaste or Nausicaa, or alternatively he is banished by Odysseus in response to an oracle foretelling that his son will kill him, and marries Circe.

Telephus

Son of Heracles and the Greek princess Auge, who is brought up by shepherds after his mother has been forced to abandon him. Once grown, he consults the Delphic oracle to discover his parentage and is sent to Mysia in Asia Minor, where he defeats a usurper and is adopted as heir by the legitimate king, Teuthras. Teuthras marries Telephus to Auge, whom he has adopted as a daughter, but fortunately her identity is revealed in time and mother and son are reunited.

Instead Telephus marries a daughter of Priam, and so is a supporter of the Trojans. In a preliminary Greek raid on Mysia before the Trojan War, he is wounded by Achilles and, when the wound festers, is told that "he that wounded will also heal." He disguises himself and goes to Mycenae, where the Greeks are planning a more major expedition against Troy.

There he seizes the infant Orestes and demands that Achilles cure him. The Greeks, warned by an oracle that they need Telephus to guide them to Troy, support him, but Achilles maintains that he has no skill as a doctor. Odysseus, however, suggests that the oracle refers to Achilles' spear, which caused the wound, and so Achilles touches the tip of the wound, which vanishes. Telephus leads the Greeks to Troy but refuses to join them.

Tellus

Roman equivalent of the Greek earth-goddess Ge.

Tenes

Ostensibly the son of Cycnus, king of Colonae near Troy, but more probably fathered by Apollo. After the death of his mother Proclea, Tenes is pursued by his stepmother Philonome, who first tries to seduce him and then, when she fails, accuses him to Cycnus. Tenes and his sister Hemithea are set afloat in a chest but the gods, and particularly Poseidon, their grandfather, protect the pair and land them safely on the island of Leucophrys. There the inhabitants make Tenes their king and rename the island Tenedos. Presently Cycnus learns the truth, punishes Philonome by burying her alive, and comes in search of his son.

When he tries to land, however, the unforgiving Tenes seizes an ax and severs the ship's cable, casting his father adrift. Achilles lands on Tenedos on his way to Troy and is warned not to harm Tenes for fear of incurring the anger of Apollo, but he tries to rape Hemithea, and kills Tenes when he comes to his sister's defense. In one story, Tenes refuses to let the Greeks land, and is killed by Achilles. Achilles' name is never again mentioned on Tenedos, and it is Apollo who guides the arrow, when Paris kills Achilles.

Tereus

Thracian king who aids Pandion, king of Athens, against the Thebans and marries the Greek princess Procne. When Procne's sister Philomela comes to visit her, Tereus rapes her, makes her his prisoner and cuts out her tongue to prevent her telling her story. The two sisters exact a gruesome revenge and are turned into birds.

Terminus

Roman god of boundaries, who punishes all unlawful seizure of land. He is represented with a human head, but without feet or arms, to show that he does not move from wherever he is placed.

Terpsichore

Muse of dancing, shown as a young woman crowned with laurel and holding a musical instrument.

Tethys

A pre-Olympian Greek sea-goddess, one of the race of Titans and wife of Oceanus. Her children are the river deities and the Oceanids, or sea-nymphs. In the war between Zeus and the Titans, Tethys, and Oceanus support Zeus and take care of his sister and consort, Hera, while the war lasts.

Thalia

Muse of pastoral and comic poetry, who presides over festivals. She is usually portrayed leaning on a column and holding a mask and a shepherd's crook.

Thamyris

Greek minstrel, and the first man to fall in love with a boy, the beautiful Hyacinthus. Thamyris wins so many singing competitions that he challenges the Muses themselves. When he loses, the Muses blind him for his impudence and remove his gift of song, and after his death he is condemned to suffer with the presumptuous in Tartarus.

Thanatos

Greek personification of death, the son of Nyx, night, and brother of Hypnos, sleep. He comes to each man or woman when the time allotted to them by the Fates or Moirae has run out, cuts off a lock of their hair to dedicate to Hades, and carries them away. Only Sisyphus manages to trick him, and suffers eternal torment in punishment.

Themis

A Titan, whose name means justice or order. She is the daughter of Uranus and the earth-goddess Ge, and the mother of Prometheus by her first husband Iapetus. She then has a liaison with Zeus, to whom she bears the Moirae or Fates and the Seasons.

She is wise and far-seeing, and perceives future events which are hidden even to Zeus. Some of this knowledge she passes to her first child, Prometheus, including the fact that the son of Thetis is destined to be greater than his father, which Prometheus uses to gain his freedom from Zeus's punishment. See Prometheus, Thetis.

Theophane

A beautiful Thracian princess, courted by many human suitors, with whom the sea-god Poseidon falls in love. He carries her off and settles her on a convenient island, where he can visit her regularly, but the suitors institute a search and find her island.

To prevent them removing Theophane, Poseidon turns her into a sheep, and when they begin eating the sheep he turns them into wolves. He himself becomes a ram and mates with Theophane in this form, and their child is a lamb with a fleece of gold, which in due course is sent by the nymph Nephele to rescue her children from the plotting of their wicked stepmother Ino. See Phrixus.

Thersites

Greek warrior in the Trojan War, the only non-heroic character described in Homer's *Iliad*, where he is ugly, sour-tongued, mean-spirited, and low-born. He accuses Agamemnon of prolonging the war in his own interests and harangues him for stealing Briseis from Achilles, until silenced by Odysseus.

In other stories, he is killed by Achilles for mocking the sudden rush of love the hero feels on seeing the face of the dead Penthesilea. In Shakespeare's *Troilus and Cressida*, Thersites is a "deformed and scurrilous" Greek, who comments sardonically on the play's theme of war, lechery, and betrayal.

Theseus

The national hero of Athens and one of the greatest of all Greek warriors, whose story has been memorably retold by Mary Renault in her novels *The King Must Die* and *The Bull from the Sea*, Theseus is best known for his killing of the Minotaur. He is the son of Aegeus, the king of Athens (or possibly

Below Theseus and the Minotaur, on a fifth-century BC Greek vase.

of Poseidon) and of Aethra, princess of Troezen, and is brought up in his mother's homeland until he is strong enough to lift a certain stone under which Aegeus has placed a sword and a pair of sandals. With these as his passports, Theseus sets out to claim his patrimony, taking the land rather than the sea route in admiration for the exploits of his kinsman Heracles.

The coast road to Athens is notorious for its brigands, and on the way Theseus is challenged by and defeats Periphetes, whose club he keeps as an emblem; Sinis, who would tear his victims in two by tying them to two trees, and is despatched in the same way by Theseus; Sciron, who kicks wayfarers over the cliffs; and Procrustes, who stretches or mutilates his victims to fit his bed. Arriving in Eleusis, then independent of Athens, Theseus finds that strangers are made to wrestle with the king, Cercyon, and then put to death. Again Theseus is the victor, and is hailed as the new king.

Finally he comes safely to Athens, where he receives a warm welcome for his exploits on the way but does not reveal himself to his father Aegeus, who is living with the sorceress Medea. Aegeus's throne is under threat from the 50 sons of his half-brother Pallas, and Medea also has her eye on the succession for her son Medus. By means of her witch's skill, she recognizes Theseus, and persuades Aegeus that he is in league with the Pallantides and should be poisoned, but Aegeus recognizes his own sword and acknowledges his son, and Medea flees from Athens. Theseus then leads an army against the sons of Pallas and defeats them, and also kills the wild bull of Crete which Heracles had brought to Greece as his seventh labor, and which was ravaging Marathon.

At this time Athens is paying an annual tribute to Minos of Crete as a punishment for the death of his son Androgeos. This tribute consists of seven (or in some versions nine) boys and seven girls who are offered as human sacrifice to the Minotaur, the half-man, half-bull offspring of the bull of Crete and the Cretan queen Pasiphae.

Either Theseus volunteers to go, or Minos insists that he should be among the party, and he sets sail for Crete, promising his distraught father that the ship that bears him safely home will carry white sails rather than the usual black. In one story, Theseus defends one of the girls from the attentions of Minos himself, who is present on the ship, and the two men confront each other, each accusing the other of being a bastard. Minos prays to Zeus to send a thunderbolt to prove his divine birth, while Theseus dives into the sea to recover a gold ring that Minos has cast overboard, and returns both with the ring and with a gold crown from Poseidon. The honors at this stage are even.

When the party arrive in Crete, however, Theseus gains a distinct advantage, for Minos's daughter Ariadne falls in love with him at sight. She determines to help him both to overcome the Minotaur and to escape from the Labyrinth in which Minos has imprisoned the creature, and gives him a sword and a spool of thread. Leaving his companions near the entrance, Theseus advances into the maze of passages, paying out the thread as he goes.

Near the center of the Labyrinth he finds the Minotaur and, after an epic struggle, kills it, returning safely to the entrance by following his thread. The Athenian youths with Ariadne at once take ship for Athens, holing the Cretan ships in the harbor to prevent pursuit. On the way home they land on the island of Dia, later called Naxos, and there, either through some bewitchment or through deliberate treachery on the part of Theseus, Ariadne is left behind. And he is so delighted to be returning that he forgets to change his sail and the aged Aegeus, watching from the cliffs, concludes that he is dead and throws himself into the sea.

Theseus is thus king of Athens as well as of Eleusis, rapidly subdues the whole of Attica, and is credited with the first development of Athens as an urban and political center. He has a role in almost every famous Greek

Below Theseus and the Centaur, by the neoclassical sculptor Antonio Canova.

legend, sailing with the Argonauts, hunting the Calydonian boar, participating with his great friend Pirithous in the battle of the Lapiths and the centaurs, and waging war on the Amazons, when he wins the Amazon queen Hippolyta as his bride. He welcomes the exiled Oedipus to Athens, and prevents Creon from forcing Oedipus's return to Thebes to lend his support against the seven armies which march on the city.

Despite his abandonment of Ariadne, Theseus marries her sister Phaedra in a treaty of reconciliation with Crete, and they have two sons, Acamas and Demophon. Soon after this Pallas and his sons make one last attempt to dethrone Theseus, but instead Theseus kills him and wipes out his entire family. For this homicide of a kinsman, Theseus is exiled from Athens for a year and takes his new family to Troezen, where Hippolytus, his son by the Amazon Hippolyta, is acting as regent. Phaedra's unrequited love for Hippolytus leads to her death from suicide and his from a curse laid by his father.

Perhaps in a gesture of scorn to the careless gods, Theseus and Pirithous, both now widowers, determine to choose brides worthy of their rank, and both decide on daughters of Zeus. First they carry off the youthful Helen for Theseus, then they descend into the underworld itself in search of Pirithous's choice, Persephone. There they are imprisoned by Hades in thrones of forgetfulness, staying until Heracles descends in search of Cerberus and releases Theseus, though not Pirithous.

When Theseus returns to Athens, he finds all in turmoil and himself deeply unpopular. Helen has been rescued by her brothers, Castor and Polydeuces, who have invaded Attica, and Athens has fallen under the rule of Menestheus, a descendant of the early Athenian king Erectheus. Theseus takes refuge on the island of Scyros, where he owns estates, but the Scyrian king Lycomedes is unnerved by the presence of so powerful a guest and, on the pretence of showing him the island, takes him to a high cliff and pushes him off.

Menestheus continues to rule until the Trojan War, in which he is killed, and Theseus's son by Phaedra, Demophon, then inherits the kingdom. In about 475 BC the Athenian general Cimon fetched Theseus's supposed

bones from Scyros and reinterred them in a temple dedicated to Theseus, whom Athenians believed had aided them against the Persians at the Battle of Marathon (490 BC).

Thetis

A Nereid or sea-goddess and mother of the hero Achilles. She is brought up on Olympus by Hera, and she shelters Hephaestus when Hera flings him down from Olympus in disgust at his lameness. When Hera, Poseidon, and Athena plot to revolt against Zeus, however, Thetis takes Zeus's part and fetches the 100-armed giant Briareos from Tartarus to support him. She also shelters the young Dionysos when he is attacked by Lycurgus and leaps into the sea.

Thetis is also outstandingly beautiful and both Poseidon and Zeus wish to

Above The sea-nymph Thetis with Peleus and Aphrodite, on the Portland Vase.

marry her, but it has been foretold that her son will be greater than his father. The gods decide that Thetis must be safely married off to a suitable human, and their choice falls on Peleus, king of Phthia. Thetis is deeply reluctant and uses her power to change shape to try to escape her suitor but, having caught her, he holds on to her until she agrees to marry him. The wedding is celebrated with immense splendor, all the gods bringing magnificent gifts.

The exception is Eris (strife), who has not been invited but comes anyway, and throws down the Apple of Discord. For a while Thetis lives dutifully with Peleus, but leaves him when he prevents her from making their son Achilles immortal. She continues to watch over him, however, and she and her sister Nereids guide him and his fellow Argonauts past the Wandering Rocks at the mouth of the Bosphorus.

Anticipating with her divine prescience the death of Achilles outside Troy, she tries in whatever way she can to prevent it, hiding him on the island of Scyros and then persuading Hephaestus to make him an infallible suit of armor. After his inevitable death, she and her sisters mourn him with such a desolate wailing that the Greek army flees in terror.

Thisbe

See Pyramus.

Thoth

Egyptian god of the moon and of wisdom, the patron deity of scribes, who is said to have given mankind the art of hieroglyphic writing. He is sometimes described as the son of the sun-god Re, but is more usually regarded as born from the head of Seth, the god of chaos. Nonetheless he is a benign and scrupulously fair deity, who is given the task of recording the souls who pass to the afterlife, and also adjudicates in the Hall of the Two Truths to see who is worthy to enter into the realm of Osiris. He is depicted either as an ibis, or in human form with the head of an ibis, or as a seated baboon.

Below Tiresias by Leonard Baskin, bronze, 1964.

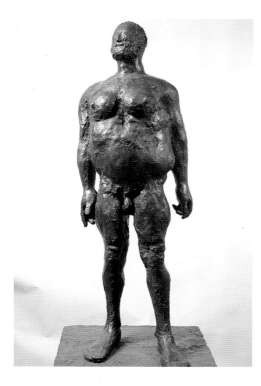

Thyestes

Son of Pelops and Hippodamia and brother of Atreus, who shares in the curse which Pelops places on his sons for the murder of their half-brother Chrysippus, Pelops's love child. Both Atreus and Thyestes are banished from their father's kingdom of Pisa in Elis, and they go to Mycenae, where Atreus marries Aerope.

Aerope, however, falls in love with Thyestes and after bearing her husband two sons destined to win fame in the Trojan War, Agamemnon and Menelaus, has two sons by Thyestes. Atreus first banishes his brother and then, in a pretense of leniency, invites him back to a banquet at which he is served the flesh of his own children. When he learns the truth, Thyestes once more goes into exile, cursing Atreus, and consults the Delphic oracle as to what vengeance he can exact.

He is advised to have a child by his own daughter Pelopea, and so he rapes her without revealing who he is. Pelopea keeps his sword and hides it and becomes the mother of Aegisthus. Meanwhile Atreus's kingdom of Argos has been seized by a famine, and an oracle has told him that this will only lift when Thyestes is brought back home.

Agamemnon and Menelaus find him at Delphi and bring him back as a prisoner to Argos, where Atreus sends Aegisthus to kill him. But Thyestes recognizes the sword with which his attacker threatens him, and reveals himself to Aegisthus as both his father and his grandfather. Aegisthus returns to Atreus and kills him, and Thyestes claims the throne.

For a time he rules peacefully, but presently Agamemnon and Menelaus drive him out with help from Sparta, and he takes refuge on the island of Cythera, where he dies naturally. His curse continues to work itself out, however, for Aegisthus becomes the lover of Agamemnon's wife Clytemnestra, and together they murder Agamemnon on his return from Troy, being in turn themselves murdered by Agamemnon's son Orestes.

Tiresias

Blind seer of Thebes, much famed for his gift of prophecy, who features in many Greek myths. There are two stories about how he loses his sight. In

Above The Titans pile up rocks in a vain attempt to scale Olympus.

one, he sees Athena bathing and she blinds him in punishment, but then in compensation gives him the gift of prophecy, the power to understand the language of birds, and a lifespan seven times the norm.

In the alternative and more bizarre version, he sees two snakes mating and lashes out at them with his staff, killing the female. He is at once transformed into a woman and remains so for seven years, when he again sees two snakes mating, this time kills the male, and becomes a man again. This unique experience enables him to settle a dispute between Zeus and Hera as to whether a man or a woman gains greater pleasure from sex. Hera maintains that the man enjoys sex more, but Tiresias declares that the woman's pleasure is nine times greater. Hera is infuriated and blinds him, and Zeus gives him long life and the gift of prophecy in compensation.

Tiresias is present in Thebes when the young wine-god Dionysos returns in triumph from his sojourn in Asia, and urges the Theban king, Pentheus, to accept the god, prophesying that his worship will become established in Delphi. It is he who reveals that Oedipus has unknowingly killed his father Laius and married his mother, thus causing the plague that afflicts Thebes.

When the seven armies first attack Thebes, in support of Polynices' claim to the kingdom, and are repulsed, Tiresias warns the regent, Creon, that

Polynices' body should not be left unburied as Creon commands. Creon's failure to listen leads to the death of his son Haemon, his wife, and his niece Antigone. Many years later the sons of the original Seven against Thebes return to the attack and this time Tiresias correctly predicts the fall of the city.

He is captured and dies soon after, on the way to Delphi to be offered to Apollo as a prize of war. His is the only shade to keep its intelligence after death and he retains the gift of prophecy. Circe sends Odysseus to the edge of the world to consult the shade of Tiresias about his homeward journey, and Tiresias, after drinking the blood of a black ewe that Odysseus offers him, forecasts all the vicissitudes he must still suffer before reaching Ithaca, and warns him of what he will find there.

Tisiphone

One of the Furies, the instruments of divine vengeance in Greek myth. She carries a whip and wears serpents wreathed round her arms instead of bracelets. Hera sends her to try to prevent Io from landing in Egypt.

Titans

Primeval Greek gods, the offspring of the sky-god Uranus and the earth-goddess Ge, whom the Greeks believed to have ruled the world before the advent of the Olympian gods,

The principal Titans are Cronos, Rhea, Oceanus, Tethys, Iapetus, Phoebe, Themis, and Mnemosyne. Some of their children, such as Helios, Prometheus, and Atlas, are also regarded as Titans, but the children of Cronos and Rhea are the first members of the Olympian race of gods, who supplant the Titans.

Zeus deposes his father Cronos in a cosmic battle for the rule of the universe, in which some Titans support the Olympian gods, while others, such as the sun-god Helios and the sea deities Oceanus and Tethys, take no part. Zeus punishes those who fight against him by throwing them into Tartarus, the lowest area of the underworld.

Tithonus

Trojan prince, son of Laomedon. Eos, goddess of dawn, falls in love with him and carries him off to her palace in the Far East to be her husband. Zeus grants him immortality, but Eos forgets also to request that he shall not age, and he gradually withers away, so she turns him into a cicada which can entertain her with its constant shrilling and shed its aged skin once a year.

Tityus

A giant who lives on the island of Euboea in Greek myth. Hera persuades him to try and rape Leto, the mother of Apollo and Artemis and the object of Hera's bitter hatred, but Artemis shoots him and Zeus flings a thunderbolt at him. He is then tied to the ground in Tartarus, with a pair of vultures constantly pecking at his liver (the source, according to the ancients, of sexual desire).

Triptolemus

Young Greek chosen by Demeter to carry her gift of grain and its cultivation to the nations of the world. She gives him a magic chariot drawn by winged serpents in which he travels the world, scattering seed, teaching the skills of husbandry, and establishing law and justice.

Triton

A Greek merman, half man and half fish, who is the son of Amphitrite and Poseidon. When the gods send a flood to punish mankind, it is Triton who orders the waters to retreat by blowing his horn or conch-shell, and this became a favorite subject for Renaissance and Baroque fountain figures.

Troilus

Trojan prince, son of King Priam, Troilus is killed by Achilles in the course of the Trojan War. The story that he falls in love with and is betrayed by Cressida (Chryseis) does not appear until the medieval period.

Turnus

An Italian prince, who is engaged to a neighboring princess, Lavinia, until the arrival of Aeneas from Troy causes her father Latinus to reconsider. The issue is to be settled by single combat, but Turnus is daunted by Aeneas's formidable reputation and persuades his sister Juturna, a water-nymph, to help him evade the Trojans. Finally Venus makes him stand and fight, and he is defeated and killed by Aeneas.

Tydeus

Son of Oeneus, king of Calydon, he is banished from his home after murdering a man and takes shelter at the court of Adrastus at Argos. There he fights another refugee, Polynices of Thebes, but Adrastus stops them and, in response to an oracle, marries them to his two daughters and undertakes to restore them to his throne. They march first on Thebes, where Tydeus acquits himself gallantly and earns the approbation of Athena.

He fights a mortal duel with Melanippus at the gates of Thebes and, as he lies dying, Athena approaches to

Below Greek armbands in the form of Tritons.

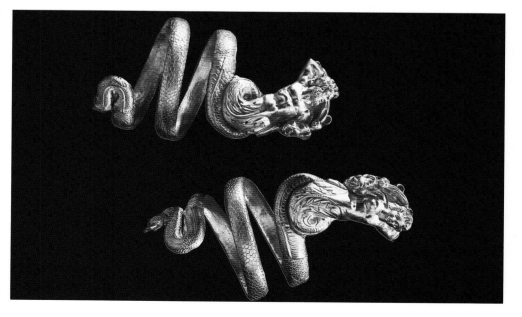

endow him with immortality. The Theban prophet Amphiarus, however, is determined to prevent this because he blames Tydeus for persuading Adrastus to undertake the disastrous expedition, which he knows will cause his own death. He therefore cuts off Melanippus's head and tosses it to Tydeus, who seizes it and devours the brains. This so disgusts Athena that she turns away, and Tydeus dies a human death.

Tyndareos

King of Sparta, whose wife Leda has Helen, Polydeuces, and possibly Castor by Zeus, as well as the several offspring, including Clytemnestra, she bears to Tyndareos. Tyndareos offends Aphrodite by neglecting to sacrifice to her, and then compounds his offense by chaining up her statue, and it is her vengeance to make not only Leda but also Tyndareos's daughters unfaithful to their husbands.

The beautiful Helen is sought in marriage by many princes, but when Agamemnon and Menelaus take refuge in Sparta after their father Atreus has been killed by his brother Thyestes, Tyndareos agrees to the marriages of Helen with Menelaus and Clytemnestra with Agamemnon. At the suggestion of Odysseus he binds all Helen's suitors by oath to support the chosen bridegroom and to protect his marriage rights, and Menelaus calls on that oath when Paris steals Helen from him.

As ordained by Aphrodite, both Tyndareos's daughters are unfaithful; Helen goes voluntarily to Troy with Paris, and Clytemnestra takes Agamemnon's cousin Aegisthus as her lover while Agamemnon is away fighting the Trojan War. Moreover, Castor and Polynices die in battle with Idas and Lynceus, leaving Tyndareos without a male heir, and so he leaves the kingdom of Sparta to Menelaus.

Typhon

A giant with 100 serpentine heads, whom the Greek earth-goddess Ge conceives with the underworld-god Tartarus, in order to revenge herself on Zeus for imprisoning Cronos and the Titans in Tartarus's kingdom. Once fully grown, Typhon makes war on Zeus and, seizing the sickle with which Zeus castrated his father Cronos, Typhon cuts away the muscles from the god's limbs, leaving him helpless.

He hides the muscles, but Hermes manages to find them and fit them again to Zeus's body.

Battle is renewed, and Typhon consults the Moirae or Fates, who tell him that the food of mortal men will give him additional strength. In fact, however, it weakens him, and Zeus gains the upper hand, chases Typhon southward to the sea off Italy and, picking up a convenient island, pins him under it. This becomes Sicily, and the immortal Typhon's fiery breath becomes the volcano of Etna, which occasionally erupts when the buried giant writhes particularly vigorously against his bonds.

In another version of Typhon's end, Zeus flings him into Tartarus, where he fathers all the malevolent winds, hence the typhoon. During the epic struggle of Zeus and Typhon, the other gods are supposed to have fled to Egypt and assumed animal shapes, one explanation of the animal forms of the Egyptian gods; the Greeks identified Typhon with Seth, who pursues and kills Osiris.

Tyro

Greek princess, daughter of the king of Elis by his first wife. Poseidon makes love to her in the form of a river-god, causing a wave of the river to curl over them as they lie together. Tyro has twins, Pelias and Neleus, but abandons them in fear of her stepmother Sidero, and is later married to her father's brother Cretheus, king of Iolcos, to whom she bears Aeson, the father of Jason. Pelias eventually supplants Aeson as king of Iolcos and kills Sidero for her cruelty to his mother.

U

Ulysses

The Roman name for Odysseus.

Urania

Muse of astronomy, and the mother of Linus by Apollo and Hymen by Dionysos. She is shown with a crown of stars, holding a globe, and surrounded by mathematical instruments.

Uranus

Primeval Greek sky-god, born of the earth-goddess Ge, who also bears him the Titans, who rule the world before the advent of the Olympian gods. Uranus grows jealous of his children, and tries to push them back into the earth when they are born, and so Ge gives her son Cronos a sickle, with

Below Three-headed Typhon from a Greek temple pediment.

V

Above Eighteenth-century engraving showing Urania, Muse of astronomy, crowned with stars.

which he castrates Uranus next time he tries to mate with Ge.

Where Uranus's blood falls on the earth, the Furies and the giants are created, while his severed genitals fall into the sea and are transformed into Aphrodite, the goddess of love, who is thus in a sense the oldest Olympian deity.

Below *The Birth of Venus* (detail) by Sandro Botticelli (1445-1510).

Venus

Originally an Italian goddess of agricultural rather than human fertility, Venus early becomes identified with the Greek goddess of love, but remains a more sober and responsible deity than the wilful Aphrodite. As the mother of the hero Aeneas, from whom the Julian house of the Emperor Augustus and his successors claimed descent, Venus was worshipped as Venus Genetrix, universal mother and creator, and had a particularly important role in the official state cult of Rome.

In the Middle Ages she becomes a more sensuous and dangerous figure, again taking on some of the attributes of Aphrodite, and is often pictured with her mirror, a symbol of self-indulgence and idle dalliance. Later medieval poets partially re-established Venus's reputation by making her a symbol of chivalrous love, but it was the Neoplatonists of the Italian Renaissance who restored her to respectability, with their belief in love as a metaphysical experience that leads to an awareness of God. The Venus of Renaissance and Baroque art reflects the positive and life-enhancing, as opposed to the destructive, powers of love.

Vertumnus

Italian god of spring and orchards, who falls in love with the garden-goddess Pomona. He woos her in the guise of a fisherman, a soldier, a harvester, and a peasant, to no avail. Finally he assumes the shape of an old woman and tells a sad tale of the young man pining for Pomona's love; the goddess softens and agrees to marry him.

Vesta

Roman goddess of the hearth, worshipped as a symbol of personal security in every Roman household. She also had her own temple in the Forum, containing a fire believed to have been brought by Aeneas from Troy, which must never be allowed to go out.

This was tended, almost until the fall of Rome, by six priestesses known as the Vestal Virgins, who were condemned to be buried alive if they lost their virginity. Forbidden to use piped water, the Vestals drew their water from the spring of Juturna in the Forum. The remains of the round temple of Vesta, built to encircle its sacred fire, can still be seen, and inspired a number of architectural delights in eighteenth-century English gardens.

Volupta

Roman goddess of pleasure, regarded as the daughter of Cupid and Psyche.

Vulcan

Italian god of fire, sometimes called Mulciber, the smelter, and identified with the Greek smith-god Hephaestus. Vulcan working in his forge, with the Cyclops as his assistants, was a popular subject in Renaissance and post-Renaissance art.

Z

Zephyrus

Greek god of the west wind, the son of Eos, goddess of the dawn. He falls in love with the beautiful young Hyacinthus, but Hyacinthus is also courted by Apollo and rejects Zephyrus, who avenges himself by causing a discus thrown by Apollo to swerve and kill Hyacinthus. Zephyrus is also the father of Achilles' immortal talking horses, Xanthus and Balius, by a harpy who was grazing in the form of a filly by the waters of Ocean.

He is perceived as a gentle and benevolent force, heralding the mild, wet weather of spring, and is sometimes identified as the husband of Iris, goddess of the rainbow. It is he who takes pity on Psyche and carries her to Cupid's castle, and he is shown in Botticelli's painting *La Primavera* breathing life into Flora.

Zetes

With Calais, the twin son of the Greek north wind, Boreas. When born, Zetes and Calais appear human, but as they grow to manhood great golden wings sprout from their shoulders. Known together as the Boreads, they are fated to die if ever they fail to catch a fugitive. They sail with Jason as two of the Argonauts, and deliver Phineus from the harpies who are persecuting him but are killed by Heracles because they persuade the Argonauts to sail on after the loss of Hylas.

Zetus

Son of Antiope and Zeus. See Amphion.

Zeus

The greatest of the Olympian gods in Greek mythology, whose Roman equivalent is Jupiter. His name is found in some form in most Indo-European languages, meaning "sky" or "heavens," and his earliest manifestation is as a weather-god. Thunderbolts remain his usual weapon and one of his commonest Homeric epithets is "gatherer of clouds," but his cult becomes generalized very early and every aspect of the affairs of the world are regarded as under his jurisdiction.

Homer calls him "the father of gods and men," though strictly he is the brother of many of the most important gods, and it is Prometheus who creates man, with the help of Athena.

In Greek myth, Zeus derives his authority from the fact that he is the only one of the children of Cronos and Rhea to survive to adulthood. Cronos has been warned that one of his children will overthrow him, and therefore swallows each one at birth, but Rhea hides Zeus, the youngest, on the island of Crete. Once fully grown, he restores his brothers and sisters to life with the help of his first wife, Metis.

The ensuing battle against the Titans, in which Cronos is overthrown, represents the triumph of the Olympian gods against pre-Greek deities.

Zeus and his two brothers, Hades and Poseidon, then draw lots to divide up the universe between them, Hades becoming lord of the underworld, Poseidon of the sea, and Zeus of the sky, while the earth and Mount Olympus, on which the early Greeks believed the gods to live, remain common territory.

The Greeks believed Zeus to have married a succession of goddesses, many of them originally earth deities. The union of a sky-god and an earth-goddess has a fundamental place in Greek myth, and may well reflect the conflation of a male-oriented Indo-European immigrant society with an established Mediterranean cult of a mother-goddess. The Titan Metis is Zeus's first partner, but when she is pregnant, Zeus is warned by Ge that the next baby will supplant him, just as he overthrew his father.

He therefore swallows Metis, thus absorbing her wisdom, and with her he also swallows the unborn child, who presently bursts fully grown from his forehead as Athena, goddess of wisdom. Themis, Zeus's next wife, is also a Titan, and bears him the Moirae or Fates and the Horae or Seasons; by

Below Zeus, in the guise of a bull, carries off Europa. Roman mosaic from Lullingstone, Kent.

Euronyme he fathers the Graces; by his sister Demeter he has Persephone; by Mnemosyne the nine Muses; by Maia the messenger-god Hermes; and by Leto the twin deities Apollo and Artemis.

There is a degree of confusion as to which of these relationships are to be regarded as legitimate and which are simply amours; when Hera becomes Zeus's last and permanent wife, she pursues Leto with retrospective jealousy, and is equally harsh to the many other lovers, both human and divine, with whom her erring and unsatisfactory husband continues to disport himself. These include Danae, mother of Perseus; Europa, mother of Minos, king of Crete; Leda, mother of Helen, Castor, and Polydeuces; Semele, mother of Dionysos; and Alcmene, mother of Heracles. Hera's children by Zeus are Ares, god of war, Hebe, and in some versions Ilithyia, goddess of childbirth.

As a universal deity, Zeus is regarded as the source of all mortal sovereignty; he is the protector of rightful authority, and thus of the king's power and the city's integrity. He is the patron of strangers and travelers, and punishes severely any breach of the laws of hospitality. In the Trojan War, he supports the Greeks because Paris seduces Helen while the guest of Helen's husband Menelaus, even though he has the support of Aphrodite. Zeus is also the interpreter of destiny, weighing the fates of men in a pair of golden scales which determine when each is doomed to die.

Despite his supreme position, however, Zeus's authority is occasionally challenged. When Hera, Athena, and Poseidon rebel against him, he is rescued only by the action of Thetis, who fetches the giant Briareos from Tartarus to support him. Finally the original earth-goddess and mother of Cronos, Ge herself, becomes weary of Zeus's high-handed behavior, and bears the race of giants to attack Olympus. She also produces a magic herb which will render the giants immortal

Above Zeus enthroned with the other gods and goddesses on Olympus. Nineteenth-century engraving.

and invincible, but Zeus prevents them from finding it by hiding the light from the sun, moon, and stars.

Even so, the gods do not have the power to destroy the giants by themselves, and need the help of the mortal hero Heracles with his poisoned arrows. After the defeat of the giants, Ge gives birth to the most dangerous of all Zeus's adversaries, the monster Typhon, who almost succeeds in destroying him, but is finally overcome with the aid of Hermes.

This final reaffirmation of Zeus's pre-eminent authority is reflected in the portrayal of him in the *Iliad* and the *Odyssey* as the majestic and impartial arbiter of life and death. The particular awe in which he was held by the Greeks is demonstrated by the fact that, as far as we know, he does not, unlike the other gods, appear as a character in any Greek drama.

160

Acknowledgments

The publisher would like to thank David Eldred for designing this book, Caroline Earle for editing it, Suzanne O'Farrell and Rita Longabucco for the picture research, and Nicki Giles for production. The following agencies provided photographic material:

The Bettmann Archive, New York: pages 6, 8, 9, 10(both), 11, 13 15(both), 18, 19(bottom right), 20(both), 21, 22, 23, 24(bottom), 25(both), 26, 27(bottom), 29, 30, 31, 32(bottom), 33(both), 35, 36(bottom left), 37, 40, 41, 42(both), 43(bottom), 44, 45, 46(top), 47(bottom left), 49, 50, 51(both), 52(both), 54(both), 56, 60, 61, 64(both), 65(both), 66, 67(both), 68, 69(top), 70, 71(both), 73, 75, 77, 78, 79, 81, 82, 83(bottom right), 84, 86, 87(both), 88, 89, 90(bottom right), 94, 95, 96, 97(top), 98, 99, 100(top right), 101, 103(bottom), 104, 105, 106, 107(left), 109(top), 110, 111(both), 112(bottom), 113, 114(top), 115, 116, 119, 120(both), 123, 124(bottom), 125, 127, 128(both), 129, 130, 131, 132, 134, 135(top), 136, 137, 138, 139, 140, 141(both), 142(bottom), 143, 144(bottom), 145(both), 146(left), 148(both), 149, 150, 152, 154(both), 157(both), 159.
Bison Picture Library: pages 38, 43(top), 46(bottom), 57, 72, 83(bottom right), 93(top), 135(bottom), 153, 158.

C.M. Dixon, Canterbury: pages 1, 2, 3(all), 5, 7, 12, 14, 16, 17, 19(bottom left), 24(top), 27(top), 28, 32(top), 34, 36(top right), 47(right), 48, 55, 58, 62, 69(bottom right), 74, 76, 80, 90(top left), 91, 92, 93(bottom), 97(bottom), 100(bottom left), 102, 103(top), 108, 109(bottom), 112(top), 114(bottom), 117, 118, 121, 122, 124(top), 126, 133, 142(top), 146(right), 147, 151, 156.
Galleria Borghese, Rome: page 53.
Metropolitan Museum of Art, New York: pages 39, 63, 144(top), 155.
Munich Antikensammlung: page 59.
National Archeological Museum, Athens: page 107(top right).